WRITERS IN
General Editor:

Writers in their Time

Published titles

GEOFFREY CHAUCER   Janette Dillon
JOSEPH CONRAD   Brian Spittles
GEORGE ELIOT   Brian Spittles

Forthcoming titles

CHARLES DICKENS   Angus Easson
THOMAS HARDY   Timothy Hands
GEORGE ORWELL   Norman Page
WILLIAM SHAKESPEARE   John Drakakis
VIRGINIA WOOLF   Edward Bishop

Geoffrey Chaucer

Janette Dillon

150th YEAR

M

MACMILLAN

First published 1993 by
THE MACMILLAN PRESS LTD
Houndmills, Basingstoke, Hampshire RG21 2XS
and London
Companies and representatives
throughout the world

A catalogue record for this book is available
from the British Library.

ISBN 0–333–54202–9 hardcover
ISBN 0–333–54203–7 paperback

Typeset by Nick Allen/Longworth Editorial Services
Longworth, Oxon.

Printed in Hong Kong

For Katherine, Rachel and Michael

Contents

Acknowledgements

I am grateful to Norman Page, the editor of the series, for his support and encouragement, to Helen Phillips and Simon Shepherd, who offered helpful comments on chapters 1 and 7 respectively, and above all to Thorlac Turville-Petre, who willingly read the whole draft and suggested many improvements.

Introduction

The aim of this book is to enable the reader with little or no prior knowledge of medieval history to read the works of Chaucer in a historical context. For this reason it frequently summarises important historical movements or events more fully described elsewhere in order to indicate the range of context that readers of Chaucer might wish to take into account.

The first two chapters together provide a general perspective for later chapters. The first outlines Chaucer's life against some of the wider issues and events of the later fourteenth century, while the second describes the conditions of literary production and ex - pectations of the audience in a manuscript culture. There is often no direct link that can be made between the events of recorded history and Chaucer's own life, yet it is important that readers should be aware, as Chaucer must have been, that they took place, so that they may judge for themselves the interactions between text and history. Although the necessity for providing the reader with brief historical information about the fourteenth century has the unfortunate effect of seeming to suggest that history can be neatly packaged and separated from literature, the aim of this book is to do just the opposite: to insist on the inseparability of text and context and on the uncertain boundary between historical and other kinds of writing.

Subsequent chapters select some of the concerns outlined in chapters 1 and 2 and develop them in more detail as contexts for reading Chaucer. There is no attempt at parity between chapters either in the amount of space they devote to historical discussion or in their approach to texts. Clearly some aspects of the fourteenth century need more explanation than others for a modern non-specialist audience; similarly, variation between close analysis of one text and comparison of several offers the reader different methods for evaluating the connections between litera- ture and history. I have consciously adopted different approaches in order to show that history shapes literary texts in a number of ways. Thus, for example, chapter 2 refers only intermittently to Chaucer's work within the wider context of relations between writers, texts and readers in fourteenth-century manuscript culture; chapter 4 uses source study within one of Chaucer's texts as a means of focusing English internationalism in the fourteenth century; and chapter 7, following a brief summary of Chaucer's reputation, compares a recurrent preoccupation of Chaucer's poetry with its manifestation in one of Shakespeare's plays in order to discuss the question of 'influence' via literary practice.

Notes to secondary sources consciously privilege historical material at the expense of the vast critical literature on Chaucer. To attempt to cover both would be impossible as well as inappropriate for a book of this size: the notes might have been longer than the text. My approach assumes a reader unfamiliar with fourteenth-century history, and the notes to chapters 1 and 2 are particularly full in order to create paths for the reader into the writings of both Chaucer's contemporaries and modern historians. I have also quoted from accessible editions and anthologies of primary sources and from translations of Latin texts wherever they exist, so that the reader may be encouraged to return to these sources where possible.

Middle English spelling is partially modernised throughout in accordance with the conventions usually adopted for Chaucer's text but not normally applied to his contemporaries, in an attempt to minimise the exaggerated distance between Chaucer and much other contemporary writing that such inconsistency in editorial practice produces for the modern reader.

1

Chaucer's Life and Times

The life of Geoffrey Chaucer is better documented than that of many a later writer. This is due to the fact that he entered service in one of the royal households at an early age and remained in public service for the rest of his life. His various duties and travels, together with the payments and gifts made to him, are therefore well documented in public records. The precise date and place of Chaucer's birth are unknown. He was born some time in the early 1340s, most probably in London. The closest reference to his birth is his own testimony when giving evidence in the Scrope–Grosvenor trial of 1386 that he was then forty years old 'et plus' and that he had borne arms for twenty-seven years.[1] He was the son of John Chaucer, a prosperous wine-merchant, or vintner, and Agnes de Copton, who later increased their prosperity through the inheritance of several properties. John Chaucer also served Edward III as deputy chief butler from 1347 to 1349 and held positions in the customs service, as had his father and other members of the family. The Chaucer family owned considerable property in the Vintry Ward in central London, an area occupied by noblemen and merchants as well as vintners. One of their holdings was in Thames Street, which ran parallel to the river one block north, and it has usually been assumed that Chaucer grew up in this house.[2]

When Chaucer was born in the 1340s Edward III was king, a young man in his late twenties, having come to the throne in 1327. England was at war throughout Chaucer's lifetime with both France and Scotland, though hostilities fluctuated between brief periods of truce. Scotland was a long-standing enemy, but the Hundred Years War with France was of more recent origins, having begun in 1337 as a result of Edward's attempt to press his claim to the French throne. The country was heavily burdened with taxes to finance the wars,[3] and invasion threatened intermittently at both extremities, from the French on the south coast, and the Scots in the northern border regions. England's greatest victory during Chaucer's early years was the battle of Crécy in 1346. Jean Froissart, the most famous chronicler of the fourteenth century, describes the campaign with characteristic emphasis on the chivalric ethic of behaviour. His is a creative writing of history, designed to honour rather than simply to document the deeds of the participants. His use of direct speech illustrates his preference for drama over the minimalism of fact, and Crécy, for him, is the record on the one hand of the English archers and on the other of Edward the Black Prince, the king's eldest son. He describes how the prince, aged sixteen, sent to his father for help in the battle. Froissart depicts Edward III, having established that his son was not actually dying, as replying in this manner:

> Sir Thomas . . . go back to him and to those who have sent you and tell them not to send for me again today, as long as my son is alive. Give them my command to let the boy win his spurs, for if God has so ordained it, I wish the day to be his and the honour to go to him and to those in whose charge I have placed him.

The wording of this response, together with Froissart's own narration of its effect, is true to the spirit of the ideals shared by the knightly class to which both Froissart and his king belonged:

> The knight went back to his commanders and gave them the King's message. It heartened them greatly and they privately regretted having sent him. They fought better than ever and must have performed great feats of arms, for they remained in possession of the ground with honour.[4]

In 1348–9, however, the fortunes of war were overshadowed by the first outbreak of plague. Estimates of how many died vary wildly, since contemporary estimates seem to have been based on a need to convey the full horror of loss rather than on a striving for accuracy, but certainly a huge proportion of the population, perhaps up to a third, died, and whole villages disappeared from the map in many places.[5] One chronicler, Thomas Walsingham, writes that 'so violently did the pestilence increase that the living were scarce able to bury the dead' and reports that many believed 'that hardly a tenth part of mankind had been left alive'.[6] Yet all we know of Chaucer and the plague is that he survived it. The only direct references to the plague in his poetry occur in the *Pardoner's Tale*, where death is said to have slain a thousand 'this pestilence' (VI.679),[7] and in the *General Prologue* to the *Canterbury Tales*, where the Doctor of Physic is described as making a profit out of 'pestilence' (I.442).

Following the ravages of the Black Death the work-force was not sufficient to the demand, and wages began to rise. The Statute of Labourers in 1351 represented an attempt by the government to fix both wages and prices at pre-plague levels, but without much success.[8] Both the attempt to intervene in the labour market and the resistance of market forces to such intervention are a reminder of how far labour relations had outgrown the feudal system by the fourteenth century. Although writers still used the old terminology of vassalage and invoked ideals of loyalty and service, there were increasing numbers of free peasants who worked for wages, and dwindling numbers of bondmen, or serfs, whose labour was tied to a particular lord by birth.[9] Numerous historians have noted the general tendency, as the fourteenth century progressed, towards the commutation of labour services for rents. The frustration of those who were still unfree in the late fourteenth century, and in an increasingly anachronistic position, was one of the factors contributing to the English Rising (Peasants' Revolt) of 1381. J. A. Raftis has made the point that the Rising was most prominent in those areas where commutation had gone farthest. 'Customary tenure', he writes 'would have no more meaning for peasants from these eastern regions than the service of knighthood for a mercenary soldier.'[10] Knighthood too, as Raftis implies, was becoming more a matter of literary nostalgia than of reality. Even the king expected to pay his soldiers now instead of calling on the old feudal ties, and soldiers right up to the level of the Black Prince were paid for their services.

Perhaps in the late 1340s or a little later Chaucer may have gone to school. Seven seems to have been an average age for children to begin elementary schooling at a song or reading school,[11] and Chaucer's *Prioress's Tale* is often singled out in this context as offering a clear picture of such an elementary school (VII.496–536). No record survives of Chaucer's schooling, but there were three grammar schools near Thames Street. St Paul's Cathedral school, which had a song school attached, was nearest. The *Prioress's Tale* describes the seven-year-old Hugh sitting 'at his prymer' (517), a book containing all the best-known prayers and devotions, and this was the usual first reader after children had learned their letters. Most recent writers on medieval education agree that children were probably still taught to read in Latin at this date, though it is possible that some children, especially those in rural areas, for example, taught in some cases by priests or parish clerks, themselves with minimal Latin, learned to read from English primers.[12] Learning to read in Latin meant in the first place learning the sounds without understanding the meaning, and it is clear that some of the pupils who never progressed beyond such rote learning could have become those clerks, and possibly teachers, of the next generation who were able to pronounce the divine service in Latin but not to understand it. Little Hugh learns a Latin song in honour of the Virgin simply by overhearing it, but when he asks a schoolfellow to 'construe' it for him, the boy's answer makes it clear that learning the song came before the ability to understand its meaning: 'I lerne song; I kan but smal grammeere' (536).

Grammar, then, was the next stage after primer and song, and gave its name to the next type of school (although some elementary schools might offer the rudiments of grammar). The grammar was of course Latin grammar, and the standard grammar book Donatus. Until about the middle of the century children were taught to construe their Latin in French, but, according to John Trevisa's famous comment (quoted on p. 38 below) the move to English as the language of instruction followed on from the Black Death of 1349. It is therefore not possible to be certain whether Chaucer was taught in French or English, although French would seem more likely, given a possible date before 1349 and the fact that Chaucer went to school in London, which would have been less badly hit than rural areas by the dearth of qualified teachers simply because its population of educated men was greater.

Texts for study were drawn from the Latin classics. William Ravenstone, master of St Paul's, left his collection of books to the school in 1358. It was a huge collection by fourteenth-century standards, of eighty-four books.[13] Although it is no more than a possibility that Chaucer attended St Paul's, this in turn raises the possibility of his access to this substantial library, which, with its predominance of classical writers, corresponds quite closely with what we can infer about Chaucer's reading from his work.

We know nothing about Chaucer's childhood, or about most

fourteenth-century childhoods. An unusually intimate first-hand account of childhood in the fourteenth century is given to us by Froissart in his poem 'L'Espinette amoureuse', which shows us a little boy damming streams and making mudpies like children of any era, and names a variety of games, some of which are still familiar, some wholly arcane.[14] It also shows the young Froissart attending a mixed school and passing little gifts of pins, apples, pears and glass rings to the girls. Chaucer's schooling, however, is likely to have been only with boys, since girls were not admitted to grammar schools, and were probably educated with boys only in a few song schools and nunneries.[15]

The earliest known document to name Chaucer is the record of purchases of clothes for him in 1357 in the household of the Countess of Ulster, wife of Prince Lionel, the second surviving son of Edward III. This suggests that Chaucer was probably employed as a page in their household. Again, although we have no detail directly relating to Chaucer's duties, we can look at the writings of other contemporaries to find out what he would have been expected to do. A French prose romance by Antoine de la Sale, *Le Petit Jehan de Saintré*, written early in the fifteenth century, supplies some detail concerning a page's life. The romance tells the story of a young widow at court attempting to seduce her little page, but the first half of the book is primarily an account of her instructions to him on good conduct and courtly behaviour, and paints a picture of the skills such a boy might be expected to develop. Young John is praised, at the age of thirteen, as

> a skilful youth and an hardy, whether for riding a full rough courser, for singing, dancing, or playing at tennis, for running, for leaping, and for all other exercises and disports which he saw the men do; in all things he sought to share joyously, albeit he was but frail and slender of stature, and ever so remained. But his heart, when he was among his fellows, was all iron and steel. For this his skill and graciousness, gentleness and courtesy, he was so well loved and bespoke of the King, the Queen, lords, ladies, and every man, that all esteemed and declared he would surely be, an he should live, one of the most worshipful gentlemen of France.[16]

In September 1359 Chaucer probably accompanied Prince Lionel, the head of the household, to the war in France, serving in

the division led by the Black Prince. The war at this stage was in a
period of English dominance, following the Black Prince's victory
and capture of the French king Jean at the battle of Poitiers in
1356. Chaucer was captured during the campaign and ransomed
by the king for £16 by 1 March 1360. In October of the same year
the records also show that Prince Lionel paid Chaucer for carrying
letters from Calais to England, probably on private business rather
than on matters relating to the peace negotiations which resulted
in the Treaty of Calais in that same month. The treaty liberated the
French king after four years of imprisonment in England, and
provided for Edward to take French hostages as surety against
payment of the French king's ransom.

Between 1360 and 1366 there is no record of Chaucer's activities.
There is no evidence that he went to university, and the fact that,
unlike many fourteenth-century writers, he was neither cleric nor
aristocrat, but from the rising mercantile class, makes this less
likely. One speculation is that he attended the Inns of Court. This
is based partly on a recognition that his appointments in later life
as controller of the customs and clerk of the king's works
demanded some skills in keeping legal documents and partly on
an apocryphal story in the preface to Speght's 1598 edition of
Chaucer's works. Speght there argues that Chaucer and Gower
would seem to have been students of the Inner Temple, 'for that
many yeres since master Buckley did see a recorde in that same
howse, where Geoffrye Chaucer was fined two shillinges for
beatinge a Franciscane fryer in Fletestreate'. Recent study of the
type of education provided for young men attached to one of the
royal households makes clear, however, that Chaucer could have
acquired such training as he might have needed for his future
career within that environment.[17]

Perhaps during this period he was also beginning to experiment
in French verse, or even in English verse, using forms borrowed
from French, though none of his surviving poems gives any
indication of such an early date.[18] He does later explicitly describe
himself as a writer of 'balades, roundeles, vyrelayes' (Prologue to
The Legend of Good Women, G.411), all forms originating in French
poetry.

Chaucer was granted a safe-conduct from Charles II of Navarre
from February to May 1366. What kind of journey this was, we do
not know. It could have been a pilgrimage, perhaps to the famous
shrine of St James of Compostela in Spain, or a political journey.

The Black Prince at this period held court at Bordeaux in Aquitaine, having been granted the principality of Aquitaine by his father in 1362, following his marriage to Joan of Kent the previous year. (The future King Richard II was born there in 1367.) Chaucer might have been visiting the court of Navarre or, beyond it, the court of Castile. The victory of the Black Prince at Nájera in 1367 restored Pedro the Cruel to the throne of Castile, and Chaucer may have been arranging for English troops to pass through Navarre or recalling English mercenaries from Pedro's opponent, Henry of Trastamara. Chaucer later incorporated Pedro into the *Monk's Tale* as the subject of a tragic fall from greatness.

In this same year of 1366 Chaucer's father died and Chaucer married. His wife was Philippa de Roet, daughter of Gilles de Roet, a knight of Hainault who had come to England with Queen Philippa. She may be the same 'Philippa Pan.' who was also recorded in the service of the Countess of Ulster in 1356, 1357 and 1358.[19] Her father was King of Arms (herald) for Aquitaine, so she may have met Chaucer in Aquitaine, perhaps at the court of the Black Prince, rather than in the Countess's household. In 1366 there is a record of a life annuity of 10 marks (1 mark representing two-thirds of £1) granted by Edward III to Philippa Chaucer, a *domicella* (lady in waiting) of the queen. It is not clear how many children the Chaucers had. There was certainly a son called Thomas, later to hold great wealth and honour in England, probably a son called Lewis (to whom Chaucer addressed his *Treatise on the Astrolabe*), and perhaps also two daughters, Elizabeth and Agnes, but the records are not conclusive.

In 1367 Chaucer himself was granted a life annuity of 20 marks by Edward III, showing that he too entered service in the king's household in this year. The two documents confirming this grant list him respectively as *'vallectus'* to Edward III and as *'esquier'* in the royal household.[20] For the rest of their lives both Chaucer and his wife continued in service with either Edward III, his son, John of Gaunt, or Edward's grandson, Richard II, who succeeded him. John of Gaunt was the third surviving son of Edward III, known by this title because of his birth in Ghent. Gaunt's first marriage, in 1359, was to Blanche, co-heiress with her sister to the enormously wealthy house of Lancaster. Since her father and sister both died soon after the marriage, leaving Blanche to inherit, Gaunt was thereafter known to his contemporaries as the Duke of Lancaster, becoming at the same time one of the richest men in

England. His son Henry, Earl of Derby, later Henry IV, used this inherited wealth and power as a lever to depose Richard II at the end of Chaucer's lifetime.

On 12 September 1368 Blanche died.[21] Her death produced the first of Chaucer's surviving dream poems, and his earliest substantial work, *The Book of the Duchess*. This is an elegy for the death of Blanche (named White in the poem) and shows an easy familiarity with currently fashionable French verse forms. It is written in the tradition of the *Roman de la Rose*, a thirteenth-century poem admired and imitated far beyond France by Chaucer's time, and also borrows from Guillaume de Machaut's *dits amoreux*, and Froissart's *Le Paradys d'Amours*, written in imitation of Machaut, the older poet. The poem may not have been written immediately following Blanche's death, but was presumably completed some time before Gaunt's second marriage in 1371.

Lionel of Clarence, Gaunt's elder brother, also died in 1368, and Queen Philippa in 1369, during the 'Third Pestilence', as the chroniclers called this outbreak of plague.[22] In 1371 John of Gaunt remarried. His wife was Constance of Castile, daughter of Pedro the Cruel. Philippa Chaucer entered Constance's service in 1372, and at about the same time Philippa's sister, Katherine Swynford, seems to have become the mistress of John of Gaunt. She finally became his third wife in 1396.

Chaucer probably accompanied John of Gaunt on an expedition to Picardy in 1369. It may have been military rather than poetic service that Gaunt was acknowledging when in 1374 he granted Chaucer a life annuity 'in consideration of the services rendered by Chaucer to the grantor' and 'by the grantee's wife Philippa to the grantor's late mother and to his consort'. A sixteenth-century heading in the Fairfax manuscript of *The Book of the Duchess* states that the poem was written at John of Gaunt's request, but there is no other evidence for this. Chaucer was perhaps also translating the *Roman de la Rose* during this period, since its influence is so strong in *The Book of the Duchess*. It was as a translator that he achieved fame outside England, and Eustache Deschamps, in the famous ballade he sent to Chaucer in 1386, addressed him as 'grant translateur'.[23]

During 1372–3 Chaucer made his first certain journey to Italy, in order to negotiate with the doge of Genoa concerning his desire for the use of an English port. An earlier record that Chaucer 'passed at Dover' in 1368 may suggest a journey to Italy, but perhaps represents a visit only to Flanders or France.[24] Scholars now consider it likely that Chaucer may have been familiar with Italian before this journey, through his father's dealings with Italian wine-merchants, and that he may have been chosen for the Italian mission because of his knowledge of Italian.[25] The fact that a few months later Chaucer was again chosen by the king to negotiate the delivery of a Genoese ship detained at Dartmouth to her Italian master offers further support for this view.

Chaucer's journey extended to Florence on this occasion, though the reason is not known. It could perhaps have been linked with Edward III's substantial loans from Florentine banking houses, such as the Bardi, which later went bankrupt as a result of Edward's failure to repay. The question of whether Chaucer met either Petrarch or Boccaccio on this visit seems unlikely to be answered, but it is probable that his interest in the Italian poets was aroused during his stay. Boccaccio's lectures on Dante were about to take place in Florence in the autumn of 1373 and were probably a talking point at the time, since the petition for the lectures was submitted in June 1373, only a month after Chaucer had left to return to England.[26] Certainly the writings of all three of these Italian poets had a strong influence on his poetry after this date. He first mentions 'Daunte' by name in *The House of Fame* (450); 'Fraunceys Petrak, the lauriat poete/ . . . whos rethorike sweete/Enlumyned al Ytaille of poetrie' (*Cant. Tales*, IV.31–3) is acknowledged some years later as the source of the *Clerk's Tale*; but Boccaccio, as is well known, is never named by Chaucer, though he is the direct source of both the *Knight's Tale* and *Troilus and Criseyde*.

In 1374 King Edward showed his satisfaction with Chaucer by granting him a daily pitcher of a gallon of wine. (This grant was renewed by Richard II on his accession in 1377, and the following year he allowed Chaucer to exchange it for a comfortable annual income of 20 marks.) On 10 May of this same year, 1374, Chaucer began to lease the dwelling over Aldgate, rent-free. Aldgate was at that time quite literally one of six gates in the city wall of London, and central to its defences.

A month later, Chaucer was appointed controller of the customs and the subsidy (a heavier tax) on wool, sheepskins and leather, at an annual salary of £10. Wool was England's main export at this time, so that supervision of those collecting the income on it, which was Chaucer's job, was probably a time-consuming task, and not the sinecure it was once thought to be. The wool taxes were one of Edward's chief resources for financing the war. Chaucer too made a substantial profit out of the tax in 1376, when he was allowed to keep the sum of £71 4s. 6d., the proceeds from wool forfeited by a certain John Kent, who had exported it without paying duty. During this year Chaucer also received payment for transacting 'secret business of the king', but no more is known about what this might have been.

1376 was the year of the so-called 'Good Parliament', in which the Commons (so called because they represented communities rather than 'the common people', and in fact largely drawn from the gentry) accused various magnates close to the king of malpractice and incompetence. The king had burdened the Commons with repeated demands for taxes to finance the war, and his demand for more from this Parliament produced outspoken retorts of injustice,

for the Commons are so weakened and impoverished by various tallages and taxes paid heretofore that they cannot bear such a charge at this time, and on the other hand all that we have granted for war we have for a long time lost because it has been wasted by mismanagement and spent dishonestly.[27]

The real power of the Commons lay in its ability to withhold taxes. In looking for a way to set out their grievances they hit upon the idea of electing a Speaker and demanded restraints on malpractice and the dismissal of corrupt ministers and of the king's mistress, Alice Perrers. Their demands were directed in the first instance against John of Gaunt, who managed state affairs during the final stage of the king's illness and the last days of the Black Prince (who died during this parliamentary session). Gaunt allowed the trials and reforms to proceed, but after the Parliament had disbanded, and the Knights returned to their shires, Gaunt simply declared the whole session invalid, arrested the Speaker, Sir Peter de la Mare, and returned those dismissed to their positions of power. The reforms had not been enacted as statutes and thus had no binding force.

Bishop Brinton used the fable of the mice who try to bell the cat in a sermon preached during the Good Parliament on 18 May 1376 in order to urge churchmen to take political action. 'Of what use . . . is it', he asked, 'to treat of matters in Parliament and publicly to denounce the law unless due correction follows upon such denunciation? . . . let us not be merely talkers but doers.'[28] The B-text of Langland's *Piers Plowman*, generally dated 1377–9, retells the same fable, with the bitterness of hindsight, showing the uselessness of attempting to bell the cat. Although Langland's approach does not seem to align him with the mice and rats, his revival of the fable a year or more after the political action urged by Brinton had failed at least suggests that this particular Parliament was not easily forgotten. In neutralising the radical acts of the Good Parliament John of Gaunt could not eradicate the popular discontent in which they originated. Instead he reinforced the hatred and distrust already focused on himself, and pushed the people towards rebellion rather than parliamentary reform.

When the next Parliament met, in January 1377, the Speaker was one of John of Gaunt's officials, and the Chancellor's opening speech has been described as 'an elaborate piece of propaganda for the monarchy . . . Lancaster's riposte to the claims of the Good Parliament'.[29] The Commons granted the first of what was to be a series of new poll taxes (4*d.* per head), on condition that Sir Peter de la Mare was released. The clergy also refused to grant the tax unless Archbishop Wykeham, victimised by Gaunt in the autumn of 1376, was restored to his rights. They attempted to force John of Gaunt's hand by summoning his protégé, John Wyclif, on a charge of heresy, but Gaunt disrupted the trial with abuse and threats against the bishops (see pp. 99–100 below). At the same time Gaunt was trying to push through Parliament a bill that would curtail the liberty of Londoners by putting the government of London into the control of the King's Marshal instead of the Mayor. The day after the trial Londoners heard that the Marshal had already assumed control in London without waiting for the passage of the bill, and riot broke out. Gaunt's Savoy palace was stormed and his arms reversed (in token of treason). He fled to the Princess of Wales, his sister-in-law, who mediated in organising a compromise. Order was uneasily restored, but Gaunt's vindictiveness against the participants in the Good Parliament was not forgotten.

More deep-rooted discontents were surfacing in open defiance as government and people became more polarised. It was in this same year that the Statute Against Excesses of the Villeins noted the number of serfs withdrawing their service from their lords and affirming themselves to be 'quit and utterly discharged of all manner serfage'. The statute expressed anxiety at the corporate activity of such men and described them as assembling in large groups to agree 'that every one shall aid the other to resist their lords with strong hand'. The move towards collective action that was to culminate in the Rising of 1381 was already fermenting around the country. The government responded predictably with an attempt to clamp down severely on the serfs and to maintain the rights of lords. Peasants could be imprisoned without bail if their lords accused them, and the statute came down firmly in favour of upholding the status quo, 'the condition of their tenure and customs of old time due'.[30]

During 1377 Chaucer was again abroad several times on royal business, including negotiation of the terms of truce with France. Froissart makes his only reference to Chaucer in this year. 'Geoffrey Chaucer' is the last name to appear in the list of those to participate in 'discussions about a marriage between the young Richard, son of the Prince of Wales, and Princess Marie, the daughter of the King of France',[31] but the marriage never took place. The most momentous event of 1377, however, was, in Froissart's words, that

> the gallant and noble King Edward III departed this life, to the deep distress of the whole realm of England, for he had been a good king for them. His like had not been seen since the days of King Arthur.[32]

Walsingham's eulogy was even more fulsome:

> Without doubt this king had been among all the kings and princes of the world renowned, beneficent, merciful, and august. . . . Certainly his fame spread so far abroad amongst foreign and remote nations that they considered themselves fortunate who were either subject to his lordship or were partly allied with him. Indeed, they did not believe there could be any kingdom under the heavens which produced so noble, so high-minded, or so fortunate a king, or could in the future produce such another after his decease.[33]

The consequence of Edward's death after the death of his eldest son was that his grandson ascended the throne at the age of ten. No official regency was announced, and Richard was technically the reigning king from his accession, but in practice a council of magnates was dominated by John of Gaunt. The Earl of March, Edmund Mortimer, who was married to Lionel of Clarence's daughter, was as close to the throne as Gaunt, since Lionel had been Gaunt's elder brother, but Mortimer died in 1381. It was the descendants of these two men, however, the future members of the Houses of Lancaster and York, who were to fight the Wars of the Roses over these rival claims to the throne via the male and female lines respectively.

A lesser consequence of Edward's death, but one that must have directly affected Chaucer, was that ordinances were immediately passed for safeguarding the city of London against invasion from the French, who were already threatening the south coast. The city gates were locked and fortified, the keys were kept by two of the residents, and each inhabitant had to swear 'that he will be ready with his harness [armour] to maintain the peace if affray arise'.[34]

In 1378 Chaucer made another visit to Italy, to Lombardy this time, to discuss matters relating to the war with Bernabò Visconti, Lord of Milan, and Sir John Hawkwood, son-in-law to Visconti, a notorious Englishman in command of mercenaries. Chaucer also made Visconti the subject of a tragedy in the *Monk's Tale*, where he receives less favourable treatment than 'worthy Pedro' (see p. 7 above), and is described as 'scourge of Lumbardye' (VII.2400).[35]

1378 was also the year of the Great Schism. The schism in the Church, which resulted in two popes, was part of a political rather than a religious dispute. It was the consequence of an attempt to re-establish an Italian pope in Rome, following the removal of the papacy to Avignon, which had taken place in 1308. After an Italian pope, Urban VI, had been elected in Rome in 1378, the French, with the support of their king, Charles V, elected another pope (Clement VII) at Avignon. Political hostilities in Europe were then exacerbated by declarations of support for one pope or the other. England affirmed its loyalty to Urban VI, the Italian pope, while Scotland, already intermittently allied to France in mutual antagonism towards England, declared for Clement VII. Although the origins of the schism may have been political, its effects were not restricted to the political arena. The Church suffered badly from this evidence of its internal division, and the authority of the pope, now that he was only one of two, inevitably looked more provisional and commanded less respect.

During the period 1378–80, following Chaucer's visit to Italy, he was probably engaged in writing *The House of Fame*, an unfinished dream-vision. It is a poem that shows the influence of Italian writing on Chaucer as clearly as *The Book of the Duchess* shows the influence of French. Chaucer had certainly read Dante before writing this poem (see p. 9 above), which meditates on the value of fame, and can also be read as a kind of *ars poetica*, meditating on the craft of poetry itself.

On 1 May 1380 Chaucer was released by Cecilia Chaumpaigne from any legal action following her '*raptus*'. This is a case that has caused much disagreement among literary scholars, most of whom are unwilling to concede the meaning of 'rape' to the term '*raptus*' where Chaucer is concerned. Such critics argue that Chaucer may have been involved instead in the abduction of an heiress, and the case of Chaucer's own father, who was abducted by an aunt at the age of about thirteen, is cited in support. (The phrase '*rapuerunt et abduxerunt*' is used in the records concerning the latter abduction.) Lawyers, however, have judged the case more harshly than literary critics. P. R. Watts, comparing the use of the word '*raptus*' standing alone with its use in other fourteenth-century legal documents, argued that it certainly meant rape, and disposed of the ward-stealing theory by pointing to the fact that Cecilia herself, rather than a guardian, released Chaucer, thus ruling out the possibility that she was a ward.[36] The records also show that money changed hands, and Watts thought that the likeliest explanation for this was an out-of-court settlement between the two parties. T. F. Plucknett, in a note published the following year, broadly agreed with Watts's reading of the documents, but suggested seduction rather than violent rape on the basis that there is nothing in the records 'to suggest that Cecilia could have convicted Chaucer of felony'.[37]

Whatever the details were of Chaucer's involvement in the capture, rape or seduction of Cecilia Chaumpaigne, it is ironic to place alongside it *The Parliament of Fowls*, which Chaucer was probably writing somewhere between 1380 and 1382. This is another dream-poem and centres particularly on questions of love and courtship, showing the Italian influence again of Dante and Boccaccio. Chaucer here uses ideas from Macrobius, Boethius and Alain de Lille to explore the ideal relation between love and nature. The climax of the poem shows three young tercel (male) eagles vying for the hand of a formel (female) eagle singled out for Nature's favour. Nature asks the formel to make her choice and she asks to postpone the choice for a year. Nature accepts her unwillingness to take a mate for the time being, and advises all three tercels to serve her faithfully for the year that she asks. If Chaucer had been involved in a liaison with Cecilia Chaumpaigne, and had then been obliged to compensate her when she became pregnant, one might read a sardonic underpinning into Nature's recommendation that the tercels should serve faithfully, and postpone the fulfilment of desire.[38]

It is hard for us to imagine Chaucer reading such a poem to the court if he had been publicly accused of rape, yet it would seem that Edward III's brutal rape of the Countess of Salisbury did not stand in the way of Froissart's determination to depict it as a courtly *amour*. The French chronicler, Jean le Bel, after describing how all Edward's attempts to win the young Countess's consent to his desires failed, goes on to tell how he got up in the night, when all her ladies were asleep,

and told [his] valets that nothing must interfere with what he was going to do, on pain of death. So it was that he entered the lady's chamber, then shut the doors of the wardrobe so that her maids could not help her, then he took her and gagged her mouth so firmly that she could not cry out more than two or three times, and then he raped her so savagely that never was a woman so badly treated; and he left her lying there all battered about, bleeding from the nose and the mouth and elsewhere, which was for her great damage and great pity. Then he left the next day without saying a word, and returned to London, very disgusted with what he had done.[39]

In Froissart's version, all of this is omitted, and the king is portrayed as 'stricken to the heart with a sparkle of fine love that endured long after',[40] contemplating dishonour but not perpetrating it. In his later Amiens edition, Froissart attempts to remove responsibility further from Edward by suggesting that the Countess light-heartedly toyed with the king's affections.

In 1382 Richard married Anne of Bohemia, and Chaucer's *Parliament of Fowls* has sometimes been seen as alluding to the negotiations for that marriage which were taking place in 1380.

Whether a contemporary audience saw a topical reference to either the king or the poet we do not know. Later works are also intriguing when set alongside the Cecilia Chaumpaigne case. The *Wife of Bath's Tale* opens with a knight convicted of rape, and similarity has been noted between the wording of Cecilia's 'quit-claim' (or release) of Chaucer from the charges and Aurelius's release of Dorigen from her promise in the *Franklin's Tale* (V.1533-6).[41]

The following year, 1381, was a momentous one. This was the year of the English Rising, often referred to as the Peasants' Revolt, despite the involvement of artisans, clergy and even some rural gentry, as well as agricultural labourers. Discussion of the causes is more complex than space allows here, but one immediate trigger was the introduction of 'a hitherto unheard-of tax', as Walsingham described it,[42] namely the poll tax. Three poll taxes were levied in the space of four years. The first poll tax of one groat (4*d*.) a head in 1377 was unpopular, to say the least, and was instituted at a time of great tension following reprisals after the Good Parliament (see p. 10 above). The second poll tax of 1379 was graduated, but started again at 4*d*. for a ploughman. At the end of 1380, however, the graduated tax was abandoned in favour of a levy of 1*s*. per head, with only a few exceptions.[43] This sudden increased tax burden on the lowest income strata, coupled with the fact that the Statutes of Labour had repeatedly attempted to keep wages at the level they had been in 1348, despite rising prices, was bound to produce a strong sense of injustice among those most hard hit. Anger against this tax was also the more bitter because it was known that part of it was intended to finance John of Gaunt's wars in Spain in pursuit of his claim to the Spanish throne.[44] Many simply refused to pay.

The beginnings of the rebellion in May took place in Essex and Kent and were specifically directed against the tax collectors. By Wednesday 12 June two groups were converging on London, encamped in the fields outside the city. They were demanding the heads of John of Gaunt and other chief ministers, and had already made clear their intention to murder the archbishop of Canterbury. Clearly their grievances were directed against both Church and State. John Ball's famous sermon on the rhyme,

> Whan Adam dalf, and Eve span,
> W[h]o was thanne a gentilman?[45]

underlined the anger felt against the wealth and privilege of the upper classes. When the rebels stormed into the city of London their targets reflected this anger. They burned or destroyed the homes of both secular and clerical magnates, they attacked lawyers and lawyers' records, they opened prisons, and they burned down John of Gaunt's Savoy palace. One chronicler, Henry Knighton, makes the point that the rebels would not tolerate looting, since the avowed aims of the rebellion were idealistic:

> One of the criminals chose a fine piece of silver and hid it in his lap; when his fellows saw him carrying it, they threw him, together with his prize, into the fire, saying that they were lovers of truth and justice, not robbers and thieves.[46]

It is noteworthy that Knighton, himself an Augustinian canon, and hostile to the rebels' cause, feels the need to record this incident in their favour while simultaneously labelling them 'criminals' (*'nefandorum'*).

Richard II, a boy of fourteen at the time of the rebellion, was intent on a policy of conciliation and met both groups of men to hear their demands. The men of Essex petitioned for an end to serfdom, the right to work under free contract (that is, without the arbitrary attempts at wage restraint imposed by the Statute of Labourers since 1351) and the right to rent land at fourpence an acre. The Kentishmen demanded the same rights, together with more sweeping attempts to eradicate the class system: all men to be equal under the king, all bishoprics but one to be abolished and the wealth of the Church to be redistributed among lay people. Richard assured them that all their demands would be met, but angry words between Wat Tyler, one of the rebel leaders, and William Walworth, the mayor of London, resulted in Walworth losing control and striking Tyler, who was then killed by a squire standing by.[47]

Richard addressed the crowd directly and led them off. A government armed force later surrounded them, but Richard pardoned them all and urged them to return to their homes. Other parts of England were in revolt by this time but within days of the London events the government was taking preventive and punitive action. Like his treacherous uncle, John of Gaunt, Richard had agreed to radical demands in order to buy off danger. Once the men had dispersed, as did the members of the Good

Parliament in 1376, Richard revoked his promises and his pardons. Although historians are agreed that in the circumstances the reprisals were not severe, the rebels lost all those freedoms that briefly seemed to have been achieved. Richard's reported reply to a deputation asking him to keep his promises encapsulates the attitude of those in power to those without it:

> Serfs you were and serfs you are still; you will remain in bondage, not as before but incomparably harsher. For as long as we live and, by God's grace, rule over the realm, we will strive with mind, strength and goods to suppress you so that the rigour of your servitude will be an example to posterity.[48]

One of the greatest difficulties in reconstructing a true picture of the rising is the universal hostility of medieval chroniclers towards the rebels. Chroniclers and other writers, by definition literate, often monks, and unlikely to have risen from the lower classes, frequently describe the rebels as base or inhuman. The monk of Westminster who wrote the continuation of Higden's *Polychronicon* describes them as 'rabid dogs'.[49] Gower allegorises the peasants as different types of beast throughout Book I of his *Vox Clamantis*, explaining his intention thus in his headnote:

> In the beginning of this work, the author intends to describe how the lowly peasants violently revolted against the freemen and nobles of the realm. And since an event of this kind was as loathsome and horrible as a monster, he reports that in a dream he saw different throngs of the rabble transformed into different kinds of domestic animals. He says, moreover, that those domestic animals deviated from their true nature and took on the barbarousness of wild beasts.[50]

Even a poem that begins in open sympathy for the causes of the revolt:

> Tax hath tened us alle,
> probat hoc mors tot validorum;
> The kyng therof had smalle,
> fuit in manibus cupidorum.
> Hit hade ful harde honsalle [fortune],

dans causam fine dolorum.
Vengeaunce nede most falle,
propter peccata malorum.

goes on to call the rebels 'rybawdus' [robbers], 'fole' [fools] and
'churles' and to denounce them as 'an uvel covent' [wicked
group].[51]

And what of Chaucer in relation to the rebellion? A few details
emerge, but nothing may be said with certainty about how these
events affected him. He was living in the house over Aldgate
during the time when the Essex men were encamped at Mile End,
in the fields beyond Aldgate, and seems to have been in London at
the time.[52] They entered London through Aldgate during the night
of Wednesday 12 June, and a certain William Tonge was later
charged with opening the gate to allow the rebels entry. They
must also have poured out again through Aldgate to meet the king
at Mile End on the Friday morning, though it would seem likely
that anyone living in such a position would have fled the house
before the Friday.

Three of Chaucer's former associates at the customhouse were
knighted for their part in helping to put down the rising: William
Walworth, the mayor of London, and two fellow-Londoners, John
Philipot and Nicholas Brembre.[53] Chaucer's only direct reference
to the revolt occurs in the *Nun's Priest's Tale*, where he describes
the din of the fox being chased by every human being and animal
on the farm in this way:

> So hydous was the noyse – a, benedicitee! –
> Certes, he Jakke Straw and his meynee
> Ne made nevere shoutes half so shrille
> Whan that they wolden any Flemyng kille,
> As thilke day was maad upon the fox.
>
> (VII.3393–7)

It is not an indictment in the mode of Gower, but it can scarcely be
construed as sympathetic to the rebels' cause.

Chaucer probably did not write the *Nun's Priest's Tale*, however,
until well into the 1390s. During the 1380s he was writing *Troilus
and Criseyde*, an early version of the *Knight's Tale* and *The Legend of
Good Women*. *Troilus and Criseyde* and the *Knight's Tale* both show
Chaucer absorbed with Boccaccio and Boethius and concerned in

particular with questions concerning free will and the status of secular love in a Christian universe. *The Legend of Good Women*, another unfinished work, describes, as its title indicates, the lives of good women. Its prologue, written in the form of a dream poem, claims that the writing of such a work was undertaken in order to redress an injustice in Chaucer's treatment of women in some of his other works. It is interesting to note that despite the narrator's claim at the end of *Troilus and Criseyde* to be writing not 'al oonly for thise men,/But moost for wommen that bitraised be' (V.1779–80), it is this work, together with Chaucer's translation of *The Romaunt of the Rose*, which the god of Love names as demonstrating his 'heresye' (Prologue to *The Legend of Good Women*, G.256) against the law of love and an undue interest in 'shewynge how that wemen han don mis' (G.266).

During the 1380s, while Chaucer was engaged in writing these works, his name was associated with a group of Lollard knights. 'Lollard' was the name given to those influenced by the ideas of Wyclif (whose teachings were publicly condemned in 1382, two years before his death), though it was also used rather loosely as a term of abuse. Sir John Clanvowe and Sir William Nevill, who witnessed Cecilia Chaumpaigne's deed of release in 1380, and Lewis Clifford, who brought Chaucer Deschamps's poem in 1386, were named as Lollards by contemporary chronicles. These knights, together with several others, formed a close-knit group and were all attached to the court by the early 1380s.[54] K. B. McFarlane makes the point that these knights were not persecuted in any way for their Lollard sympathies and argues that 'the knights' views found more than an echo in many hearts'.[55] He views the knights' position as one of moral revolt against the practices of the contemporary Church, rather than one of theological heresy, and more recent critics have endorsed the view that many Wyclifite ideas were shared by fundamentally conservative writers who would not have seen their positions as dissident in any way.[56] Certainly this view could explain Chaucer's friendship with these men, and the absence of persecution.

In February 1385 Chaucer was given leave to appoint a permanent deputy at the customs office. Paul Strohm (and T. F. Tout before him) have argued that Chaucer's loss of his posts in customs were associated with the increased power of the anti-Ricardian faction in the years leading up to the Merciless Parliament in 1388, thus demonstrating a close link between

Chaucer's fortunes and the king's.[57] He may have already moved to live in Kent before then (though he did not give up the Aldgate lease until 1386) and was in October 1385 made a justice of the Kentish peace commission, a position he retained until July 1389. The French were threatening invasion in 1385 and had a huge force assembled in the Channel ports in 1386, when Chaucer was elected as one of two knights of the shire representing Kent in the House of Commons.[58] When Parliament was summoned on 1 October, rumours of invasion had been rife since May. Troops, still unpaid, who had been called up because of the French threat, were marauding round London and the south of England giving free rein to the old habit of pillage acquired from French wars to fill their time and their stomachs.[59]

This was an important parliament, later known to historians as the 'Wonderful Parliament'. As in the Good Parliament of 1376, feelings ran high about the king's favourites. Lords and Commons together demanded the dismissal of Michael de la Pole, Earl of Suffolk, and John Fordham, Bishop of Durham, from the offices of chancellor and treasurer respectively. Richard's fury as negotiations proceeded led him to threaten to seek help from the king of France against his rebellious people, but he was swiftly reminded of Edward II's fate in a speech made by his uncle, Thomas of Woodstock, the Duke of Gloucester. The implicit threat of deposition was enough to make Richard give way, and the chancellor and treasurer were duly dismissed. Deposition, when it finally came in 1399, was not a new challenge to Richard's authority.[60]

Chaucer's wife Philippa was admitted to the fraternity of Lincoln Cathedral in February 1386, alongside various members of the royal family. John of Gaunt was already a brother of the cathedral and King Richard and Queen Anne were made members in 1387 when they visited the cathedral. The last payment of Philippa Chaucer's annuity was recorded in 1387. She presumably died in that year, since Chaucer claimed only his own payment from November 1387, whereas before that date he normally collected both their payments at the same time. He may also have begun work on the earliest of the *Canterbury Tales* by this time, and it has been argued that the *Prioress's Tale* of St Hugh of Lincoln, the child martyr, was written for the occasion of the king's visit to the cathedral.

The following year, 1388, was a dangerous one for many in

court circles. The parliament called in February of this year is known as the Merciless Parliament. Five lords accused, or 'appealed', several of King Richard's favourites of treason, hence becoming known as the Lords Appellant. They were successful in bringing these favourites to execution, and K. B. McFarlane has argued that from this time on Richard was plotting his revenge against the five.[61] Gaunt's son, Henry of Derby, the future Henry IV, was one of them. Of those executed, one man, Nicholas Brembre, was known to Chaucer from his days at the customs office, and two more had served with Chaucer on the Kentish peace commission. Yet Chaucer as usual survived the political upheaval without mention. His only prominence in the records of this date is as the subject of two suits for debt.

In 1389 Richard II appointed Chaucer clerk of the king's works. This was a high-ranking office and Chaucer was one of only two laymen appointed to it during Richard's reign.[62] It made Chaucer directly responsible for carrying out the king's wishes as regards building and repair works to some of his most important properties, including the palace of Westminster, the Tower of London and later St George's Chapel, Windsor. The latter two underwent important repairs during Chaucer's term of office, and his expenditure on the Tower accounted for more than half his total expenditure as clerk of the works. It was a post that also brought him into contact with men like the master mason Henry Yeaveley, famous for his later alterations to Westminster Hall and his construction of Richard II's tomb in Westminster Abbey. As clerk of the works, Chaucer was also in control of the erection of the lists and seating scaffolds for the tournaments at Smithfield in May and October 1390, to which the king invited knights from abroad to participate. This was the most elaborate tournament of Chaucer's lifetime, and Froissart records it in great detail.[63]

In September of the same year Chaucer was attacked by outlaws and robbed. The robbers were convicted, but the records are unclear, and there may have been more than one robbery. Certainly other writers at this time complained about the dangers of the open road and the numbers of those living outside the law. There were several reasons for this. Serfs escaping from their masters were forced to live as outlaws; so too were free peasants infringing the Statute of Labourers. In addition, soldiers were returning home to find the effects of plague and economic pressures had reduced, and in some cases obliterated, their properties or tenancies. Hoccleve, writing some twenty years later, laments the poor treatment such veterans received:

> Now al forgete is the manly labour
> Thorgh whiche ful ofte they hire foos afferde;
> Now be tho worthi men bet with the yerde
> Of nede, allas! & non hath of hem routhe;
> Pyte, I trowe, is beried, by my trouthe.[64]

Chaucer left his appointment as clerk of the works in June 1391, possibly wounded after the robbery, and still with £87, a very large sum of money, owing to him. He then became deputy forester at the royal forest of North Petherton in Somerset, but it is not clear whether he lived in the forest during this period or not. From this time and until the end of his life, he presumably continued to work on the *Canterbury Tales*.

In 1394 Queen Anne died at the age of twenty-seven. Richard's grief was overwhelming, and he had part of Sheen Palace, where she had died, destroyed. In his distress he struck the Earl of Arundel for arriving late at her funeral. Her death left Richard childless and the succession uncertain.

Chaucer received in 1393 a gift of £10 from the king 'for good service' and in the following year an annuity of £20, suggesting that he continued to enjoy the king's favour. He seems to have managed to maintain good relations with John of Gaunt and his family alongside his service to the king during this period, since he received a gift of fur to trim a scarlet gown from Henry of Derby, during the period 1395–6. Henry, however, was banished in 1398, when Richard took his revenge on the appellants in the form of exile, imprisonment or execution. It was Richard's seizure of Henry's inheritance on the death of Henry's father, John of Gaunt, in 1399, which provoked his return to England and his deposition of Richard.

Chaucer seems to have survived unscathed through this reversal as through so many others. King Henry renewed his various grants from Richard and added another 40 marks annually (about £26). Chaucer's last known poem, the 'Complaint to his Purse', can be dated by its reference to Henry as 'verray king', and Chaucer conspicuously acknowledges both elements of Henry's claim to the throne, election and descent: Henry, he says, is king 'by lyne and free eleccion'.[65] Whether Chaucer was really convinced of the validity of Henry's claim or simply keeping on the right side of the reigning monarch we shall never know, though Chaucer's responses to changes in contemporary politics seem to have been consistently pragmatic. The very absence of explicit statement on such topics in his writing can also be read in this light. In literal terms, at least, his poetry does not engage with topical events or controversy. The implicit and understated nature of the links between his works and the times in which he lived is probably the direct result of his own position in public life, and he clearly took care to avoid being seen as extravagantly partisan either in his life or on the page. The consequences of explicit commitment to a single political line are clearly demonstrated by the executions of 1388.

In December 1399 Chaucer took a lease on a house in the precincts of Westminster Abbey. Records show payments to him continuing up to June 1400, and after that there are no records of him. He was buried in the Abbey, partly because he was one of its tenants, but perhaps also because it was becoming customary for the king's servants to be buried near him. Richard had had courtiers and friends buried in the chapels surrounding the high altar from 1395 onwards, and Chaucer's burial at the entrance to St Benedict's chapel may indicate public acknowledgement of the death of one of Richard's valued servants. Tradition reports the date of his death as 25 October 1400, but the inscription on his tomb is now illegible.

2
Literary Production and Audience

Possibly the single most important distinction between the conditions of production for writers before and after the late fifteenth century is the distinction between manuscript and print. In Chaucer's time all writing of any kind was copied in manuscript, and this had important consequences for the nature of the text as well as for the nature and expectations of the audience. Most obviously, the copying of manuscripts was slow and laborious and inevitably meant that the number of copies produced, compared with print runs, was small. On the other hand, the practice of reading aloud manuscript works to a group of people meant that the audience was certainly much wider than the number of manuscripts produced, so that it is impossible to establish with any certainty the size of audience for a given text.

Prior to the fourteenth century, most copying of manuscripts was done by monks. It is not surprising, therefore, to find a predominance of religious and didactic works written down in that period. The monastic scriptorium continued to be a central agent in the production of books during the fourteenth century, but at the same time a commercial interest was becoming evident in the emergence of lay scriptoria, or 'bookshops', as they are sometimes called. The term 'bookshop' is laden with modern preconceptions, a point that will be further explored in this chapter. In the meantime it should be understood as a commercial, lay centre for the compiling, copying and physical making of books, not as an outlet purely for the sale of books.

How early such secular centres of production came into being is a source of some dispute. Laura Hibbard Loomis claimed in 1942 that the Auchinleck manuscript, dated 1330–40, was the earliest evidence of such a mode of production.[1] Her view has been very influential, although A. I. Doyle has argued that the manuscript is too expensive to have been aimed at the general reading public and suggests the court of Edward III as a more probable context.[2] Whatever the origins of this particular manuscript, it is clear that commercial means of production had multiplied by the second half of the century. Whether or not there were physical centres for the production of books, there were certainly 'stationers' working in London during the fourteenth century, craftsmen who co-ordinated the different stages of production in the making of books.[3] As long ago as 1935, J. S. P. Tatlock argued that 'no one familiar with Chaucer manuscripts doubts that they were written mostly by professionals. The probability is also that most of them were written for and sold by bookdealers.'[4]

More recently, changing conditions in the fourteenth century have been described as amounting to a 'book revolution'. John Burrow has summarised the development of a quicker form of handwriting, the increasing use of paper instead of parchment and the introduction of the pecia system, whereby several scribes could make copies simultaneously from one manuscript. 'By the fourteenth century', he writes, 'commercial book-producers were achieving in their shops something as near to the mass-production of books as was possible before printing.'[5] Further evidence of an expanding book-trade is provided by the increasing need evidenced during the fourteenth century to distinguish between those scribes who copied books and those who copied legal documents, the scriveners, who broke off to form their own guild in 1373.[6]

One of the aspects of the word 'bookshop' that stands between us and an understanding of the medieval book trade is our ana-chronistic notion of it as a place already filled with books, from among which we expect to make our choice. This misconception is further fuelled by the frequency with which an illustration from British Library MS Cotton Tiberius A VIII has been reproduced or referred to as a picture of a medieval bookshop. If it were such an interesting piece of sociological evidence it would represent, as James Westfall Thompson admitted, 'the only known illustration of the interior of a medieval bookshop before the invention of printing'[7] and would lead us to imagine not only that books were displayed for sale on open stands, but that bookshop assist-ants were commonly female. The picture, however, illustrates an allegorical text, Lydgate's *Pilgrimage of the Life of Man*, and depicts the female personification Hagiograph, meaning, as Lydgate explains, Holy Scripture, showing her books to the Pilgrim (Mankind). There are no grounds for supposing that the illustrator would have drawn on contemporary commercial models to construct such an image. Although Hagiograph does sell things in the poem, they are not books, but allegorical mirrors, ointments, knives and combs. The illustration clearly aims to represent her allegorical meaning by surrounding her with the books of Holy Scripture, not by depicting her as a bookseller.

It is likely that in the fourteenth century, most, if not all, books were produced to order. The expansion of the book trade, then, presupposes an expansion of readership, and of the book-buying public. The fourteenth century is generally recognised as a period when the growth of literacy as well as the easier availability of books created a new audience drawn from the middle classes, and this new audience necessarily had some influence in its turn over the production of books, not only in terms of their quantity, but also in relation to their content. This expanded audience, however, was not standardised in its tastes to the extent that the book-buying public is now. Publishing, advertising, reviews and educational institutions nowadays conspire to produce the widespread acceptance of literary canons, but in the medieval period there was no literary establishment and no national press, so that reading habits necessarily remained local and disparate. One has only to compare the alliterative poetry predominating in the north and west of the country with the French-derived metres of Chaucer's poetry to see this stratification. This is not to suggest that people from one part of the country knew nothing of what was being written in another part. Chaucer clearly was aware of the existence of alliterative poetry, because he jokes about its regional nature. 'I am a Southren man', says his Parson in the *Canterbury Tales*, 'I kan nat geeste "rum, ram, ruf" by lettre' (X.42–3). It was not, however, fashionable to write in this style in Chaucer's literary milieu.

A medieval stationer would be unlikely to try to predict his customers' needs by producing ready-made books and then trying to sell them, when he could rely on the customers coming to him to order exactly what they did need. He might keep stocks of texts in very heavy demand, such as the primer (see p. 4 above), together with leaflets, or fascicles, of individual works or groups of works to be bound up later according to order, but generally the

finished products were left to the audience to dictate.[8] Perhaps
sometimes small fascicles were sold separately. This could explain
the very low valuation placed on books found in the stocks of two
bankrupt grocers in the 1390s to which Malcolm Parkes draws
attention in discussing the influence of new, cheap methods of
production on the nature of the fourteenth-century audience. As
Parkes writes, 'books were always a luxury in the Middle Ages,
but the production of cheaper books meant that they could
become a luxury for poorer people'.[9]

One of the most common types of book in Chaucer's time was
the anthology. This reflects the relative expense of books and the
fact that an individual might well possess only one book. In this
case he or she would want it to represent a kind of library in itself
of everything useful or interesting, from pure entertainment to
physical remedies or spiritual edification. Chaucer's reference to
his own (or his narrator's) possession of 'sixty bokes olde and
newe' (Prologue to *The Legend of Good Women*, G.273) is very
unusual for this period. The determining factor in compiling an
anthology was, as we have seen, individual taste, so that range is
likely to have been the principle of selection more often than unity
of theme or authorship. Manuscripts of the *Canterbury Tales* are
frequently bound with other miscellaneous poetry and prose, and
even in one manuscript with a prescription for toothache. Com-
pilations of this kind are too numerous to mention and include
many of the most famous manuscripts of the period.[10]

This broad range of interests persists from the early Middle
Ages to the fifteenth century. M. T. Clanchy offers Matthew Paris
in the twelfth century as an example of an individual capable of
vast range in his written works and suggests, as an introduction to
the variety of works bound together in the thirteenth century,
looking at Oschinsky's description of manuscripts containing
treatises on accountancy and estate management.[11] One of the
manuscripts she lists, for example, includes a treatise on hus-
bandry, a poem written to help the reader learn French, a moral
poem, an encyclopaedia called *L'image du monde* and various
proverbs.

Robert Thornton and John Paston are two of the most famous
fifteenth-century anthologisers. There are extant, for example, two
such miscellaneous collections put together by Robert Thornton, a
country gentleman, for his own use, and copied by him personally; and the Paston letters document the process by which John

Paston commissioned his scribe to copy out the different works to be included in his 'Grete Boke'.[12]

Sometimes a manuscript does seem to have a subject: the Vernon manuscript, for example, is a miscellany of religious works and is one of the few manuscripts to give itself a title, which is in itself suggestive of a specialist intention. At the head of the list of contents is written: 'Here bygynnen the tytles off the book that is cald in latyn tonge Salus [animae] and in englyhs [sic] tonge Sowlehele [the health of the soul]'.[13] There was also a move in the fifteenth century towards collecting the works of famous poets such as Chaucer or Gower. Medieval readers, however, clearly saw nothing peculiar in finding prayers, poetry, obscene stories and herbal treatments for minor ailments together in one book and were themselves influential in producing such diversity within one set of covers.

The dominance of individual taste and the absence of the paraphernalia by which a literary standard is created combined to produce a more flexible attitude towards literature than is possible in present-day conditions. Many of the questions readers ask now of the texts they read would not have made sense to a fourteenth-century reader. Terry Eagleton, for example, begins his book on literary theory with the question 'What is Literature?'[14] For a medieval reader, however, the type of communal value-judgement implied by the question would have seemed alien. The word 'literature' is first recorded in 1375, but not in its current sense of privileged writing. It meant simply an acquaintance with letters or books (close to the modern meaning of 'literacy'), and its modern meaning did not develop until the nineteenth century. It is symptomatic of the medieval alternatives that were employed in the absence of such a term ('book', 'making', 'enditing') that they suggest merely words on the page without any accompanying ideological assumptions about status.

Individual writers sometimes tried to imitate the comprehensiveness of the encyclopaedic volume in their own works. The *Canterbury Tales* itself might be seen as an example of such a work striving for range and diversity. The Ellesmere manuscript of the *Tales* has the following colophon: 'Here is ended the book of the tales of Canterbury compiled by Geoffrey Chaucer of whos soule Iesu Crist have mercy, Amen', suggesting that the scribe perceived the work as a compilation.[15] Although we noted earlier that the *Canterbury Tales* was frequently bound with all variety of other works, we should also note that it is often bound alone; but the range it offers within its framework makes it in some ways analogous to a miscellany. The proliferation of genres within the *Canterbury Tales*, as well as beyond it, illustrates a willingness to set morally improving works alongside comic bawdy and to allow the written word to teach and play alternately or even simultaneously. Such range similarly suggests an absence of any classification that might define certain subjects as literature and exclude others.

Alongside this propensity for anthologising and the relative disregard for the author it implies should be set scribal habits, with all that they imply. Copying by hand is clearly more open to error than modern typesetting, and it is sometimes evident that scribes were copying texts that they did not understand. In any case the scribe, unlike the machines of the modern printing business, was himself a reader of the text, and, as such, concerned with other readers. It was this concern which often led him to become a co-writer of the text. Richard de Bury, Bishop of Durham, in his *Philobiblon* [The Love of Books], complains about scribal interference in the transmission of manuscripts. Books themselves are the speakers in the following extract:

> Our purity of race is diminished every day, while new authors' names are imposed upon us by worthless compilers, translators, and transformers, and losing our ancient nobility, while we are reborn in successive generations, we become wholly degenerate. . . . Alas! how ye commit us to treacherous copyists to be written, how corruptly ye read us and kill us by medication, while ye supposed ye were correcting us with pious zeal.[16]

Here, however, an implicit ideology in the medieval approach to literary texts does become evident. While medieval readers may not have shared a definition of literature that would have excluded certain texts on grounds of content, they did approach texts differently according to a linguistic standard. Latin texts were usually revered as authorities, and copied without intentional alteration. Richard de Bury has Latin books in mind when he writes, and his complaint is directed against the accidental corruption of such texts. Works in English, however, were clearly perceived quite differently, almost as common property. Copyright laws did not exist before publishers, and anyone could copy a text for any purpose. A fourteenth-century scribe copying from an English exemplar was therefore quite likely to rate the conservation of the author's original text (if indeed that was what he was copying in the first place) lower than the necessity for correcting what he thought were errors or explaining to the audience what he thought the author really meant to say.

Chaucer seems poised between the medieval and the modern worlds in his attitude towards his own text. On the one hand he at least plays the game of recognising the reader's right to improve the text when he beseeches the reader of *Troilus and Criseyde* to amend as he thinks fit,

> And put it al in youre discrecioun
> To encresse or maken dymynucion
> Of my langage;
>
> (III.1334–6)

yet in a brief poem written directly to his scribe, rather than the general reader, he takes a very different line:

> Adam scriveyn, if ever it thee bifalle
> Boece or Troylus for to wryten newe,
> Under thy long lokkes thou must have the scalle [scaly condition of the scalp],
> But after my makyng thow write more trewe;
> So ofte adaye I mot thy werk renewe,
> It to correcte and eke to rubbe and scrape,
> And all is thorugh thy negligence and rape [haste].

The closest parallels to this concern for the purity of the text occur not in the work of other fourteenth-century English writers, but in the writings of Petrarch and Boccaccio or later English writers.[17]

Scribes were not alone in being untroubled by the reverence for the author's fixed text that preoccupies modern editors. Authors as well as scribes in the medieval period show a tendency to rewrite, which may suggest that they too were concerned with readers and perhaps rewrote in some cases in response to audience reception. The modern editor is faced with the problem of how to attribute any variant with certainty to either author or scribe. Langland's *Piers Plowman* is one extreme case. Until recently, there were thought to be three texts of the poem, A, B and C, indicating successive stages in Langland's revision of the poem. The extant manuscripts, however, and there are over fifty of them, do not divide neatly into exact copies of these three identified states, but sometimes represent gross variations. Some recent scholars have argued that one of these variations is a separate authorial version pre-dating the A-text: a Z-text. Existing variations between the manuscripts thus make it possible for a new argument of this kind still to be made, but at the same time highlight the difficulty of differentiating between scribal alteration and a change in authorial intention.[18]

The manuscript context of literary works thus demonstrates the relative importance of readers in determining both the shape and the text of medieval books, as compared with the importance of the author and the publisher in our own times. Medieval readers evidently valued content more highly than authorship, as the predominance of anonymity in the period confirms. The notion of assembling a collection around a particular author was still unborn in the fourteenth century and it was not until the fifteenth century that collections of Chaucer's works were assembled. Caxton printed *Troilus and Criseyde* without naming Chaucer as the author, and, though he noted in the prologue to the second edition of the *Canterbury Tales* that Chaucer had written many other works 'in ryme and prose', he did not think it of sufficient interest (or a sufficient selling point) to name them.[19] Some authors incorporated their signature into the work in enigmatic form. Langland and Usk are well known examples, and more recently a previously anonymous text has been attributed to one John Clerk on such an acrostic basis.[20] But the very fact that such secret signatures can remain hidden to readers for so long suggests that the signature was of more interest to writers than it was to readers.[21]

It might seem that there are parallels to be drawn between the privileging of the reader over the author in recent literary theory with the circumstances of anonymity in the medieval period. In a book on Chaucer, however, it has to be acknowledged that Chaucer's poetry marks the beginning of a very different attitude. Chaucer went to comparatively great lengths to remind the reader within one text of his authorship of others. His listing of some of his own works in the Prologue to *The Legend of Good Women*

(*G.*405–20), the Prologue to the *Man of Law's Tale* (II.57–76) and the Retractions to the *Canterbury Tales* are well known. As A. C. Spearing has pointed out, however,

> We, looking back on Chaucer . . . confront an acute paradox. He is the first English poet to exist as an 'author', the first to be known by name as the father of a body of work; and yet throughout his career he seems to be striving towards the culmination achieved in *The Canterbury Tales*, the relinquishment of his own fatherhood, the transformation of his work into a text.[22]

Spearing also notes the parallel with recent theoretical writing, specifically Barthes's description of the text as 'not a line of words releasing a single "theological" meaning (the "message" of the Author-God) but a multi-dimensional space in which a variety of writings, none of them original, blend and clash'.[23] This is a conception of the text more fully examined in chapter 4 below.

In striving to establish a canon of his writings, Chaucer can be seen struggling against the fourteenth-century context in which he finds himself. Medieval works in English did not usually have titles, and the titles by which we know them today have generally been conferred by modern editors. This absence of titles is yet another quality of medieval writing which echoes the 'unfixed' nature of both text and context. Literary works did not have a stable text, could be bound with any other kind of writing, were not usually attributed to a particular author and did not normally have names. Chaucer's references to his works therefore do not follow the same pattern on every occasion. He refers to the poem named by recent editors as *The Book of the Duchess* only once by that name himself, in the Retractions to the *Canterbury Tales* (X.1086). Elsewhere he calls it 'the Deth of Blaunche the Duchesse' (Prologue to *The Legend of Good Women*, *G.*406) or 'Ceys and Alcione' (Introduction to the *Man of Law's Tale*, II.57). If the work we now know as *Troilus and Criseyde* had been so named by Chaucer, critics might well have based on such a name theories concerning the need to balance the interests of these characters or to see it as the tragedy of two people. As it is, we have nothing beyond the work itself to direct us. Chaucer is flamboyantly inconsistent. He calls it 'Troilus' in the poem to Adam Scriveyn above, 'the book of Troilus' in his Retraction (X.1086) and

'Creseyde' in the Prologue to *The Legend of Good Women* (G.431). Context may well be an important factor in the naming, as this last example suggests, since in this poem it is a female speaker, Alceste, who is referring to the work, and does so to emphasise her view that Chaucer has 'mysseyde' (rhymed with 'Criseyde') in his writings about women.

Context was not, of course, confined to the work itself, or its manuscript setting, but very often extended to its public performance, and hence its audience, since many works, both secular and religious, were orally performed. Chaucer's (or any other reader's) reading aloud of *The Legend of Good Women* might well proceed very differently according to whether there were actually women present at a given reading.[24] The context of performance was necessarily a highly fluid variable in the audience's interpretation of a text. Perhaps the image first conjured up to modern readers is that depicted in the famous illustration to the Corpus Christi Troilus manuscript, where a performer (not necessarily Chaucer, or even a poet, though both are commonly stated to be the case, and not a reader either, since there is no visible book in front of him) recites to an assembly of lords and ladies of the royal court. Froissart tells, however, of the pleasures of reading aloud in a more intimate context to please the Count of Foix:

> every night after suppper I used to read . . . to him. While I was reading no one presumed to speak a word, for he insisted that I should be heard distinctly, and not least by himself. When I reached some point which he wanted to discuss, he was always eager to talk it over with me.[25]

There is also a further, and very important, context for reading aloud: that of illiteracy. Margery Kempe, writing in the fifteenth century, describes how her confessor read to her from the *Life of St Bridget* to help her come to terms with her own visionary experiences. Her own book is dictated to an amanuensis, because she herself can neither read nor write. The extent of literacy in the fourteenth century has obvious bearing on the nature of the audience, and certainly a proportion of the audience for literary texts may have been illiterate in some sense.[26] The question of literacy necessarily overlaps with that of language and both must be examined in some detail in order to understand the potential range of a fourteenth-century audience.

Literacy is not a clear concept either in medieval usage or in the work of present-day writers on the medieval period. It can be understood in various ways, and even in modern everyday use there can be ambiguity as to whether it implies the ability to read only, or also to write. This is further complicated in the medieval period by the fact that the Latin word *litteratus*, or its English equivalent 'lettered', frequently referred only to competence in Latin, and would have excluded anyone able to read or write in a vernacular language.

Prior to the fourteenth century literacy was easily equated with the ability to read Latin. The literate class was then composed primarily of the clergy (the numbers of the aristocracy remaining comparatively small). So closely was literacy associated with clerical status that a man could prove his entitlement to be tried in the ecclesiastical (and more lenient) court by reading a piece of Latin, and thereby escape hanging. The beginning of the fiftieth psalm[27] was so commonly used as the test that it came to be known as the 'neck verse'. Ben Jonson claimed benefit of clergy in 1598 to escape the death penalty, and the privilege was not officially abolished until 1827.[28]

A 'clerk' (or in Latin *clericus*) in medieval usage could mean either an educated man or a man in holy orders. Michael Clanchy, discussing the overlap between the words *clericus* and *litteratus*, notes that though there is evidence conflicting with 'the medieval axiom that laymen are illiterate and its converse that clergy are literate', medieval terminology 'preserved intact the appearances of these fundamental axioms while acknowledging the realities of daily experience, where some clergy were ignorant and some knights knew more of books than brave deeds'.[29] Clerics themselves, naturally enough, were often keen to preserve the impression that literacy was too difficult for the laity to master, as Richard de Bury's sneering dismissal suggests: 'the laity', who, in his view, 'look at a book turned upside down just as if it were open in the right way, are utterly unworthy of any communion with books'.[30]

It is clear, however, that there was an expansion in education during the fourteenth century. Grammar schools multiplied and some of these provided education free of charge. Small elementary schools, such as might be run on a charitable basis by the parish priest for local children, provided the necessary grounding to enable children to progress to a grammar school. The grammar from which the schools took their name was Latin grammar, as noted on p. 4 above, though the language of instruction changed to English around the mid-century. Teaching at the universities, however, was conducted in Latin.

During the fourteenth century, due to the combination of increased literacy and cheaper books already outlined in this chapter, there is evidence that more people possessed books than ever before. A man of Chaucer's class would not have possessed sixty books at any time before the fourteenth century, and the bankrupt grocers (p. 28 above) would have been unlikely to own any at all. Although an increasingly wide range of the population was attaining some degree of literacy during the fourteenth century, the majority of books owned, according to contemporary records, were still in Latin and devotional in content. After Latin, French books would seem to have been most frequently owned, with books in English coming a poor third.[31] It needs to be emphasised, however, that many of the records are themselves monastic, and thus list a particular class of book owners who would be naturally predisposed towards Latin devotional works. If individual monks did possess secular or vernacular works, they would be unlikely to have listed them among the official holdings of the monastery. Noblemen, who would be more likely to have owned English books, may not have thought them important enough to record.[32]

Latin had been for centuries the language of education and international scholarship, the language of the Bible, the clergy and the universities, and it remained throughout the Middle Ages the expected form of the written word. French had become the spoken language of the court after 1066 and remained the prestige vernacular in England until the end of the fourteenth century. Writers did not choose either vernacular without particular reason, and the commonest reason was the wish to reach a non-Latinate audience. Many French texts are translations from Latin, and English texts are quite often in turn translations from the French, suggesting the acknowledged hierarchy of this trio of languages in England (see further pp. 71–4 below).

The language used in written texts addressed to nuns clarifies the changing status of Latin, French and English in England. As Eileen Power has pointed out, 'their learning was similar to that of contemporary laymen of their class, rather than of contemporary monks',[33] so that fluctuations in their linguistic competence may provide a guide to the abilities of the lay aristocracy. Whereas the male clergy continued to read and write in Latin, women, who did not have equal access to education, and were debarred from the grammar schools and the universities, were unlikely to know Latin by the fourteenth century. By the end of the thirteenth century bishops were writing to their nuns in French, and by the fifteenth century in English. Nuns, then, needed devotional reading matter in one of the vernacular languages. Richard Rolle and Walter Hilton, for example, writing in the fourteenth century, both chose English as the language in which to compose their treatises for anchoresses who had been nuns.[34]

Up to about the middle of the fourteenth century it would seem that many of the male literate population were familiar with the three languages used in England. The number of surviving macaronic lyrics that combine two or three of them suggest this, and Elizabeth Salter has drawn attention to the number of verse miscellanies of the late thirteenth and early fourteenth centuries that 'mingle French and English pieces indiscriminately'.[35] But Langland, writing in the late fourteenth century and likely to have been educated himself in the first half of the century, is scornful of 'this newe clerkes' who cannot read a letter in any language but Latin or English.[36]

The decline of French was probably hastened by a growing hostility towards France and things French in the wake of the Hundred Years War, begun in 1337. The Chancellor's opening speech in the parliament of 1377 formulated hostilities partly in a linguistic context, expressing fear that the French and other enemies were trying to 'destroy our lord the king and his realm of England, and drive out the English language'.[37] This motif had already figured in Edward III's speech to the commons, and was to surface again in the parliament of 1388. Elizabeth Salter argues for a growth of nationalism during the fourteenth century, citing prefaces that assert pride in England and English. The Auchinleck manuscript, she argues, produced between 1330 and 1340, is 'the first large collection of medieval verse to show a solid preference for English over French'.[38] Derek Pearsall, in his introduction to the facsimile of Auchinleck, argues similarly that it 'marks the first significant emergence of a new class of readers'.[39]

Turning to the spoken language, it needs to be made clear from the outset that there can have been no one in England, apart from recent immigrants (from Flanders, for example), who did not know English in this period. However well an educated man might read or converse in Latin or French, English was the mother tongue, and probably more familiar than any other, at least to children of any class. Trevisa's much quoted comment is crucial. He translates Higden's statement from *c.*1342 that

> chyldern in scole, agenes the usage and manere of al other nacions, buth [are] compelled for to leve here oune longage, and for to construe here lessons and here thinges a Freynsch, and habbeth suththe the Normans come furst into Engelond. Also gentil men children buth ytaught for to speke Freynsh fram tyme that a [they] buth yrokked in here cradel, and conneth speke and playe with a child hys brouch [child's trinket]; and oplondysch men wol lykne hamsylf to gentil men, and fondeth [try] with gret bysynes for to speke Freynsch, for to be more ytold of.

Even in Higden's time, then, English is perceived as 'here oune longage' and French as a language that needs to be taught. Trevisa adds his own remarks about the changed conditions in 1385, at the time of writing:

> Thys manere was moche y-used tofore the furst moreyn [Black Death of 1349] and ys seththe [since] somdel ychaunged . . . in al the gramerscoles of Engelond childern leveth Frensch, and construeth and lurneth an Englysch, and habbeth therby avauntage in on side and desavauntage yn another. Here avauntage ys that a lurneth here gramer yn lasse tyme than childern wer ywoned [accustomed] to do. Disavauntage ys that now childern of gramerscole conneth no more Frensch than can here lift heele, and that ys harm for ham and a scholle [if they should] passe the se and travayle in strange londes, and in many caas also [many other circumstances]. Also gentil men habbeth now moche yleft for to teche here childern Frensch.[40]

Trevisa connects the change in passing with the Black Death, and it is clear that the numbers dying of plague during the fourteenth century must have had a considerable impact on the numbers and quality of remaining teachers at any level. If literacy nevertheless increased, at least in proportion to the total population, it would seem that the promoting of English over French made literacy accessible over a wider range of society.

It has, however, been common for scholars to assume that French was still the natural spoken language of the court. Janet Coleman, for example, states that the language of Richard's court was French, even though on the same page she quotes Henry of Lancaster apologising for too little acquaintance with the French language in his *Livre de Seyntz Medicines*, in 1354, a generation earlier, and adds in a footnote the lines from *Arthour and Merlin* referring to noblemen who know no French.[41] It is imperative to make the distinction here between the written and spoken language, and Henry's apology surely must suggest that the language in which he chooses to write a serious treatise is not the one he is most familiar with. Froissart's well-known remark that King Richard himself spoke and wrote French very well[42] suggests similarly that this was not the language that came first to his tongue. When Henry IV made his claim to the English throne in 1399 he did so in English, which is hard to explain if he is assumed to have been speaking French as a member of Richard's court up to 1398.

It is probable that English was the more natural spoken language in courtly circles even before Richard's reign. Richard's father, the Black Prince, is said to have spoken English with the English knights and French with the French knights in his court at Bordeaux. Richard's grandfather, Edward III, had the English motto 'it is as it is' embroidered on his bed of state in 1342, and adopted English mottos at festivities in 1358 and 1360.[43] It has even been argued that English was the more natural spoken language of the aristocracy as early as the twelfth century, though this is harder to prove and inherently less likely.[44]

It is important to take account too of the extent to which language was a political arena in late fourteenth-century England. The dominance of Latin over the written word had for centuries underlined the gap between those with access to knowledge and power and those under their authority. Latin had been the language of both Church and State, as well as of intellectual debate, and formed an effective barrier to exclude the unlearned. It was in the 1380s that the need to have the Bible in English became a focus of popular concern, and not merely a topic for academic debate. Wyclif, himself an academic and master of

Balliol College, Oxford, understood that the unwillingness of the established Church to make the Bible available in English was based on a resistance to the idea that ordinary people should be at liberty to interpret the truth of the 'bare text' of Scripture. Partial translations into English and a complete Anglo-Norman Bible already existed, but only in the hands of nuns and noble families. Wyclif referred to this existing class distinction in his plea for an English translation:

> the worthy reume of Fraunse, notwithstondinge alle lettingis [obstacles], hath translatid the Bible and the Gospels, with othere trewe sentensis of doctours, out of Lateyn into Freynsh. Why shulden not Engliyschemen do so? As lordis of Englond han the Bible in Freynsch, so it were not agenus resoun that they hadden the same sentense in Engliysch; for thus Goddis lawe wolde be betere knowun, and more trowid.[45]

Queen Anne was reputed to have owned a partial English translation, a copy of the 'al the foure Gospeleris with the doctoris upon hem', but the story that Archbishop Arundel (a notable persecutor of Wyclifites) had inspected these and found them to be 'good and trewe' is told in a vernacular defence of Bible translation and may well be distorted by partisan motives.[46]

Both the writers quoted above refer to the 'doctors', that is, the standard glosses or interpretations of the biblical text built up by the Church over hundreds of years. If the inaccessibility of the Bible in English gave the clergy power to relay its content to lay people as they saw fit, then the glosses maintained a unity of interpretation among individual preachers. Wyclif and his followers wanted access to the actual words of Scripture for all (the phrases 'bare text' or 'pleyn text' recur in Wyclifite texts), but the established Church foresaw a challenge to its authority in the opening up of dispute over meaning. As one writer put it, 'Holy writ in Englische wole make cristen men at debate, and sugettis to rebelle ageyns her sovereyns.'[47] The real crux of the dispute was not so much translation itself as who gained access to the Bible through such vernacular translation.

To write in English at this time, therefore, especially on theological topics, could be seen as a political statement. Robbins overstates the case when he writes that 'to break away from Latin or French and use English was a major act of rebellion',[48] because he ignores the importance of context. In the context of Bible translation, as has been shown, it undoubtedly expressed dissent, and there was from the earlier fourteenth century an established tradition of satire and complaint in English.[49] But the vernacular generally in the fourteenth century, even in religious manuscripts, was increasing in respectability, and this overall context cannot be ignored. Where Chaucer is concerned, to argue that his choice of English should be seen as 'a major act of rebellion' would be to place him in a radical tradition to which he does not belong. This is not to say that his poetry never enters into the political arena, as later chapters will make clear, but his choice of English for all his works cannot be seen as primarily propagandist or subversive. He addresses the relatively leisured and educated audience that until recently had expected to find its entertainment and instruction in French and Latin texts, and his choice must be seen as reflecting the increasing status and authority of the English language in his lifetime. After all, English could only become a weapon genuinely threatening to political and ecclesiastical authority after it had gained some degree of authority itself.

English in Chaucer's lifetime was at a point of transition between oral and written cultures. Chaucer's poetry is full of references both to a live audience and to a solitary reader. He often begins by talking about books he has been reading, usually Latin books, 'authorities'; but he also regularly ends with a direct or implicit question, leaving the reader to interpret the relevance of the authorities cited, or the audience to debate the answer to the question. The framework he devised for the *Canterbury Tales*, which wrote an audience into the text, allowed questions of performance context and audience response to become an explicit concern of the written word.[50] It seems appropriate to end this chapter, which has examined the potential range and expectations of a medieval audience, by considering the specific nature of Chaucer's immediate audience.[51]

The most explicit indicators within his poetry are those dedications and envoys naming individuals to whom the work is addressed. Chaucer's short poems in particular abound in such envoys, which broadly point to three, sometimes overlapping, categories of audience: royalty; knights and esquires attached to the court; and fellow-poets.

Envoys to the poems 'Fortune' and 'The Complaint of Venus'

address themselves to 'princes' in the plural.[52] 'Lak of Sted-
fastnesse' addresses an unnamed prince, but two manuscripts link
it with Richard II in different ways;[53] and there can be no doubt
that 'The Complaint of Chaucer to his Purse' makes clear reference
to Henry IV (see p. 23 above). Compliments to Queen Anne can be
discerned in *Troilus and Criseyde*, when Criseyde's beauty is
affirmed 'Right as oure firste lettre is now an A' (I.171), and in the
earlier of the two prologues to the *Legend of Good Women*, where
the god of love commands the writer:

> And whan this book ys maad, yive it the quene,
> On my byhalf, at Eltham or at Sheene.
>
> (F.496–7)

The fact that this reference is omitted in the later version makes it
likely that the compliment was personally directed to Queen
Anne, and removed following her death in 1392.

Chaucer adopts an easier, more intimate tone in the poems he
addresses to members of the court circle such as Vache, Scogan
and Bukton. He uses the familiar second-person pronoun, 'thou',
to Sir Philip de la Vache, a knight of the chamber, in the 'Balade de
Bon Conseyl' (usually entitled 'Truth'). Scogan and Bukton,[54]
knights or esquires in positions of royal service similar to
Chaucer's own are teased as equals, Scogan for the 'blasphemy' of
giving up his lady because she ignored him and Bukton because
he is considering taking a wife. In 'Lenvoy de Chaucer a Scogan'
Chaucer playfully imagines the vengeance of love falling on 'alle
hem that ben hoor and rounde of shap' [grey and stout], like
Scogan and himself, and pictures Scogan answering his poem with
similar banter: 'Lo, olde Grisel [Greybeard?] lyst to ryme and
playe!' The tone of the envoy to Bukton is similar, as Chaucer
advises Bukton to read 'the Wyf of Bathe' before he ties himself to
a wife.

This second group of those in royal service, however, can be
subdivided, as Paul Strohm has pointed out, into gentlemen who
were also clerks and clerks who were barely gentlemen at all.
Those directly addressed in the poems fall into the upper echelon
of this class, but we can also identify individual members of the
lower tier who were among Chaucer's audience. Usk and Hoccleve, for example, both employed as clerks, tell us through their
own poetry of their acquaintance with Chaucer's work. Chaucer's

audience in his own lifetime can thus be seen extending in a radius outwards from the court, with the king at the centre and clerks employed in the medieval equivalent of the civil service on the perimeter.

The fellow poets whom Chaucer invokes do nothing to disturb or expand this description. Gower and Strode, to whom Chaucer dedicates *Troilus and Criseyde* (p. 93 below), and Oton de Graunson (alluded to in 'The Complaint of Venus') fall safely within the circle outlined above. Implicit clues to audience, such as the punning allusions to John of Gaunt linking him with the *Book of the Duchess*, or the Corpus manuscript illumination (see p. 34 above)[55] also confirm a court environment within which the poetic tone ranges from respectful tact towards superiors to playful familiarity with social equals and near-equals.

The main point of Paul Strohm's argument in his study of Chaucer's fifteenth-century audience, however, is that this immediate circle was almost completely dispersed by 1400. Those who read Chaucer's poetry in the decades immediately following his death 'were at once more widely distributed geographically and more disparate socially than Chaucer's primary audience, and more narrow in their taste for particular facets of Chaucer's poetic achievement'.[56] The changing nature and responses of Chaucer's audience after his death will be the subject of further discussion in chapter 7. Chapters in between will necessarily return to the question of audience many times, if only because Chaucer's writing is so unusually self-conscious about it, conceptualising it both as immediate and historical. Even as he writes, he invites his immediate audience to rewrite for him and anticipates the 'miswriting' and 'mismetring' of future audiences (*Troilus and Criseyde*, v.1793–6).

3

Four Estates

The commonest way of describing the structure of society in medieval literature was to divide it into three 'estates' or social groupings: those who prayed, those who fought and those who laboured. In the words of the Dominican preacher John Bromyard:

> God has ordained three classes of men, namely labourers such as husbandmen and craftsmen to support the whole body of the Church after the manner of feet, knights to defend it in the fashion of hands, clergy to rule and lead it after the manner of eyes. And all the aforesaid who maintain their own status are of the family of God.[1]

Women, if a writer deigned to consider them at all, were grouped by themselves as a fourth estate, determined by gender rather than social status, and usually positioned last in any list.[2] Writers, themselves most commonly male and members of the clergy, like Bromyard, treated this structure as though it were a God-given necessity, a moral dictum rather than a sociological observation. Chaucer's Parson, despite the fact that he is part of a work that elsewhere questions this approach, agrees with Bromyard: 'God ordeyned that som folk sholde be moore heigh in estaat and in degree, and som folk moore lough, and that everich sholde be served in his estaat and in his degree' (X.770). Sovereignty, according to the Parson, was ordained to force human beings to follow this command, since without degree 'the commune profit myghte nat han be kept, ne pees and rest in erthe' (772).

Keeping to your estate, which was obviously politically convenient, was presented as 'right' in all senses of the word. Bishop Brinton, preaching on the text 'Rich and poor, alike in one' (Psalms 49.2), argued that 'equality' between the classes must be shown in their behaviour: 'rich and poor ought to be alike as one, that is in supporting each other and in praying each for his neighbour'. The 'ought' underlines the moral imperative. Both rich and poor are necessary, he continues,

> For if all were poor, no one would be able to support another. If all were rich, no one would labor, and thus the world would collapse. Thus the rich exist on account of the poor and the poor on account of the rich. The rich must offer alms, and the poor must pray.[3]

The only consolation for the poor is that they have no riches to stand between them and the kingdom of God, and patient endurance of poverty prepares their souls for salvation.

The history of the fourteenth century shows that the lower classes did not willingly accept the social status framed for them as a moral paradigm by so many written authorities. Sumptuary laws from 1363 onwards strove to fix hierarchical theory in practice by regulating people's dress according to their estate, although it is clear that social class was in fact far more volatile than the lawmakers were willing to accept.[4] Similarly the labour statutes of late fourteenth-century government underline the fact that, while some of the rich may have given alms to the poor for the sake of their own souls, their corporate interest was to be seen in legislation that attempted to freeze income levels for the labouring classes and in increasingly heavy taxation, particularly via the new poll taxes, which targetted lower sections of the population than ever before, taxing even those with little or no property. The demands of the 1381 Rising for a redistribution of wealth, fair rents and fair wages, and an end to all lordship beneath that of the king make it clear that there were those who realised that their estate was not God-given, but politically maintained.

Predictably, a gap between ideals and practical realities was visible at all levels of society. It is perhaps most glaring in relation to the labouring estate, since the notion that peasants should be content to labour for the profit of their betters is inherently implausible, but clearly the estate of knighthood also fell short of the chivalric ideal in practice. In reality knighthood presented a financial and administrative burden particularly oppressive in time of war. A knight was responsible for providing and maintaining his own equipment, and prolonged military service could bankrupt a knight with relatively little land or power to his name.

This situation is highlighted by Edward III's provision of a home for poor knights in 1353.[5] Edward did not hesitate nevertheless to try to force the rising middle classes to take up knighthood, and seven orders for 'distraint of knighthood' were issued during his reign.[6] These attempted to compel those with landed income of £40 a year or more to become knights, imposing fines on those who refused. The low esteem in which such forced knights were held is revealed by the *Gest of Robyn Hode*, when Robin taunts a knight with this ignoble background:

> 'I trowe thou warte made a knyght of force,
>   Or ellys of yemanry',

and he replies indignantly, that he is 'none of those':

> 'An hundred wynter here before
>   Myn auncetres knyghtes have be.'[7]

Gradually, during the latter part of the fourteenth century, orders for distraint of knighthood seem to have evolved into a method of raising income, rather than a real attempt to create new knights. Richard II showed his anger with the citizens of London, who in 1392 refused to pay such fines, by suspending the city's liberties.[8] The chivalric ideal portrayed in contemporary literature must be read against the background of such sordid political realities.

Even this brief look at the historical background underlines the point that the estates cannot be described, as fourteenth-century estates theory seems to suggest, as isolated units. They are revealed in their interaction. Looking at Chaucer's approach to the estates via their interaction is, however, harder than it might seem, partly since many of his texts tend to isolate classes in the traditional way, and partly also since peasants are as a group very underrepresented in his writing. For the purposes of this chapter I propose to consider the estates in two groups of two. The two sections that follow will discuss knights together with peasants and women together with the clergy. Although Chaucer does not write much explicitly about the interaction of knights and peasants, they define each other in unspoken ideology, linked by the history of their feudal relations and their interdependent financial status. The pairing of women with the clergy is grounded upon the same ideological interdependence: just as it is the male clergy by whose 'authority' the dominant literary tradition of anti-feminism is constructed, so do women, as the objects excluded by clerical vows of celibacy, help to shape the definition of the clergy.

A different strategy will operate in each section of this chapter, so that the discussion of knights and peasants will range over a number of texts, whereas the consideration of women and the clergy will be focused on one text, in which relations between the two are fully and consciously explored by Chaucer.

KNIGHTS AND PEASANTS

Since Chaucer's portrayal of the peasantry is so limited in scope, it may be as well to begin by raising the question of why that should be. It is notable, first of all, that only *The Parliament of Fowls* and the *Canterbury Tales* among his works mention the lower classes at all. In *The Parliament of Fowls* it is questionable whether the range of social classes represented by the birds really includes the labouring classes. If the birds' parliament were closely modelled on a fourteenth-century parliament, then no lower classes would be present, since the House of Commons was composed of middle-class gentry and upwards. If, however, we think of the parliament as simply a metaphor for a gathering of all the birds, which Chaucer after all says it is (ll. 310–11), then the seed-fowl are ranked lowest (ll. 328, 512), and may represent the peasantry.[9] The turtle-dove, as representative of this class, speaks only once, and then only to pronounce the folly of giving an opinion unasked on a subject one knows nothing about. The voice of the establishment is here clearly usurping the space apparently allocated to the lowest class, and the implications of what is said for the role of the lower classes in the process of government are self-evident: leave it to those who *really* know.

Turning to the *General Prologue* to the *Canterbury Tales,* it becomes clearer that there is a problem in defining the peasant class. Should all who labour be described as peasants, even though they may be wealthy and free, or should the term be used specifically of those who work the land, perhaps even only those who are tied to the manor by the remnants of the feudal system? The Ploughman is the only figure who could be called a peasant in relation to the second category, and Chaucer does not tell us whether he is free or unfree.[10] The description of the Ploughman typifies the conservative ideal constructed for the peasant by his social superiors:

> A trewe swynkere and a good was he,
> Lyvynge in pees and parfit charitee.
> God loved he best with al his hoole herte
> At alle tymes, thogh him gamed or smerte,
> And thanne his neighebor right as hymselve.
> He wolde thresshe, and therto dyke and delve,
> For Cristes sake, for every povre wight,
> Withouten hire, if it lay in his myght.
> His tithes payde he ful faire and wel,
> Bothe of his propre swynk and his catel.
>
> (*GP*, 531–40)

Not only is he true to his estate and content to labour, but he is even content to labour for no wages. Langland's *Piers Plowman* presents the same idealised and conservative view of the ploughman's role in society, but, as Jill Mann has argued, Langland and other estates writers include description of the peasant's suffering, which Chaucer omits. The most important feature of Chaucer's Ploughman, she argues, is that he is the Parson's brother, and both these figures are isolated from the other pilgrims, existing in a separate and idealised sphere not grounded upon the observed workings of society.[11]

There is no other representative of the rural peasantry in the *General Prologue* at the level of the Ploughman, and apparently no member of the villein class at all. This is perhaps because the unfree peasant was becoming increasingly anomalous in Chaucer's time and in his particular part of the country. Studies of the 1381 Rising have made clear that those southern and eastern counties where the rebellion was most active were exactly those where the disintegration of the feudal system had progressed furthest (see p. 3 above), and in cities it did not exist at all. Villeins were deemed to be free after residence in a chartered town for a year and a day. Lee Patterson, however, has rightly warned against idealising medieval towns as islands of democracy in a feudal sea, pointing out that the dominance of a mercantile 'patriciate' in the city paralleled the feudal power structures in rural areas.[12] The dominant group in the *General Prologue* is the 'middle' class, stretching from the yeoman, the miller and the cook to the wealthy doctor, the lawyer and the franklin (a landowner, but not one of the aristocracy); and the dominance of this group in Chaucer's text mirrors Chaucer's own urban environment and the economic expansion of the middle class within it which characterised the fourteenth century. The differences between the social structures of town and country thus help to account for Chaucer's relative lack of interest in the rural, feudal peasantry.

Lee Patterson has also discussed the question of whether millers, for example, are or are not peasants. While he admits that millers, 'since they are neither tenants of land nor tillers of soil . . . cannot technically be considered peasants', he nevertheless argues that it is important to see the Miller as representative 'not of the bourgeois mercantile world of the cash nexus but rather of the aggressive rural economy'.[13] Patterson's discussion of the status of millers, including their participation in the Peasants' Revolt, seems, however, to work against the rigidity of his own distinction between the bourgeois and rural worlds, and to uncover instead the parallels between artisans and labourers in both city and country, subjected equally to the control of a more powerful class. It could be argued that the definition of 'peasantry' should be expanded to include the lower end of the 'middle class' of Chaucer's *General Prologue*, since the emergence from specifically feudal bonds did not bring with it an escape from economic subjection or exploitation.

Chaucer's few peasants, according to the narrower rural definition, are sparsely and stereotypically represented. They are enshrouded in that same aura of idealism that enshrouds the Ploughman, to the point of becoming allegorical types. Chaucer is interested in their symbolic potential, not in their inner lives. The poor widow who keeps the cock Chauntecleer and a few hens in the *Nun's Priest's Tale*, for example, is ideally patient, her simple life contrasting emblematically with Chauntecleer's vain posturing, and probably, given the tale's many parallels with the Fall of Man, intended to stir echoes of the voluntary poverty embraced by Christ and the apostles.

The epithet 'patient' is inseparable from the character of Griselda, the peasant girl in the *Clerk's Tale*, and the allegory informing that tale is made explicit in the Clerk's closing words. Here Griselda is offered as a type of patient mankind obediently

suffering all the trials God may impose. The extremity of Griselda's poverty, together with the biblical allusions in Chaucer's
description of her, help to point the reader in the direction of an
emblematic rather than a sociological reading of her. She is 'born
and fed in rudenesse, / As in a cote or in an oxe-stalle' (IV.397–8),
and when she is made to return to her humble origins the echo is
of Job, 1.21:

> 'Naked out of my fadres hous,' quod she,
> 'I cam, and naked moot I turne agayn.'
> (871–2)

The tale is not allegorical either in the version of Petrarch,
Chaucer's acknowledged source, or that of Boccaccio, Petrarch's
source, both of which are critical of Walter. Petrarch's letter to
Boccaccio, however, provided Chaucer with the cue to allegorise
the tale, since Petrarch states:

> My object in thus rewriting your tale was not to induce the
> women of our time to imitate the patience of this wife, which
> seems to me almost beyond imitation, but to lead my readers to
> emulate the example of feminine constancy, and to submit
> themselves to God with the same courage as did this woman to
> her husband.[14]

Interestingly, although Griselda considered in isolation is
undoubtedly symbolic – her class a moral rather than a sociological signifier – that distinction is sometimes deliberately blurred
by Chaucer when he writes about her relation to Walter, the
marquis who is also her husband. Although Chaucer deliberately
sets up an allegorical reading of the tale, he equally deliberately
problematises such a reading. He makes it difficult for the reader
to identify Walter with God, as the allegory requires, by allowing
the Clerk to harp on his human failings. He lays blame on him in
the third stanza, for example, for following his own pleasure
without heeding other concerns, so that when he decides to test
Griselda, the narrator's accusations come as no surprise. The clerk
stresses the arbitrary nature of Walter's desire 'to tempte his wyf,
hir sadnesse for to knowe' (452), and openly gives his own
opinion:

> I seye that yvele it sit
> To assaye a wyf whan that it is no nede,
> And putten hire in angwyssh and in drede.
>
> (460–2)

Throughout the tale, despite the clear allegorical and non-realist slant, Chaucer inserts remarks that direct us to consider events simultaneously from a human and social point of view, so that as well as seeing God tempting the patient soul we also see, perhaps more vividly, a husband treating his wife cruelly and a powerful lord testing the extent of his power over one of his humblest and most powerless creatures.[15]

The presentation of knights in Chaucer's texts regularly introduces a sceptical tone. The sequence of the *Clerk's Tale*, which moves from a description of Walter as 'gentylleste yborn of Lumbardye' (72) and 'ful of honour and of curteisye' (74) to questioning and even open condemnation of his behaviour is echoed elsewhere. Gentle birth, as Chaucer repeatedly makes clear, is no necessary indicator of inherent moral worth. The knight in the *Wife of Bath's Tale* rapes a maiden and his punishment is to seek an answer to the question of what women most desire. He promises to marry the old hag who tells him the answer, but is then unwilling to make love to her, partly because she is 'loothly' and old (III.1100), but also because she is 'comen of so lough a kynde' (1101), that is, of humble birth. This creates the context for the longest speech in Chaucer's works on the nature of 'gentillesse', a word originally denoting aristocratic birth, but used in Chaucer's time to connote moral virtue also. The loathly lady's reply to the knight underlines the point that although language may imply that the two are identical, they are not. Knights are no more likely to behave well than those of low birth, as this knight proves. She reproves him for his arrogance, assuring him that 'genterye/Is nat annexed to possessioun' (1146–7) and that, whatever a man's birth, 'vileyns synful dedes make a cherl' (1158).

January, the 'worthy knyght' (IV.1246) of the *Merchant's Tale*, is little better. Although he does not rape the young May, he effectively 'buys' her as his wife, wanting to secure his ownership of young flesh now that he is sixty. The more disgusting his behaviour becomes in the tale, the more consistently does Chaucer repeat and undermine the concept of a 'noble knyght'. 'Somme clerkes', he writes,

> holden that felicitee
> Stant in delit, and therfore certeyn he,
> This noble Januarie, with al his myght,
> In honest wyse, as longeth to a knyght,
> Shoop hym to lyve ful deliciously.
>
> (IV.2021–5)

It is following this sardonic linking of the concept of appropriate
knightly conduct with the pursuit of pleasure that January
conceives the idea of building a walled garden for sexual play, a
garden that is to be the setting for the worst sins of all three
protagonists in the tale.

Even where Chaucer's knights are not frank contradictions of all
that is noble, their behaviour may be open to doubt, particularly
where words like 'noble' and 'worthy' are clustered. The *Franklin's
Tale* opens with a knight who strives to go beyond the
conventional definition of honourable marriage by offering to
share the 'maistrie' (748) with his wife. This seems to be offered as
an ideal within the context of love, but as soon as Arveragus, after
over a year of happy marriage, casts his thoughts to other contexts
by which a knight's honour is defined, the problems begin. He
decides

> to goon and dwelle a yeer or tweyne
> In Engelond, that cleped was eek Briteyne,
> To seke in armes worship and honour –
> For al his lust he sette in swich labour.
>
> (V.809–12)

Military activity, the active seeking of war simply for the sake of
'worship and honour', becomes his only desire and he leaves
Dorigen, his wife, for two years. It is this gap of time that presents
Dorigen with the problem of how to evade the attentions of
another lover and leads her to make the playful promise that is to
bind her. When Arveragus returns to find Dorigen in great
distress, his concern is with the knightly principle of honour,
which requires both that his wife should keep her promise and
that his own reputation should be maintained. He insists that
Dorigen must go to Aurelius, as she has promised. The principle
as he states it ('Trouthe is the hyeste thyng that man may kepe' –

1479) sounds a worthy one, but the threat that follows has the tones of Walter's tyranny:

> 'I yow forbede, up peyne of deeth,
> That nevere, whil thee lasteth lyf ne breeth,
> To no wight telle thou of this aventure—
> As I may best, I wol my wo endure—
> Ne make no contenance of hevynesse,
> That folk of yow may demen harm or gesse.'
>
> (1481–5)

What is the knightly principle of 'trouthe' worth if it is grounded upon tyranny and deceit? The tale smooths over the cracks by showing Arveragus's 'nobility' leading to a domino sequence of noble acts which resolve the difficulty, but its very smoothness is conspicuous after the intensity of anxiety and grief that has been allowed to develop around Dorigen's promise. The strong sense of fictionality, the aura of fairy-tale, which pervades the ending acts as a reminder to the audience that it is only in tales that moral problems are resolved in this easy and highly patterned way. Questions of blame, of how knights and ladies *should* behave and whether their ideals are viable, are left hanging.

Satiric undertones are audible again in the presentation of knighthood in the *Knight's Tale*. David Aers has already shown how Chaucer queries the violence that underpins the rule of Theseus,[16] but it is important in this context to look at the presentation of the two knights, Palamon and Arcite, and to take account of the ambivalent approach to them that Chaucer adopts. These two brothers-in-arms, divided by love, are equal in honour. Their rigid adherence to the codes of their estate, however, is simultaneously idealised and satirised. Their rivalry in love and arms is the stuff of romance, their knighthood a necessary condition of their participation in a romance, their equality necessary to create the moral dilemma for the reader; and yet Chaucer often seems to be smiling at the absurdities inherent in the depiction of knighthood in romance. When they first see Emily and fall in love, their quarrel quickly degenerates to childish bickering ('I loved hire first' – I.1146, 'I loved hire first er thow' – 1155), and it is Arcite himself who compares them with dogs fighting over a bone (1177–80).

The scene that presents their chance meeting in the wood after seven years of separation seems also gently satirical in its approach. The narrator first pokes fun at the volatility of lovers in a most unromantic image: they are, he says, 'Now up, now doun, as boket in a welle' (1533). Although each of them, on seeing the other, is pale and shaking with rage, or fierce as a lion, they postpone battle to the next day because Palamon is unarmed, and when they return they help to arm one another 'As freendly as he were his owene brother' (1652) before again attacking one another like 'a wood leon' (1656) and 'a crueel tigre' (1657).

When Theseus comes upon them fighting in the wood, mockery of the knightly code escalates. Whereas the two knights themselves postponed their battle by one day until both were armed, Theseus postpones battle for a year and orders them to return with a hundred knights each for a full-scale tournament. Elaborate building works then follow in the construction of the lists for this great event as the day of the tournament approaches. Chaucer's tone in describing the nobility of all the participants is characteristically hovering. The extremes of his praise bring together idealisation and scepticism:

> And sikerly ther trowed many a man
> That nevere, sithen that the world bigan,
> As for to speke of knyghthod of hir hond,
> As fer as God hath maked see or lond,
> Nas of so fewe so noble a compaignye,
>
> (2101–5)

and the rhyme on 'name' and 'game' that follows again yokes ethical principles with playfulness:

> For every wight that lovede chivalrye
> And wolde, his thankes, han a passant name,
> Hath preyed that he myghte been of that game.
>
> (2106–8)

What tone would Chaucer the performer have adopted in addressing these next lines to his audience?

> For if ther fille tomorwe swich a cas,
> Ye knowen wel that every lusty knyght

That loveth paramours and hath his myght,
Were it in Engelond or elleswhere,
They wolde, hir thankes, wilnen to be there.
(2110–4)

Is he openly calling on his audience to identify with the lust for
honour, or asking them to stand back from their own talk of
honour to see it as potentially absurd? The written text offers no
easy answers, only the possibility of conflicting performances
based on establishing different kinds of relationship with the
audience, whether through shared ideals or a shared joke.

As the tournament begins, a herald announces detailed rules
approved by Theseus, which seem to restrict the degree of
violence, and the people respond joyfully:

'God save swich a lord, that is so good
He wilneth no destruccion of blood!'
(2563–4)

The cry goes up: 'Do now youre devoir, yonge knyghtes proude!'
(2598), but what follows is a blood-bath. The impersonality of the
narrator's account may be read either as calling upon traditional,
heroic descriptions of battle, or as recalling such heroic traditions
within a context that allows them to be seen as self-parody:

There is namoore to seyn, but west and est
In goon the speres ful sadly in arrest;
In gooth the sharpe spore into the syde . . .
Out goon the swerdes as the silver brighte;
The helmes they tohewen and toshrede;
Out brest the blood with stierne stremes rede;
With myghty maces the bones they tobreste.
(2601–11)

The victims form an inventory of unidentified third-person pro-
nouns:

He rolleth under foot as dooth a bal;
He foyneth on his feet with his tronchoun,

> And he hym hurtleth with his hors adoun;
> He thurgh the body is hurt and sithen take,
> Maugree his heed, and broght unto the stake . . .
>
> (2614–18)

The code of honour, despite its elaborate rules appearing to protect the participants, results in bloodshed on an epic scale. This is neither new nor surprising in chivalric literature. The question is whether Chaucer intends his audience to accept this unthinkingly or to question it. A stream of phrases boasting that no knight suffered any loss of honour is set alongside the death of Arcite:

> Ne ther was holden no disconfitynge
> But as a justes or a tourneiynge;
> For soothly ther was no disconfiture. . . .
> It nas arretted hym no vileynye;
> Ther may no man clepen it cowardye.
>
> (2719–30)

The effect is as dubious as that of a double negative in different speech registers: it may either intensify or cancel out its own sense. Injury, even fatal injury, is trivial, it seems, so long as honour is intact; but the tale seems simultaneously to embrace and to undermine this ethic.

The *Knight's Tale* does not, I think, offer such a unified attack on the military ethic as Aers suggests. Theseus's long Boethian speech (2987–3066) at the end of the tale does not seem to me to continue the undermining process which pervades the tale up to that point, but rather to attempt to resolve the difficulties of political and social interaction by viewing them from the distance of eternity, so that the particulars are dissolved in the generalisations of philosophy. It is the *Miller's Tale* that again begins to unpick the code of honour informing the *Knight's Tale* with a set of characters who parody the knightly dilemma from the angle of a lower social class. The implication is that while the social class of the characters may determine the linguistic register and perspective of a literary artefact, beneath the distinctions of language the concerns are the same. It is language that idealises or undermines actions that are comparable from one class to another. As the Manciple says in his tale:

I am a boystous man, right thus seye I;
Ther nys no difference, trewely,
Bitwixe a wyf that is of heigh degree,
If of hir body dishonest she bee,
And a povre wenche, oother than this –
If it be so they werke bothe amys –
But that the gentile, in estaat above,
She shal be cleped his lady, as in love;
And for that oother is a povre womman,
She shal be cleped his wenche or his lemman.
And, God it woot, myn owne deere brother,
Men leyn that oon as lowe as lith that oother.
(XI.211–22)

The clearest corrective in the *Canterbury Tales* to the chivalric ideal is presented in Chaucer's own *Tale of Melibee*. This tale is notable for its refusal to begin by presenting its main protagonist as a 'noble' or 'worthy' knight. It avoids both the social indicator (knight) and the conventional epithets which associate that class with praiseworthy conduct. The tale begins: 'A yong man called Melibeus, myghty and riche, bigat upon his wyf, that called was Prudence, a doghter which that called was Sophie' (VII.1). We know, then, that Melibee is rich and powerful, so why doesn't Chaucer describe him as a 'noble knight'? The characters are allegorical, as their names reveal, but allegory does not prevent the presentation of class-based characters in the *Clerk's Tale*. The answer, I think, lies in the tale's attempt to establish a different meaning for the word 'noble', one that does *not* depend on class.

The tale, like the *Parson's Tale*, is distinguished from the rest of the tales by being told in prose, and, again like the *Parson's Tale*, its concerns are primarily moral. The story is told in a mere seven lines: Melibee goes out one day leaving his wife and daughter safely shut in the house, but his enemies break in, beat his wife and kill his daughter. The lengthy 'tale' that follows consists of a discussion between Melibee and his wife as to whether it is right for him to take vengeance upon his enemies. Prudence finally persuades Melibee that violence is no solution and that he must forgive his enemies. This conclusion thus offers a very different definition of honour from that of the *Knight's Tale*, and explicitly rejects the association of honour with 'good' behaviour in battle. The discursive seriousness of this tale does not admit even the

possibility that battle can ever be a good, so that differentiation of
the methods of warfare is irrelevant. This may be a political as
well as a moral statement, given the futility of the contemporary
war with France.[17]

Honour in this context consists in recognising the inadequacy of
battle to solve anything. Although the young people in the tale
advise Melibee to make war, the old and wise remind him of its
terrible consequences:

> For soothly, whan that werre is ones bigonne, ther is ful many a
> child unborn of his mooder that shal sterve yong by cause of
> thilke werre, or elles lyve in sorwe and dye in wrecchednesse./
> And therfore, er that any werre bigynne, men moste have greet
> conseil and greet deliberacion.
>
> (1040–1)

This is also what Prudence argues throughout, and it is she who is
described from the beginning as 'noble', but by virtue of her moral
standpoint rather than her social status. When Melibee proposes to
use his wealth and power to overcome his enemies his wife
reminds him that riches can only be considered as a good 'to hem
that han wel ygeten hem and wel konne usen hem' (1552). If
fortune changes, the rich man is left, as Arcite is in the grave,
'alloone withouten any compaignye' (1559; I.2779).[18] Honour is
not the natural partner of riches or of war, as Prudence points out:

> And therfore seith a philosophre, 'That man that desireth and
> wole algates han werre, shal nevere have suffisaunce,/for the
> richer that he is, the gretter despenses moste he make, if he wole
> have worshipe and victorie.'
>
> (1650–1)

Victory, in any case, as Prudence goes on to show, is in God's
hands, not in the control of men.

Melibee explicitly raises the conventional concept of honour that
dominates the *Knight's Tale*, the concept of honour as reputation.
'Wol ye thanne that I go and meke me? [humble myself]', he asks,
'. . .for sothe, that were nat my worshipe' (1684). The paradox
that the tale announces, however, is that it is in just such
swallowing of petty pride that true honour does consist. Honour
is the only thing that Melibee cares about, as his wife knows –

'Ther nys nothyng in this world that he desireth, save oonly worshipe and honour' (1761) – and what she must teach him is that honour does not lie where the chivalric code would locate it, in vengeance, victory or trial by battle, but in mercy and the love of God.

WOMEN AND CLERGY

Women and clergy in the fourteenth century stand at opposite poles in terms of both education and power. Whereas the clergy composed by far the greatest proportion of the literate population, women as a group were least likely to be literate. A few aristocratic girls received an education either from private tutors or from nunneries, and there is some evidence that literate mothers may have taught their children to read, but the learning of nuns themselves had greatly deteriorated by this time (see pp. 36–7 above). Most nuns no longer read Latin, and many of the vernacular religious works that survive were addressed in the first place to nuns.

Nunneries were for the most part poorer and less powerful in the community than monasteries, so that even a woman who rose to be abbess, unless it was in one of the few great houses such as Shaftesbury or Barking, wielded little power outside her own enclosed and all-female community. The bishop was responsible for the convents in his see, so that all female religious communities were subject to male control. Nevertheless a nunnery could offer a woman a kind of freedom, in that it allowed her to escape from the necessity of marriage. The Paston letters, from the fifteenth century, give a vivid picture of the pressures brought to bear upon girls who resisted marriage, or resisted what was in the parental view the 'right' marriage economically. Elisabeth Clere, writing of her young cousin's unwillingness to marry the ageing widower chosen for her by her parents for financial reasons, describes how she is forbidden to speak to any man, even to her mother's servants, and 'hath sin Eastern the most part be beaten once in the week or twice, and sometime twice on o day, and her head broken in two or three places'.[19]

Women were not allowed to celebrate mass and so could not become members of the secular clergy, which was one of the

accepted routes to political power in the medieval state. They
were also explicitly excluded from higher education. Both of these
prohibitions derived from the scriptural authority of St Paul, who
had forbidden women to preach or teach, and insisted on the
necessity of their obedience to men.[20] One of the areas in which
bishops were vigilant in their correction of nuns was in their
refusal to allow them to educate boys over the age of eight. Nuns
might be allowed to educate girls and very young boys, but given
the strictures of St Paul, it was considered inappropriate for them
to be in a position other than that of subservience towards the
male beyond his earliest childhood. Virginity was indeed considered the highest female vocation – but unfit nevertheless to
remain in a position of superiority to the juvenile male after his
eighth year.

The Beguine movement, originating in Northern Europe in the
late twelfth century, focuses the clerical attitude towards women
very clearly.[21] The Beguines were women who chose to live a life
dedicated to God without entering the enclosure of a convent
or taking vows. Established nunneries required dowries from
women wishing to enter their communities, and so were in
practice only available to women of gentle birth, but any woman
could choose to become a Beguine. Although, as the movement
developed, Beguine convents were founded, in the early days the
women lived scattered throughout a town and met together at
mass. All Beguines vowed obedience to the ecclesiastical authorities, but the established clergy, hostile in any case to new lay sects
offering a challenge to orthodoxy, was particularly suspicious of a
lay women's movement, and frequently harassed and persecuted
the Beguines.[22]

It is not difficult to find other evidence of the gendered quality
of the Church's response to female unorthodoxy. *The Book of
Margery Kempe*, for example, in which Margery describes her
visions of God and the way they stimulated her to flamboyant
public weeping, gives numerous illustrations of the particular
disgust that her gender provoked. She was repeatedly accused of
sexual misconduct as well as heresy, laymen feared that she would
lure away their wives with her, and the vicar of Norwich, on first
hearing that she wanted to speak with him about God for an hour
or two, responded with straightforward disbelief: 'Benedicite.
What cowd a woman ocupyn an er tweyn owyrs [one or two
hours] in the lofe of owyr Lord?'[23]

Insistence upon clerical celibacy was of course an important component of the Church's attitude towards women. To the celibate male, the female represents temptation incarnate, a view given further authority by the Book of Genesis. It is a truism of critical writing on the fourteenth century that it is dominated by two images of woman: Eve and Mary, the temptress and the virgin, the extremes of sin and virtue. The ideal woman, as depicted by saints' lives, for example, was a virgin who endured in the name of God all tortures that the world might inflict upon her (although the titillating quality of descriptions of how such women are stripped and whipped to bleeding clearly raises questions about the double standards of celibate male authors). At the same time, however, female saints' lives, often explicitly addressed to a female audience, do fulfil a female yearning for power, in that they show the saint dominating, and refusing to be dominated by, the wicked male tyrant who torments her. In the end, the woman of such stories will rise to eternal glory, while the wicked pagan man will perish horribly. Caroline Walker Bynum, in a detailed study of medieval religious women, has also shown how women used food practices, particularly refusal to eat, as a way of gaining control over both themselves and their circumstances.[24]

Virginity, at once powerful (over pagans) and submissive (to God), may be seen as the ideal towards which nuns and anchoresses aspired, but the more common image of woman in medieval literature is that of Eve, the weaker vessel, a mere derivative of Adam's rib and ready to betray him at the first opportunity. A strong tradition of anti-feminist literature, going back to the writings of the early Church fathers, depicted women as lecherous, greedy, envious, deceitful, frivolous scolds, a distraction to men from their higher thoughts. Since most of the educated population were male and in holy orders throughout the Middle Ages, it is hardly surprising that such a tradition should have flourished.[25]

Ironically, however, the literary stereotype of the cleric in Chaucer's time is little better. Clerics in one form of holy orders were frequently hostile to other orders, and did not hesitate to put their views in writing. The satiric traditions informing the depiction of monks, friars, pardoners and priests are dominated by the same sins as the anti-feminist tradition: lechery, greed and hypocrisy. Just as the female in literature is so often presented as lustful, adulterous and prepared to go to any lengths to deceive her husband or extort money from him, so her partner both in extortion and copulation is very often a member of the clergy. Chaucer's *Shipman's Tale*, for example, shows this combination with comic directness.

Women and the clergy interact within the framework of the *Canterbury Tales* as well as within individual tales, most conspicuously in the *Wife of Bath's Prologue*. The Wife of Bath's first words formulate an open challenge to the clergy:

> Experience, though noon auctoritee
> Were in this world, is right ynogh for me
> To speke . . .
>
> (III.1–3)

To renounce 'auctoritee', meaning the written word, and most often, of course, the written word of the Church, is to deny the whole anti-feminist tradition and everything written about a woman's place. To replace it with experience, which is merely personal and individual, is to oppose it with all that tradition scorns, and at the same time, of course, to enact the very stereotype of woman that tradition constructs. The Wife's belligerence casts her simultaneously as the harridan of anti-feminist literature and as the woman who fights the constraints of male stereotyping. As in the *Knight's Tale*, and so often in his writing, Chaucer takes pleasure in creating a clash of perspectives.

The Wife's choice of subject is also one that confronts clerical authority: marriage. She challenges clerical tradition in asserting that she has had five husbands and immediately doubles the insult by citing scriptural authority for taking more than one. Given the Church's position on women teaching, it goes without saying that women were not expected to interpret the scriptures, far less quarrel with the authority of the existing glosses.[26] The Wife, however, without naming Jerome (writer of the Vulgate, the standard medieval Latin Bible, as well as one of the founders of interpretative glossing), explicitly disagrees with his reading of the marriage at Cana as an indication that Christ intended men and women to marry once only, and refers first to the Samaritan at the well (John 4.6, 18) to argue that no number is defined and then to God's command 'to wexe and multiplye' (28; Genesis 1.28).

Susan Schibanoff has shown that it was not the Wife of Bath's sexual mores so much as her defiance of the Church's claim to be sole interpreter of the Scriptures that shocked at least one of Chaucer's fifteenth-century readers.[27] By studying a different kind of glossing, not the traditional and authoritative glossing of Scripture but the marginal annotation of contemporary scribes copying two manuscripts of the *Canterbury Tales*, Schibanoff uncovers two very different responses to the Wife of Bath from fifteenth-century readers. The Ellesmere scribe, according to Schibanoff, 'cheers the Wife on'[28] by echoing and augmenting the highly selective text she compiles in favour of female sovereignty in marriage, whereas the Egerton scribe struggles with her for control of the text by citing biblical texts that refute her position. Schibanoff perhaps exaggerates the positions suggested by the two sets of glosses, but her point remains valid that 'it is not the Wife's sexuality per se that draws the Egerton glossator's heaviest fire but her "textuality", her insistence on the right to interpret Scripture'.[29]

The presumption of the Wife of Bath both in claiming the right to an opinion concerning the meaning of the Scriptures and in openly offering her opinion in the company of the clerical members of the pilgrimage is a battle-cry that cannot go unnoticed. In challenging written authority she challenges not only the clergy *per se*, but the implied male monopoly on the perception of truth:

> Men may devyne and glosen, up and doun,
> But wel I woot, expres, withoute lye,
> God bad us for to wexe and multiplye
>
> (26–8)

The word 'men' in Middle English is often used to mean 'people', as occasionally still in Modern English, but the listening audience begins to become aware of it as a gendered pronoun in the Wife's speech. Oral delivery foregrounds the word by virtue of the fact that it is placed at the beginning of a line and creates a pattern of stress that reverses the normal iambic rhythm. As the Wife continues her diatribe, her view of experience as a struggle between men and women becomes more insistent, and when the pronoun 'Men' next appears in the same position, it is quite clearly set against 'womman':

> Men may conseille a womman to been oon,
> But conseillyng is no comandement.
> He putte it in oure owene juggement.
>
> (66–8)

Even St Paul, she argues, cannot order women to be virgins if it is not God's decree:

> Poul dorste nat comanden, atte leeste,
> A thyng of which his maister yaf noon heeste.
>
> (73–4)

The Wife of Bath's anger against men is inseparable from her anger against 'clerks' (in both senses: educated men and men of the Church),[30] since 'clerks' form a male hegemony that excludes women. Her argument is with men, who have written the Bible, glossed it, told lay congregations how to think about it, used it to give authority to a negative image of womankind and attempted to maintain a monopoly on literacy so that their power is unassailable. The point about gender is underlined in that her scorn for men and their books reaches a peak in her discussion of exactly those organs that differentiate the male and female genders. 'Tell me also', she asks, 'to what conclusion/Were membres maad of generacion?' (115–16) Whatever the glosses say, she argues, experience tells us that genitals were not made only 'for purgacioun/Of uryne' (120–1) and 'eek to knowe a femele from a male' (122). She mockingly frames her argument within the limits of orthodoxy ('So that the clerkes be nat with me wrothe' – 125) when she suggests that they were made for both functional and pleasurable ends. As she points out, men have themselves admitted this in their books (notably the Bible and its glosses):

> Why sholde men elles in hir bookes sette
> That man shal yelde to his wyf hire dette?[31]
>
> (129–30)

Her attack against clerks in both senses may temporarily be separated into two strands: the one against the Church and the other against the Book (and books). It must be emphasised, however, that the separation is artificial, since the two are by definition interwoven (Christianity is a religion of the Book, and glossing is both a religious and a literary activity). Let us first isolate the specifically religious implications of the Wife's *Prologue*. Critics have often noted parallels between the Wife's discourse and that of preaching.[32] Certainly her construction of arguments based on quotations from Scripture and the glosses follows the standard procedure of a medieval sermon, and two of the clerics in the pilgrim audience hear it as such. The Pardoner interrupts her to tell her she has talked him out of taking a wife, and calls her 'a noble prechour' (165). The Friar, who also interrupts her to complain of her 'long preamble' (829), later mentions her contribution to the problems of 'scole-matere' (1272), and recommends that both he and she should 'lete auctoritees . . ./To prechyng and to scoles of clergye' (1276–7). Both these statements suggest that the Pardoner and the Friar see the Wife of Bath as trespassing on clerical territory, and the fact that they interrupt her enacts their unwillingness to allow roles to be reversed and to accept the 'preaching' of a lay woman. Like the Egerton glossator, they cannot ignore her explicit challenge to clerical authority.

It is evident that medieval churchmen guarded their territory jealously against lay attempts to usurp their rights. In the words of one fifteenth-century sermon:

they lovyn non multiplicacion of Goddis lawe, for they wolde nout ben askid ne opposid; and for manye of hem ben wol lewyd [ignorant], therfore they wolden kepin the peple in overdon lewydnesse, that hemself in here lewydnesse myghte semyn wyse.[33]

Latin was one instrument used by the learned to exclude the unlearned from the possibility of dialogue, and it was cherished on occasion for its very powers of obfuscation. Robert Basevorn, writing as early as 1322, comments on the tactics of university preachers:

Many uneducated men would usurp the act of preaching except that they see this great finesse to which they cannot attain. And for the same reason, when [English university preachers] preach to lay people they give their theme with its division in Latin, because it is difficult for the ignorant to do this.[34]

Lydgate, himself a monk, writing poetry during and after Chaucer's lifetime, openly admits to changing from English to Latin when he wishes to exclude the non-clerical element in his audience.[35] John Trevisa, in his *Dialogue between a Lord and a Clerk* in 1387, shows an educated layman and a cleric in dispute about the need for English translations. The lord wants Latin works translated into English so that more people can understand them, whereas the clerk wants them kept in Latin, partly out of the snobbish belief that not all such people (that is, those with a knowledge of English but not Latin) need to have access to the knowledge contained in Latin books, and partly out of a wish to retain control, so that 'hy that understondeth no Latyn mowe axe and be informed and ytauht of ham that understondeth Latyn'.[36] Trevisa, himself both clerk and translator to an aristocratic patron, Sir Thomas Berkeley, both is and is not the clerk of the *Dialogue*. Writing the *Dialogue* presumably under Sir Thomas's watchful eye, he allows the clerk to put forward arguments against translation, but makes him capitulate quite suddenly to the lord.[37]

The Lollards, followers of Wyclif from the 1380s onwards, were unorthodox both in their preference for English over Latin and in their elevation of women to higher levels of literacy and power. They actively ignored St Paul's restrictions on women's participation in the Church, and encouraged women to learn how to read and to teach others what they had learned. Henry Knighton, himself in holy orders, shows the mixture of scorn and paranoia typical of the established Church when he argues that Wyclif, in translating the Bible into English, has made

> that which was formerly the province only of learned clerks and those of good understanding . . . common and open to the laity, and even to those women who know how to read. As a result the pearl of the gospel is scattered and spread before swine.[38]

Giving lay people access to Holy Scripture is bad enough, but giving it to women is even more contemptible. Bishop Pecock, writing c.1449, was particularly scornful of Lollard women 'whiche maken hem silf so wise bi the Bible . . . and avaunten and profren hem silf whanne thei ben in her jolite and in her owne housis forto argue and dispute agens clerkis'.[39]

The statute enacted in 1401 to allow the burning of Lollards, *De Heretico Comburendo*, demonstrates the increasing fear on the part of both religious and secular authorities of books and teaching in the hands of subversives. The Lollards, says the statute, 'make unlawful conventicles and confederacies, they hold and exercise schools, they make and write books, they do wickedly instruct and inform people'.[40] One of the signs by which a Lollard was to be recognised was his or her possession of books in English, and the writer of the fifteenth-century sermon quoted on p. 65 above, though not a Lollard, expresses his fear of persecution as a result of his choosing to write in English.[41]

It has been suggested that the Wife of Bath was intended as a portrait of a Lollard,[42] but, regardless of whether or not Chaucer's intention was so specific, it is clear that she formulates a challenge to the religious establishment, both by her adoption of its didactic methods to her own ends, and by her gender. Equally clearly, the interruptions of the Pardoner and the Friar enact their refusal to accept her intervention. The Wife's quarrel is not as narrow as the Lollard cause: it is not a quarrel with particular aspects of religious doctrine, but a quarrel with men and their books. And it is not only a quarrel with religious men and religious books but with literacy itself and male attempts to restrict it, since it is access to and control over the written word that determines the structure of power. The Wife of Bath is subversive, certainly, in her attitude towards the clerical establishment, but her challenge is more radical and wide-ranging than that of Lollardy.[43]

The Wife depicts each of her first four marriages as a struggle for power between the genders. She boasts that in every case she finally 'hadde the bettre in ech degree' (404), and often the contest is a linguistic one: 'for by my trouthe, I quitte hem word for word' (422). Her fifth husband, however, is 'a clerk of Oxenford' (527) who has now left university, but uses his learning to dominate her. He cites classical examples of husbands who left their wives because they sought too much freedom, and quotes from the Bible to the effect that a man should not allow his wife to wander about. His particular taunt is to read 'nyght and day,/For his desport' (669–70) in a 'book of wikked wyves' (685) which makes him laugh out loud. The authors listed as appearing in the book are of course those same pillars of the anti-feminist tradition whose arguments have appeared throughout the *Prologue*. The battle with this husband, then, is a battle with his book.

The Wife knows, however, that books are not 'authorities' in the absolute sense that clerks would have it, but the products of their authors (see further chapters 4 and 5 below). The Bible has less to say about good wives than about bad ones, but this, she implies, illustrates a truth about male authorship rather than about the nature of the female, for it is

> an impossible
> That any clerk wol speke good of wyves [women],
> But if it be of hooly seintes lyves.
>
> (688–90)

Clerical authors cannot help but reveal their own subjectivity in their writing, hence:

> The clerk, whan he is oold, and may noght do
> Of Venus werkes worth his olde sho,
> Thanne sit he doun, and writ in his dotage
> That wommen kan nat kepe hir mariage!
>
> (706–10)

All the traditional approaches to women in literature derive from this same clerical hegemony of authorship. A book, a supposed 'authority', is no more than a reflection of its author, argues the Wife, so that if women could become literate and enter the world of the written word, literary tradition could be rewritten:

> By God, if wommen hadde writen stories,
> As clerkes han withinne hire oratories,
> They wolde han writen of men moore wikkednesse
> Than al the mark of Adam may redresse.
>
> (693–6)

The Wife does not only refuse to be defined by the Bible, the Church fathers and the satirists of anti-feminist tradition. She also mocks the determinism of astrology, another male-constructed authority foisted by the learned on the unlearned. Her account of how the position of the stars at her birth has obliged her to be open in her sexual favours (604–20) parodies, as H. Marshall Leicester has pointed out, pretentious clerkly explanations of female behaviour. By reminding us of the human fallibility of astrological 'authority' (as of the glossing of Scripture), 'she is identifying astrological explanation itself as not a discourse of matters of fact but a discourse of power, a use men make of the stars to keep women down'.[44]

Her refusal to be defined by existing male literary discourses goes beyond simple disobedience and a refusal to be 'corrected' (661) in her behaviour. She assaults both man and book physically, tearing three leaves out of the book and punching Jankin in the face so that he is knocked backwards. The rest of the story is well-known. Although Jankin hits back, the Wife plays dead to make him penitent and then hits him again. When he gives her total 'soveraynetee' (818) over his house, his land, his tongue and his hand, she makes him burn his book. The Prologue demonstrates, quite literally, a blow against men and against male domination of literacy, education and the literary tradition.

Whether Chaucer offers this blow for our approval is another question. It has often been argued that, because the Wife embodies the attributes of the typical harridan of anti-feminist satire, she turns the weapon of the book against herself. This view, however, has to be set against the fact that Chaucer gives the Wife self-awareness. She consciously performs the part of the literary type, acknowledging her sources or camping up the details as she proceeds, particularly when she addresses her fellow-women, as in this instance:

> Ye wise wyves, that kan understonde.
> Thus shulde ye speke and bere hem wrong on honde,
> For half so boldely kan there no man
> Swere and lyen, as a womman kan.
>
> (225–8)

When she reports her tirades against her first three husbands, she does so in a way that makes clear that they are planned devices, carefully constructed rhetorical strategies for manipulating husbands. A character who consciously enacts the stereotype of the wicked wife cannot at the same time be accused of being no more than the stereotype, though the stereotype remains visible too.

The importance of the Wife of Bath in her time lies in the fact that she exists, not in a Lollard tract, but in a vernacular work aimed at an audience which included the literary 'establishment', the court and the rising middle classes. The original audience, in other words, included that same group of the rich and powerful who were becoming so suspicious of vernacular literacy as an agency for the spread of heresy and sedition. A work of this kind demands that such an audience reconsider the meaning of its stereotypes. As long as the monster of anti-feminist satire remained externalised in male-authored texts, she might be identified as a kind of truth. A text such as the *Wife of Bath's Prologue*, however, which presents the monster in the first person, as a figure who then engages seriously with the grounds for accepting one authority and rejecting another, directs its audience towards the recognition of caricatures as reflecting their authors as well as their objects. The wickedness of the wicked woman does not entirely disappear, but it is made to reveal truths about men as well as about women. The parameters of social estate, approached as fixed by so many earlier texts, are here shown to be humanly and fallibly constructed.

4

Continental England

ENGLAND AND WESTERN EUROPE

The audience to whom the Wife of Bath may have come as something of a shock was an audience conditioned by over two hundred years of familiarity with French and Latin as the languages of prestige literature in England. Even before 1066, England's links with the Continent were strong. The spread of Christianity had created an international community of shared belief, the Holy Roman Empire, so that different countries speaking different languages were united in their allegiance to Church and Empire. Messengers travelled to and from the Emperor and the Pope and all Christian countries in their domain, royal families intermarried, scholars and artists moved between different European courts and pilgrims travelled to shrines all over the continent.

Latin had long been recognised as the language of international scholarship, and the accepted medium of interchange between different cultures. Although England had a highly developed vernacular literature during the Anglo-Saxon period, it was also part of this international, Christian and Latin culture. Invasion and settlement were of course also influential on the development of English culture, and by the end of the ninth century the Scandinavians were firmly established in England alongside the existing mix of Germanic and Celtic inhabitants.

When William of Normandy laid claim to the English crown in 1066, however, he saw himself not as an invader, but as the true inheritor of the land by birth. Earlier intermarriage between the English and the Normans made his claim a reasonable one, and he may perhaps have seemed culturally no more 'foreign' to the English nobles than Edward the Confessor (reigned 1042–66), who had himself been brought up in Normandy. Politically, however, his accession did inflame nationalistic feeling against him as an interloper in England, and the Anglo-Saxon Chronicle berates him for not behaving like an English king and allowing his foreigners to oppress the people.[1]

William's accession changed the political context to which England belonged. No longer was the king of England restricted to that role alone. William was Duke of Normandy as well as King of England, and England became part of the Anglo-Norman and Angevin empire. A significant transfer of land and office in England to Norman magnates took place during William's reign, so that the extent of Norman influence in England increased dramatically. Positions of power were now filled by Normans rather than by Englishmen, and the language of government changed from English to Latin.

Although English never fell out of use, and probably remained the only language of the vast majority of the population, that section of the population was composed of those without access to literacy or power. Since the powerful and literate increasingly chose Latin or French, especially in the context of the written word, the influence of these languages was out of all proportion to the numbers using them. A thriving tradition of Anglo-Norman literature developed in England, and alongside it a burgeoning of translation. Translation from Latin into French, or from French or Anglo-Norman into English suggests the hierarchy operating in England during the twelfth and thirteenth centuries: while Latin remained the language of international authority and learning, French became the prestige vernacular and English was the least likely of the three to be the chosen language of composition for written texts. The twelfth-century Canterbury Psalter demonstrates this hierarchy visually. It presents the Latin text in large and beautiful script, using elaborately ornamented capitals; two further versions of the Latin text in slightly smaller script, still with ornamented capitals; Latin glosses in an even smaller script in the margins and interlined with the main Latin text; and finally, in the same size script as the glosses, but interlined merely with the secondary Latin texts, English and French translations.[2]

There are exceptions, however, which are difficult to explain except in the context of a fusion rather than a conquest of cultures. *Ancrene Wisse*, for example, a text addressed to three sisters adopting the solitary life of the anchoress, was written first in English, and later translated into Anglo-Norman and Latin. These women could read French,[3] yet the author nevertheless chose to write a Rule for them in English. A similar case in point is the poem *The Owl and the Nightingale*, written in English and apparently addressed to a learned and powerful audience, amongst whose members might be someone influential enough to take action concerning the poem's plea for preferment for a certain Nicholas of Guildford. The poem may, of course, be modelled on an Anglo-Norman source, but such a source has never been found. More importantly, the poem is bound in the two manuscripts where it occurs with an Anglo-Norman debate poem, the *Petit Plet*, and the coexistence of the English and the Anglo-Norman poems within the same covers suggests their suitability for the same audience.

It would be false to make a sweeping class distinction about the audience for English, as opposed to Anglo-Norman texts.[4] Rather we must read them against the background of a trilingual culture. Although it is true to say, as above, that writers increasingly chose to write in French or Latin, the most significant element in this statement is that of choice. It is clear that many educated men in twelfth- and thirteenth-century England were literate in two or three languages, and made their choice according to the immediate contexts of place and audience. Jocelin of Brakelond, for example, describes how Abbot Samson in the twelfth century 'was a good speaker, in both French and Latin, . . . could read books written in English most elegantly, and . . . used to preach to the people in English, but in the Norfolk dialect, for that was where he was born and brought up'.[5] Layamon, at the beginning of his *Brut*, cites sources in Latin, French and English. Although this does not offer hard evidence that Layamon, a parish priest, knew all three languages, it does suggest that he thought his audience would find his claim to such knowledge plausible, and there is internal evidence to support his claim.[6]

Not only are texts in all three languages sometimes found together in the same manuscripts, as in the case of *The Owl and the Nightingale*, but individual texts may move between different languages, assuming a familiarity with two, or even three on the part of the audience. Consider, for example, the poem cited on pp. 18–19 above, or this verse from one of the Harley lyrics:

> Scripsi hec carmina in tabulis;
> mon ostel est en mi la vile de Paris;

may y sugge namore, so wel me is;
Yef hi deye for love of hire, duel hit ys.[7]

Throughout the period in which Norman influence was at its most intense in England, there was a wider context in which an increasingly powerful Latin international culture worked to prevent any sense of nationalism from developing into parochialism, at least among intellectuals. Western Europe was crossed by a network of 'paths of art and devotion'.[8] Richard de Bury describes how his passion for book collection crossed geographical boundaries:

> we secured the acquaintance of stationers and booksellers, not only within our own country, but of those spread over the realms of France, Germany, and Italy, money flying forth in abundance to anticipate their demands; nor were they hindered by any distance or by the fury of the seas, or by the lack of means for their expenses, from sending or bringing to us the books that we required.[9]

Scholars moved freely between universities and cathedral schools and, though Dom David Knowles overstates the case in describing 'the whole of educated Western Europe' as 'a single undifferentiated cultural unit',[10] cultural and intellectual exchange was clearly active and wide-ranging.

Within this same European context, France was becoming increasingly dominant. The cathedral school of Chartres and the abbey of Bec in Normandy were at the centre of intellectual life in the twelfth century, as was the University of Paris in the thirteenth century. It is important to note, however, that these intellectual centres were not insular or narrowly nationalistic, but attracted scholars from all over the continent in a mutual interchange of learning. Thus Anselm in the eleventh century, born in Aosta, moved from Bec to Canterbury; John of Salisbury in the twelfth century from Paris to Benevento, Canterbury and Chartres; Duns Scotus in the thirteenth century, born in Dumfries, from Oxford to Paris and Cologne; and William of Ockham (in Surrey), in the fourteenth century, from Oxford to Avignon and Munich.[11] The fact that so many manuscripts of Wyclif's Latin works survive today in the libraries of Prague and Vienna is indicative of the strong cultural exchange between England and Bohemia during the lifetime of Richard II's first wife, Anne of Bohemia. Similarities between Wyclif's thought and the ideas of John Hus, who inspired the Hussite movement in Bohemia, have long been recognised.

The paths of cultural interchange were set in motion by patrons as well as by scholars themselves. Charles V of France, for example, invited Tommaso Pisano, an astronomer and physician, the father of Christine de Pisan, to the French court, and his acceptance meant that his whole family eventually became resident there. Christine was herself invited a generation later by Henry IV to come to England, but did not accept the invitation.

The Church also promoted this international mobility. The two great orders of friars, the Franciscans and the Dominicans, originated at the beginning of the thirteenth century and quickly sent their members all over Europe. Both orders were founded upon the ideals of poverty and preaching, though the Dominicans from the beginning made study an essential part of their Rule, whereas St Francis insisted that his Rule should never be glossed, and Franciscan preaching concentrated on penance and moral reform rather than doctrine. By mid-century, however, there was little perceptible difference between the two orders. Friars became known generally for their learning and their skill in preaching, and the handbooks they compiled as aids to preaching show that they used material from a range of sources, combining popular stories and lyrics with scripture and patristic reference, and interweaving Latin with the vernacular. They differed from previous movements, as Gordon Leff has pointed out, in not being monastic: 'their emphasis was upon going into the world, not withdrawing from it; their aim was the salvation of others, not directly that of their own souls; theirs was a social mission rather than a personal regime'.[12] Their active interests in both the towns and the universities, their sense of the combined importance of academic study and popular preaching, meant that they shaped cultural expectations at a variety of social levels. As Beryl Smalley concluded in her study of English friars in the early fourteenth century, 'when Chaucer mocked at the friars, he was biting the hand that fed him. They educated his audience.'[13]

Pilgrimage also fostered cultural exchange. The *General Prologue* of Chaucer's *Canterbury Tales*, with its range of pilgrims cutting across boundaries of class and culture, suggests the variety of people who might choose to travel in this way. Although Chaucer's pilgrims are all English pilgrims travelling to an

English shrine (the joke about the Prioress's French serves to underline the gap by Chaucer's time between the kind of French spoken in English nunneries and the language of Paris), journeys to European shrines were not uncommon. *The Book of Margery Kempe*, the autobiography of a determined pilgrim, shows Margery visiting shrines as far afield as Rome, Aachen, Santiago and the Holy Land.

The supremacy of the pope in matters of Church government throughout Europe was another factor contributing to international relations. Papal taxes, appointment to clerical offices, negotiations to secure papal backing in affairs of state were part of the business that helped to maintain a steady flow of embassies to and from the Curia. When, in 1308, the pope moved to Avignon, this intensified French cultural dominance in Europe, and Avignon became a great centre of scholarship. Petrarch is probably the most famous of those who worked in and around Avignon during the fourteenth century, but every country needed to have its representatives in the Curia and to cultivate links with the papacy.[14]

Political events shaped rather than inhibited the exchange of cultures. Royal marriages, for example, were made in order to cement alliances or forestall hostilities. Edward III was the son of an English king, Edward II, and a French princess, Isabella, and it was his descent from Isabella that gave some basis for his claim to the French throne. His mother betrothed him to Philippa, daughter of the Count of Hainault, Holland and Zeeland, in return for troops to help her invade England with Mortimer, and the marriage took place in 1328, a year after Edward's accession following his father's enforced abdication. Philippa's connections with the Low Countries were useful to Edward both in terms of trade (English wool was an indispensable import for the weavers of Flanders) and later in terms of political support against France in the Hundred Years War. Her kinship with Robert of Anjou, patron to both Petrarch and Boccaccio, created opportunities for greater contact with Robert's great court in Naples, perhaps the foremost cultural centre in Europe during the first half of the fourteenth century.[15]

With every royal bride came an entourage of attendants from her country of origin, bringing with them books, skills and materials from that culture. Chaucer's future wife, another Philippa, was from a Hainaulter family who came to England with the new queen. The career of the great chronicler Jean Froissart, an exact contemporary of Chaucer, shows how the mobility of artists and scholars was connected to movements in royal families: he tells us at the end of his *Chronicle* that he came to England in 1361; Philippa accepted him as a member of her household, where he remained until the Queen's death in 1369; and after her death he returned to The Netherlands, where, apart from brief visits to France and England, he seems to have remained until his death.

Predictably, both of the marriages of Richard II also had clear political objectives. In marrying Anne of Bohemia he was marrying the daughter of the Holy Roman Emperor and strengthening England's ties with Rome. Since this marriage was made during the time of schism, when two popes competed for allegiance and authority, this was a way of counterbalancing France's strength in having one of the popes based at Avignon. As Gervase Mathew has pointed out, the marriage brought no dowry, but afforded instead the opportunity of breaking the old alliance between the Emperor and the French royal house of Valois, as well as of acquiring international prestige.[16] Richard even seems to have entertained the notion of becoming Holy Roman Emperor himself. His second marriage, to Isabella, daughter of Charles VI of France, brought a huge dowry, a prolonging of the truce with France and the assurance of French aid against rebellious subjects.

Not only marriage, but war itself acted in a curious way to intensify cultural exchange. The fact that the king of England was also duke of Gascony when Edward III came to the throne was one of the causes of the Hundred Years War, and Edward's eldest son, the Black Prince, held court at Bordeaux after he became Prince of Aquitaine in 1362 (see p. 7). As a result, his son, the future Richard II, was born there in 1367 and spent his earliest years in France, until his father returned to England in 1371. In the same way political events had led Richard's grandfather, Edward III, to spend over a year from 1325 to 1326 at the French court with his mother Isabella while she plotted with Mortimer to overthrow her husband Edward II. The courts of France were not 'foreign' environments to medieval English kings.

French kings had less reason to be resident at the English court, but the Hundred Years War also created this opportunity. The French king, Jean le Bon, together with some of his most powerful noblemen, was captured by the Black Prince at the battle of Poitiers in 1356. He and his men spent four years in captivity in

England, not in dungeons, but participating fully in the life of the English court. When the terms of peace were finally agreed in the Treaty of Brétigny of 1360, forty hostages, including the king's two sons and his brother, set sail for England in his place as surety against the payment of the king's ransom. Some were to remain ten years or more. One, Enguerrand de Coucy, married Edward's daughter Isabella in 1365 and was granted freedom to return to France, together with the restoration of his inherited lands in England. Despite the fact that war had created the circumstances that led to this prolonged French presence at the English court, relations between the two groups were generous and courteous, even intimate. It is perhaps indicative of these relations that not only did the French king find political justification for returning to captivity in London in 1364, but that when he died there three months later Edward gave him a funeral on the grand scale at St Paul's.[17]

The French captives found no difficulty in buying French books during their stay in England, and their commissions stimulated the production of lavish manuscripts in French. (One of the hostage French princes was Jean, later Duc de Berri, the most famous and extravagant book collector of his time.) English aristo-cratic libraries of the fourteenth century showed a strong preference for French texts in their secular reading matter (though Latin devotional texts usually outnumbered secular books). A roll of issues and receipts from the privy wardrobe during the reign of Edward II shows that the king's collection of 160 books served as a kind of circulating library among his immediate circle of family and friends, and that French romances were prominent within this collection (though the term 'romance' was used much more widely at this time).[18] Edward's queen, Isabella, is well-known for her interest in secular literature and her acquisition of luxury books. Repeated liaisons with the French royal family, whether through marriage or through the fortunes of war, helped to keep this preference for French reading matter within aristocratic circles alive even after English had probably become the primary spoken language for all classes (see pp. 88–9 above). The upsurge of English writing in the late fourteenth century did not happen as a result of falling French literary prestige, but, partly at least, as an attempt to emulate French writing within the native vernacular of England. Any consideration of English writing in the late fourteenth century must take into account the number of texts that are translations or adaptations from French sources.

CHAUCER AND INTERNATIONALISM

Chaucer's life and writings demonstrate a wide-ranging pattern of internationalism. London, where he was born, was even then a national and international crossroads. The fourteenth-century Gough map shows a concentration of routes towards London, confirming its status as a great centre of business and trade. All kinds of reasons might bring outsiders to London, from buying and selling to law-suits and parliamentary sessions. The Paston letters show that the men in the family were frequently away from their estate in Norfolk, and when they were absent they were most commonly to be found in London. Various country gentlemen or high-ranking churchmen would have had houses in London as well as elsewhere in England and there was also a steady stream of people moving to become resident in London, particularly from eastern counties. Chaucer's own family originally came from Essex.

London also had large numbers of overseas immigrants, notably Flemish and Italians. Chaucer's father, as a vintner, would have had regular dealings with Italian wine-merchants, and it may have been through his father's business that Chaucer learned to speak Italian. His mercantile background, then, would have brought him into contact with different languages and cultures even before he became attached to the household of Elizabeth de Burgh, Countess of Ulster. From this point onwards his contacts with the mixture of nationalities at court, together with his travel abroad both as a soldier and as a diplomat, and his marriage, combined to make his cultural milieu truly international.

What we know of his reading confirms this breadth of influence. We can map the paths of his reading through contemporary French and Italian writers, earlier French writing, medieval and classical Latin writers, as well as English works, via sources and allusions within Chaucer's own writing. His choice of English may perhaps have been influenced by familiarity with the writings of Dante and Petrarch on the use of the vernacular. While there is no clear evidence that Chaucer had read these texts, his

reading matter was sufficiently international and wide-ranging for
it to have been likely.

He seems to have been known to the French poet Deschamps
first and foremost as a translator, since the refrain of Deschamps's
poem to Chaucer is '*Grant translateur, noble Geffroy Chaucier*', and
indeed a brief glance at Chaucer's collected works will show the
prominence of translations. Not only did Chaucer translate into
English two of the great classics of his time, the *Roman de la Rose*
(possibly not completely) and the *Consolation of Philosophy*, but
many of his more original works also incorporate long passages
closely based on French, Italian or Latin sources. His subject matter, his poetic forms, his stylistic devices, his diction and syntax,
everywhere display their indebtedness to continental, particularly
French, traditions.[19]

Chaucer lived and worked in an environment emphatically
European in outlook, yet the strength of Chaucer's attachment to
European literature marks him out from his English contemporaries. As Elizabeth Salter has suggested, his attempts to bring
together contradictory elements from different sources may be
partly responsible for the exploratory and unresolved quality of
his work.[20] The choice of *The Parliament of Fowls* as the subject for
particular study in the rest of this chapter is dictated by its
characteristic combination of multiple sources and ambiguous
effects.

THE PARLIAMENT OF FOWLS[21]

> The lyf so short, the craft so long to lerne,
> Th'assay so hard, so sharp the conquerynge,
> The dredful joye alwey that slit so yerne:
> Al this mene I by Love, that my felynge
> Astonyeth with his wonderful werkynge
> So sore, iwis, that whan I on hym thynke
> Nat wot I wel wher that I flete or synke.
>
> (*PF*, 1–7)

The opening stanza of the poem announces its debts to tradition in
a number of ways. First, the control of syntax, which organises the

whole of the stanza into one long sentence, is imitated from French and Latin models; second, the stanza form, known as rime royal, is very similar to the Italian form *ottava rima*, used by Boccaccio; and third, the subject is love, a subject that had dominated French secular poetry since the troubadour lyrics and the *Roman de la Rose*. As the poem progresses, Chaucer explicitly names some of his sources: '"Tullyus of the Drem of Scipioun"' (31), 'Macrobye' (111) and 'Aleyn, in the Pleynt of Kynde' (316). He also mentions that the music for the closing roundel 'imaked was in Fraunce' (677). These four specified sources point in the directions of classical Latin, fourth- and twelfth-century medieval Latin, and contemporary France, yet they represent only a fraction of the debts the poem actually owes.

From the second stanza onwards, however, the narrator cultivates the reader's sense of the poem's dependence on other texts. He admits that his experience of love is not first-hand, but derived from books, and reminds the reader again in the third stanza that he is himself a tireless reader. At this point he suddenly becomes specific, and not only refers the reader to a particular book that he chanced to discover at a particular time, but also confides that he began to read it with a particular objective, 'a certeyn thing to lerne' (20). This is tantalising, since though we now know that the narrator was looking for something specific from this book, he does not tell us what it is, but digresses to make the general remark that

> out of olde bokes, in good feyth,
> Cometh al this newe science [knowledge]that men lere.
>
> (24–5)

Ideas may seem new in their time, he suggests, but they develop out of the learning already inscribed in older books. The individual book has authority, but it is an authority based on other authorities. Authority is not singular, but plural, an amalgamation of multiple texts. This sounds straightforward enough, but what the poem goes on to do is explore the problems of juxtaposing authorities that refuse to be easily amalgamated.

The reference to 'a certeyn thing' leads the reader to believe that the poem has a specific and singular quest, but does not identify the quest. This goads the reader into attempting to identify the 'thing' that the narrator seeks, thus forcing him to experience the poem as a quest, just as the narrator experiences his own reading as a quest. The reader, or audience, then, is led back to more books, and to a dream, not to a single destination. It is a dis-locating experience, which dissolves the apparent singularity of the quest into multiplicity. The flickers of different sources are like visions of the grail that direct towards, but do not finally represent, the thing itself.

The importance of seeing the poem's different sources as exploring and questioning one another, rather than turning to any single one as the key, is clearly demonstrated in ll. 29–84, a section that masquerades as a straightforward summary of the *Somnium Scipionis*. The narrator's description of the book seems at pains to be accurate and precise:

> This bok of which I make mencioun
> Entitled was al ther, as I shal telle:
> "Tullyus of the Drem of Scipioun."
> Chapitres sevene it hadde, of hevene and helle
> And erthe, and soules that therinne dwelle.
>
> (29–33)

Yet neither Cicero nor Macrobius wrote in chapters, nor do they anywhere refer to hell. Chaucer deliberately rewrites a pagan description of afterlife in Christian terms, so that the two per-spectives do not appear in opposition as true and false, but rather as different approaches to the same truth. This reading of one source by the light of another is at its boldest in the direct speech Chaucer gives to Scipio to summarise his truth (73–84). Embedded within apparent quotation from Cicero is Dante's description of the fate of the lecherous in the second circle of Hell. The passage does not privilege one source over another, but deliberately enmeshes the two, so that the pagan and the Christian per-spectives are seen to overlap.

The following stanza begins with another echo of Dante and ends with a conspicuous echo of Chaucer's own translation of Boethius in the enigmatic couplet that forms the last reference to the waking mind of the dreamer:

> For bothe I hadde thyng which that I nolde,
> And ek I ne hadde that thyng that I wolde.
>
> (90–1)

The couplet alludes to Book III, Prosa 3 of Boethius's *Consolation of Philosophy*, where Lady Philosophy demonstrates to the figure of Boethius that the innate dissatisfaction of the individual is proof that the individual is not self-sufficient. Within the context of *The Parliament of Fowls*, the lines recapitulate the emphasis on the particularity of the poem's quest by their repetition of the word 'thyng', as at l. 20, so that the summary of the *Somnium Scipionis* is framed at either end by the pressure to find both within the *Somnium* and within *The Parliament of Fowls* a specific answer to a specific question. The fact that the sources so far interwoven point to similar questions about the place and purpose of mankind in the world and similar philosophies concerning the need to work towards 'commune profit'[22] and the binding of God and the natural world in universal harmony (made audible in the music of the spheres – ll. 59–64) predispose the reader to expect that Chaucer's poem too will explore these same issues.

At this point the narrator, before beginning the account of his dream, reminds the reader that dreams can be visions of truth, descending as from above upon the dreamer, or they can be mere reflections of the dreamer's own experience and subjectivity:

> Can I not seyn if that the cause were
> For I hadde red of Affrican byforn
> That made me to mete that he stod there.
>
> (108)

Although such division of dreams into significant and incidental was well-established by Chaucer's time, and stemmed directly from Macrobius's own pattern of divisions, the reference here serves to remind the reader again of the merely contingent authority of individual dreams and particular texts. Any one dream, or any one poem or book, may seem to make an absolute statement, but its statement must be tested against other dreams and other texts, apparently equally valid in themselves. The narrator invites the reader to listen to his dream, then, in a spirit of open-mindedness, to bring to this text an awareness of all that is 'other' to it and yet part of its fabric.

The present reader of this chapter may already be asking the question, 'Did Chaucer expect his readers to know all these other texts to which he refers?' One way of responding to this is to note

that he certainly sent out as many signals as possible to his readers
that his text incorporates other authors, including the explicit
naming of some. These signals act in the same way as Eliot's notes
to *The Waste Land*: while not identifying every allusion, they force
the reader to recognise that here is a piece of writing which
demands to be read in the context of other writing. The conscious
use of enigma by both writers is a further incentive to the reader
to hunt out the unstated allusions in search of illumination. The
difference, however, is that Chaucer's allusions are more
consistently directed towards very familiar texts, the great or the
popular classics of his time (given the qualification that books
were in any case accessible only to the educated minority in the
fourteenth century).

Africanus, the dream-guide, stands at the end of a long line of
such guides in dream-literature, but the fact that the narrator
'borrows' this guide from the very book he has most recently been
reading casts doubt on whether he is to be seen as a figure of
independent authority or a mere reflection of the dreamer's
reading matter, and Chaucer makes sure that his readers consider
this doubt. He also treats the relationship between guide and
dreamer as slightly comic, and such manipulations of tone
frequently set the poem at an oblique angle to its sources. When
the dreamer is brought to the gate of another world, as dreamers
so often are in literary texts, he is paralysed by the inscription on
the gate (127–40), with its huge implications for the opposing
consequences of his choice. Africanus not only notes the dreamer's
error in thinking that the choice applies to him, when in fact it is
only intended for lovers, but seizes him and pushes him in. This is
a relationship very different from that between the awed and
fearful Scipio and the stern, yet consoling Africanus of his dream,
or between Dante and Virgil before the gate of Hell (which serves
as a model, again much altered, for Chaucer's gate here).[23]

Dante's gate does not offer alternatives, but a single message of
despair. Chaucer's gate, however, leads not to Hell, but to a
walled garden. It is a garden indebted to a web of traditions going
back to both classical sources and the Bible, but linked most
immediately, for a fourteenth-century reader, with the garden of
the *Roman de la Rose*, a text that D. S. Brewer has described as 'no
less than the *matrix* of the *Parlement*'.[24] The highlighting of this
source, together with Africanus's insistence that the inscription
over the gate is directed at lovers, reminds the reader that 'Love',

as the first stanzas of the poem declared, is an important aspect of the poem's quest.

Yet the importance of seeing the theme of love within the wider context of the theme of universal harmony announced in the prologue is signalled by Chaucer's description of the birdsong in the garden in terms of angelic harmony (190–1) and by the fact that the narrator also hears stringed music of such

> ravyshyng swetnesse
> That God, that makere is of al and lord,
> Ne herde nevere beter, as I gesse.
>
> (198–200)

The idealised, non-natural characteristics of the garden (there are no extremes of temperature, no day and night, no sickness, no age; joy within it is beyond expression) signal that it is no simple, natural garden, but related to nature rather in the way that God is related to His creation. The garden contains the paradigms of human happiness, but not the forms they take in the fallen world; not, that is, until the narrator finds the Temple of Venus within the garden.

Inside the temple the signals to the reader abruptly move into a negative register. The narrator hears the sighs of sorrowful love, engendered by jealousy; sees the god Priapus as he was discovered at the point of attempted rape of the nymph Lotis; discovers Venus in a dark and secret corner, provocatively half-draped in transparent clothing, 'in disport' with Richesse (260); and finds the rest of the temple dominated by depictions of sorrowful and tragic love. The modern reader experiences some confusion in formulating a response to this presentation of decadence within the temple of Venus, in a poem that celebrates St Valentine's Day. It is instructive to look both at the source for this passage and at what follows in the poem.

The immediate source for the Temple of Venus, and one that Chaucer has been following closely from the beginning of his description of the garden, more closely even than the *Roman de la Rose*, is Boccaccio's *Teseide* (also the source for the *Knight's Tale*). Elizabeth Salter, in a close analysis of the relationship between Chaucer's and Boccaccio's texts in this section of the poem, has argued that Chaucer borrows above all a richness of imagery which suspends moral judgements, 'an interest in the shape of beauty, rather than its meaning'.[25] But Boccaccio wrote explanatory glosses to accompany his poem, and, as Professor Salter herself points out, the glosses offer clear moral directives. 'This Venus', Boccaccio writes,

> is twofold, since one can be understood as every chaste and licit desire, as is the desire to have a wife in order to have children, and such like. This Venus is not discussed here. The second Venus is that through which all lewdness is desired, commonly called the goddess of love.[26]

Chaucer's manuscript of the *Teseide* may not have contained the glosses, but the tradition of exposition they present was not original to Boccaccio, and we may assume that Chaucer, and at least some of his readers, would have been familiar with it. Given the clear contrast in the poem between the temple and the garden, and between Venus and Nature, it is difficult to avoid the conclusion that such contrasts function as moral imperatives. We have the evidence of *The Faerie Queene* that Spenser at least, closer in time to Chaucer than we are, read them as such.[27]

The figure of Nature, whom the narrator encounters on emerging from the Temple of Venus, is given a clear moral label: she is the 'vicaire of almighty Lord' (379). Chaucer explicitly refers the reader to the twelfth-century Latin writer, Alain de Lille, for further details about her. The citation of sources here becomes a kind of shorthand, whereby the individual text consciously sets itself at the centre of a web of ideas expounded in other texts (Jean de Meun and Boethius are also central points of reference here). The reader is explicitly directed towards an intertextual reading of the single text, which produces at this point a strongly positive role for Nature as God's deputy on earth. This view of Nature allows space for an affirmation of good within the created world that is at odds with the contempt of the world incorporated from Macrobius at the beginning of the poem (64–6).[28] The intertextual relations of the poem, then, open up complexity and debate for the poem's readers. Secular love is not necessarily futile and mis-directed, as the Temple of Venus might suggest, but may be given an acceptable moral context by Nature. Nature, as her name implies, sets the pursuits of secular love within the framework of the greater good of the natural world, streamlining individual desire in the direction of the love that binds the universe into a whole. Boethius, cited here in Chaucer's translation, offers one of the best descriptions of this natural love:

> al this accordaunce [and] ordenaunce of thynges is bounde with love, that governeth erthe and see, and hath also comandement to the hevene. And yif this love slakede the bridelis, alle thynges that now loven hem togidres wolden make batayle contynuely, and stryven to fordo the fassoun of this world, the which they now leden in accordable feith by fayre moevynges. This love halt togidres peples joyned with an holy boond, and knytteth sacrement of mariages of chaste loves; and love enditeth lawes to trewe felawes.[29]

The concept of a Christian universe created and bound together by love is predicated upon the belief that there is value in the things of this world. Earthly life cannot be dismissed on account of its inherent flaws; instead a scale of nature must be understood which takes account of all created things, but recognises the superior virtue of some over others. This 'principle of plenitude'[30] celebrates the diversity and multiplicity of creation, as St Thomas Aquinas explains:

> It is necessary that God's goodness, which in itself is one and simple, should be manifested in many ways in his creation: because creatures in themselves cannot attain the simplicity of God. Thus it is that for the completion of the universe there are required divers grades of being, of which some hold a high and some a low place in the universe. That this multiplicity of grades may be preserved in things, God allows some evils, lest many good things should be hindered.[31]

Celebration of the variety of creation necessarily implies the virtue of procreation. The choice of Nature as vicegerent of God underlines the blessedness of fertility, and it is in order to regulate and celebrate this fertility that the assembly of birds is summoned. The variety of birds represents the diversity of Nature, and they assemble for the purpose of choosing mates, thereby to propagate their own diversity.

The assembly is not only a gathering, however, but, as the title indicates, a parliament, a debate.[32] The cross-fire of dispute between different sources that has pervaded the subtext up to this

point now becomes explicit in the poem's form, and the particular
dilemma of the formel is openly debated. Plurality of viewpoints
begins to form the literal content of the poem, and the influence of
the secular poetic form known as the *demande d'amour* [love
question] is conspicuous. In its use of more contemporary poetic
sources, the poem is again characterised by its alterations of tone
and combination of forms in a way that leads to pervasive
questioning. D. S. Brewer has shown how unusual it was to link
the two forms of 'love-vision' and *demande d'amour*, and how the
essence of the *demande d'amour*, which was to pose a dilemma,
focused on a choice between two loves different in nature but
equal in kind, is changed in *The Parliament of Fowls* to become an
uneven contest in which the first tercel is self-evidently the best of
three very similar lovers.[33]

This subversion of a familiar genre, together with Chaucer's
avoidance of the flippancy characteristic of the genre, leads the
reader again into blind alleys that demand a self-questioning
response. The familiar pegs of genre by which readers orient their
responses to literary texts are twisted or pulled out, so that
reading or listening to this poem becomes a process of constant
revision and reorientation. Although for the modern reader this is
a purely private thought-process (or perhaps, in the context of an
educational institution, the subject of formalised seminar
discussion), it is not unlikely that a performance of the poem in
Chaucer's time intentionally stimulated spontaneous open debate
amongst the audience. Festive courtly gatherings (such as the Pui
and the slightly later *Cour Amoureuse*, founded in Paris on St
Valentine's Day, 1400) supply possible settings for such a mixture
of performance and discussion.[34] The fact that the debate is left
unresolved is typical of such poetry. The eccentricity of *The
Parliament of Fowls* lies not in the formel's postponement of a
decision, but in the fact that the outcome is so loaded in favour of
the first tercel. If discussion followed among Chaucer's contemporaries, it might have centred on the significance of this deviation
from genre expectations rather than on the formel's decision.

It is important to note too that the formel's decision does not
end either the dream or the poem. There is yet another genre to be
introduced: the roundel. This is a French verse-form, usually set to
music, so that in the context of this poem we are inevitably
reminded of the music of the spheres. This in turn suggests the
idea of order and would seem to signal that order is affirmed and

problems resolved. Both the content and the form of the roundel
support this. The song praises the joys of mutual love and
celebrates the return of summer sun after 'wintres wedres' and
'longe nyghtes blake', reminding us that the cycle of procreation is
linked with the seasonal cycle in a harmonious universe. The
repetition of the refrain, and its framing of the roundel both at its
beginning and its end, emphasise resolution, closure and certainty.

But does the poem really offer such synthesis? Are all doubts
resolved and all contradictions erased? Does the poem unify all
perspectives to endorse the straightforward teaching of Scipio's
dream that we should love the common profit if we hope to
achieve eternal bliss? If it does, then why does Chaucer list the
poem among those 'enditynges of worldly vanitees, the whiche I
revoke in my retracciouns' (*Cant. Tales*, X.1084)?

The roundel ends the dream with emphasis on unity within
itself, but the very fact that it constitutes yet another genre
incorporated into this amalgam of poetic and philosophical shapes
highlights the poem's plurality. And though the roundel closes the
dream, it is not yet the end of the poem, which refuses such
closure. The last stanza shows the narrator still unsatisfied. He
hoped to learn 'a certeyn thing' from his first book, and the dream
seemed to be a response to his search, but his first response on
waking is to turn, almost frantically, to other books:

> I wok, and othere bokes tok me to,
> To reede upon, and yit I rede alwey.
> I hope, ywis, to rede so som day
> That I shal mete som thyng for to fare
> The bet, and thus to rede I nyl nat spare.
>   (695–9)

The word 'read' is repeated four times in five lines, reminding us
of what the poem has already demonstrated, the multiplicity of its
intertextual reference. The narrator, of course, is not very bright,
and may simply have missed the message conveyed to him by the
dream; but the effect of the final stanza, regardless of the
narrator's dullness or otherwise, is to make the reader return to
her own reading to ask the questions: Does the dream convey a
singular message? Can the authorities Chaucer cites be syn-
thesised to create a unity? The ending directs us to questions
rather than answers, and in doing so redirects us into the poem

and its preoccupation with other texts. The sequence, then, is from
the apparent closure of the roundel, through the open-endedness
of the narrator's uncertainty, and back into the experience of the
poem, where the multiplicity of reference creates a web of
interconnecting perspectives, like mutually reflecting mirrors,
leading away from the idea of an absolute, or as the narrator
would say, 'a certeyn thing'. The reader is invited to consider the
variety of approaches from an informed but sceptical distance,
rather than to profess commitment to any single one.

In its highlighting of plurality the poem imitates as well as
explores the principle of plenitude. Aquinas's description of
creation (see p. 87 above) might be applied to *The Parliament of
Fowls*, were it not that Chaucer's own repudiation of the poem in
the *Retractions* suggests that this would be to sacramentalise
something essentially more frivolous. What the poem offers in
place of certainty is freedom and experimentation: it is not an act
of faith, but an act of play.

5

'Greet altercacioun': The Influence of Philosophy

FOURTEENTH-CENTURY LEARNING

As Chapter 4 showed, the study of ideas in the Middle Ages was conducted in Latin within an internationally mobile cultural context. The academic establishment was composed of male clerics (even members of the other two professions, medicine and the law, usually held at least minor offices within the Church, though they were not necessarily ordained) with the result that philosophers were almost of necessity theologians. The importance of the Christian hegemony underpinning intellectual exploration up to the fourteenth century cannot be overestimated. Reasoning could take place only within the confines of faith: if it overstepped these limits it was promptly denounced as heresy. The fourteenth century is significant, in terms of the development of philosophy, as the age when a few thinkers begin to suggest the existence of a possible gap between reason and faith, and it is perhaps symptomatic that its two most influential thinkers, Ockham and Wyclif, were accused of heresy.

A brief survey of the developing conditions for study during the thirteenth century is important in establishing a context for fourteenth-century philosophy. Two thirteenth-century developments are particularly relevant: the growth of the universities and the establishment of the orders of friars. Before the thirteenth century the great centres of learning had been abbeys and cathedral schools. The word 'school' in this context is not used in the modern sense to imply a place where children were taught (though many cathedrals did have schools in this modern sense too, some of which survive to this day), but to describe an environment in which the greatest scholars of the day, the 'masters', or 'schoolmen', wrote and lectured to younger scholars. The philosophy that developed in these schools is sometimes described as 'scholasticism', and has been defined in various ways, both by its subject and by its method. Gordon Leff argues, for example, that it is 'essentially the application of reason to revelation', while David Knowles understands it to be 'a method of discovering and illustrating philosophical truth by means of a dialectic based on Aristotelian logic'.[1]

The great monastic and cathedral schools were in many cases the starting points for later universities. The University of Paris, for example, grew directly out of the cathedral school of Notre Dame. As the definition of a university gradually became formalised, it came to denote a place of study where many masters taught, and which included at least one of the advanced faculties of theology, law and medicine.[2] Lectures, terms and degrees gradually became fixed and standardised, and an emphasis on logic replaced the earlier literary emphasis of the twelfth-century schools. The seven liberal arts, divided into the *trivium*, consisting of grammar, rhetoric and dialectic, and the *quadrivium*, comprising arithmetic, geometry, astronomy, music, had formed the basis of secular education in the West since the ninth century, but in practice this range had become narrowed down by the increasing preoccupation with dialectic in the thirteenth century.

The method of training that evolved, however, continued to place a very high value on the work of earlier philosophers and theologians. The *Sentences* of Peter Lombard, for example, was regarded as an indispensable authority and was built into courses of study throughout Europe. The student of theology was required to spend two years lecturing on the *Sentences*, and both Ockham and Wyclif in the fourteenth century produced commentaries (derived from their lectures) on the Lombard's work in accordance with this requirement.

A school was in existence at Oxford by 1115 and was organised as a university by the time Gerald of Wales read his *Topography of Ireland* there, in about 1188. Gerald describes his presentation of the work thus, writing of himself in the third person:

he determined to read it before a great audience at Oxford, where of all places in England the clergy were most strong and pre-eminent in learning. And since his book was divided into three parts, he gave three consecutive days to the reading, a part being read each day. On the first he hospitably entertained the poor of the whole town whom he gathered together for the purpose; on the morrow he entertained all the doctors of the divers Faculties and those of their scholars who were best known and best spoken of; and on the third day he entertained the remainder of the scholars together with the knights of the town and a number of the citizens.[3]

This tells us not only that teaching at Oxford was organised into faculties by this date, but also that Oxford was already perceived, at least by Gerald of Wales, as the centre of learning in England.

Unlike the University of Paris, where philosophy and theology had virtually ousted mathematics, Oxford had established a reputation for important work in the mathematical field following the work of Robert Grosseteste in the thirteenth century. Merton College was particularly noted for the work of its scholars on natural science and mathematics: 'Philosophical Strode',[4] one of the dedicatees of Chaucer's *Troilus and Criseyde*, and 'Bisshop Bradwardyn' (*Nun's Priest's Tale*, VII.3242), who was a noted mathematician as well as a theologian, were fellows of Merton.[5]

The friars, established in the early thirteenth century (see p. 75 above), dominated the study of theology from the mid-century onwards. Robert Grosseteste, who became the first Oxford lecturer to the Franciscans when they arrived there around 1229–30, was elected bishop of Lincoln in 1235, and was the last great theologian in secular orders for almost a century. From *c*.1250 to *c*.1350 the friars led the field. The chair at Paris was repeatedly occupied by friars (Bonaventure, Aquinas, Kilwardby, Pecham) and many more of the great names in medieval philosophy emerged from their ranks: Roger Bacon, Adam Marsh, Haymo of Faversham, John of St Giles, Alexander of Hales, Duns Scotus, William of Ockham. Not until after Ockham's time at Oxford did scholars of the first rank, such as Bradwardine, Fitzralph and Wyclif, begin to emerge from the secular clergy, and then a degree of hostility on their part towards the friars is evident. Fitzralph is to be found complaining bitterly about the friars in one of his sermons. It is on their account, Fitzralph argues, that the student body at Oxford has reduced in size from 30,000 to 6,000, because parents fear to lose their children to the friars if they send them to the university (friars were accused of trapping young children into unwittingly swearing oaths that bound them to become friars). In addition, says Fitzralph, they are responsible for

> more grete damage that undoth and distruyeth the seculers of al maner faculte. For these ordres of beggers for endeles wynnynges that thei geteth by beggyng . . . beth now so multiplyed in coventes and in persons, that many men tellith that in general studies unnethe is y-founde to sillyng [for sale] a profitable book of the faculte of art or of dyvynyte, of lawe canoun, of phisik, other of lawe civil, but alle bookes beth y-bouht of freres. So that in everech covent of freres is a noble librarie and a grete; and so that everech frere that hath state in scole siche as thei beth now, hath an huge librarye.[6]

Academic rivalry between the friars and the seculars was endemic in the great centres of medieval learning.

Thirteenth-century philosophy has often been described as working towards synthesis, the harmonisation of faith with reason; fourteenth-century philosophy, on the other hand, is critical of the thirteenth-century synthesis, and beset by doubt as to how much reason *can* know of faith. 'It is preoccupied', as Leff puts it, 'with the limits, rather than the scope, of reason'.[7] The fourteenth century has often been seen as the age that ushered in the 'secularisation' of philosophy, by which is meant not the loss of faith, but the confinement of the operations of reason to the secular arena. And hand in hand with the growing divide between faith and reason comes the gradual segregation of Church from State. The old doctrine of the 'two swords', Church and State indivisible, is breaking up, and the fourteenth century is characterised by the criticism of corruption in both.

Despite this break-up of synthesis, many of the subjects of philosophical debate and the terms of discussion can still be traced back to Plato and Aristotle. The most influential thinkers on the course of medieval philosophy, even to the end of the fourteenth century, were Augustine (354–430) and Boethius (*c*.480–525).

Their ideas on subjects such as free will, grace, material being and the nature of God shaped the thinking of later philosophers, and it is notable that Chaucer, who shows no sign of direct familiarity with the works of either Ockham or Wyclif in his own century, names Augustine more than once and translates Boethius's *Consolation of Philosophy* in its entirety. The ideas of Ockham and Wyclif, which are singled out for discussion next, frequently explore problems already examined by Augustine or Boethius or both.

WILLIAM OF OCKHAM

William of Ockham was born around 1285 in Ockham in Surrey.[8] He became a Franciscan as a boy, and studied and lectured at Oxford between about 1309 and 1324, writing most of his major theological works during the period 1318–24. He was known to his contemporaries as *venerabilis inceptor*, indicating that he did not proceed to the status of doctor in theology. He may have been prevented from holding a chair by Thomas Luttrell, chancellor of Oxford University until perhaps early 1322,[9] since Luttrell went to Avignon the following year and there denounced Ockham's writings to the pope. Ockham was summoned to Avignon, probably in 1324, where his trial for heresy dragged on for four years. Since the inquiry was not concluded, however, Ockham's teachings were never formally condemned. But during his stay at Avignon, Ockham became involved in the debate over poverty which divided the Franciscan Order (hingeing on the question of whether Christ and his apostles did or did not possess property),[10] and fled Avignon in 1328 with the General of the Franciscans, Michael of Cesena, to seek the protection of the emperor against the pope. He was immediately excommunicated, and remained excommunicate for the rest of his life. In taking sides with the emperor against the pope, he became embroiled in political as well as theological controversy, and his writings after this date concentrate on the question of the rightful division of power between Church and State. He died around 1347–9, at the height of the Black Death.

Ockham was a brilliant and influential logician whose thinking was based on the belief that logic must be ruthlessly applied to empirical experience, but could not operate in the realm of spiritual absolutes. He distinguished firmly between matters that could be known and matters that must be taken on faith. His creed may be understood as a passionate devotion to reason, with the essential qualification that reason is useless beyond the limits of the known. The authority of reason must be taken very seriously indeed, but must always defer to the word of God:

> I consider it to be dangerous and temerarious to force anyone to fetter his mind and to believe something which his reason dictates to him to be false, unless it can be drawn from holy scripture or from a determination of the Roman Church or from the words of approved doctors.[11]

His theory of knowledge revolutionised philosophy in that he began from the basis of observation rather than from the assumption of an abstract reality behind individual forms, a change of approach that has been described as 'almost as epoch-making as the Copernican revolution in astronomy'.[12] For Ockham the individual form was the only reality, and all knowledge was based upon the experience of singular, individual forms. The concept of an abstract category to which individual forms belonged, or, in the terminology of medieval philosophers, a 'universal', was not, according to Ockham, inherent in things themselves, but created in the mind of the observer. It was a mental picture, a _'fictum'_. In Ockham's words, 'no universal is existent in any way whatsoever outside the mind of its knower'.[13]

There are therefore two kinds of knowledge: empirical knowledge (which Ockham calls 'intuitive'), and abstractive knowledge, which is concerned with understanding, and deals in propositions rather than facts. This second kind of knowledge, which defines the operation of reason, is grounded upon words rather than things, since concepts have no external existence beyond the mind. It is Ockham's concern to distinguish words and concepts as signs, not things in themselves, which defines his thinking as 'nominalist', as opposed to 'realist'.

From this rigorous application of logic to epistemology, it follows that most theological truths cannot be demonstrated, but lie beyond the scope of reason. Ockham does not discuss such questions as the immortality of the soul or the nature of God, since he believes these truths to be held on faith alone. His God exists but is unknowable and omnipotent. God is simple, uniting being, knowledge and will as indistinguishable from one another, but his radical simplicity is unfathomable to human reason. On the question of God's foreknowledge, for example, Ockham writes

> that it has to be held without any doubt that God knows all future contingent facts evidently and with certainty. But to explain this evidently, and to express the manner in which He knows all future contingent facts, is impossible for any intellect in this life.[14]

Ockham explains his understanding of the first article of the creed, 'I believe in God the Father almighty' thus: 'Anything is to be attributed to the divine power, when it does not contain a manifest contradiction.'[15] Nothing is certain, then, except God's absolute power.

God's existence is in fact the only necessity, since all other apparently necessary truths in the material world can be displaced by Him at will. All that exists that is not God must be by definition radically contingent in its nature, subject to change if God wills it. Even the moral law, as Ockham says, is the result of God's arbitrary decree, and could be different if God so willed it.

Although it may be argued that Ockham himself was not a sceptic, it is easy to see how his thought gave rise to scepticism in matters of belief. Truths formerly held to be demonstrable to reason now looked open to doubt, and the individual seemed to be the only fixed point, unrelated in any systematic way to other individuals. Gordon Leff has argued that Ockham's doctrine of intuitive knowledge, far from 'implying a world of merely discrete individuals . . . ensures knowledge of their interconnection',[16] but it would seem that Ockham's followers did not read his work with this emphasis. As Knowles has argued, Ockham's work was instrumental in helping 'to disperse the conception of an ordered, interlocking universe'.[17] God's will could no longer be perceived as a point of reference, but only as a source of uncertainty.

Ironically, despite the absolute power of God's will, its unknowability threw enormous emphasis on to man's free will, and followers of Ockham were labelled by Thomas Bradwardine the 'Modern Pelagians', after the old Pelagian heresy, which set a higher value on man's free will than on the grace of God. Bradwardine, whose *De Causa Dei* was written specifically to re-

fute the *moderni* with its insistence on the power of grace, gives us
to understand that university teaching in his youth was already
saturated with the influence of Ockham:

> I rarely heard anything of grace said in the lectures of the
> philosophers . . . but every day I heard them teach that we are
> masters of our own free acts, and that it stands in our power to
> do either good or evil, to be either virtuous or vicious.[18]

After 1327, Ockham's writing concentrated on polemical issues
arising out of his dispute with Pope John XXII over evangelical
poverty.[19] Himself excommunicated by the pope, he considered
the pontiff to have lapsed into heresy in his interpretation of
plenitudo potestatis, the doctrine of absolute papal power.
According to a repeated dictum of Ockham's, God's law is the law
of liberty (*Lex evangelica est lex libertatis*), and the pope was in error
to think that he could oppress Christians in the name of such
power. Since Christ held dominion over nothing, claiming neither
temporal possessions nor jurisdiction, the pope's claim to such
power as Christ's vicar on earth was heretical. The pope, as a man,
was capable of sin. The only difference, in Ockham's view,
between a pope and other men was that a pope, on account of his
position, 'sins more gravely, perniciously, and dangerously than
any other Christian'.[20]

All human sovereignty, whether over things or people, Ockham
argued, was the result of the Fall. The temporal institutions of
power, therefore, whether of Church or State, could not be seen as
direct manifestations of divine law, but must be understood as
morally neutral, individual examples of rule which might or might
not choose to pursue the common good. In line with Ockham's
epistemology, observable reality is by definition singular and
individual. The universal church, accordingly, did not coincide
with the visible manifestations of ecclesiastical authority on earth,
but was defined as the communion of all individual believers
throughout time, bound in faith. Individuals, such as Pope
John XXII, could excommunicate themselves from the universal
church by their own error. The ultimate authority for Christian
truth, therefore, could not come from temporal, individual
churches or prelates, but only from the Bible itself. Such a view
was radical in its implications, undermining the necessity for the

ordained hierarchy of the Church. It opened up a route that Wyclif was to follow to its logical conclusion.

JOHN WYCLIF

Wyclif was born a generation after William of Ockham, probably around 1335–8, and was a contemporary of Chaucer.[21] He became a fellow of Merton in the 1350s, and was Master of Balliol by 1360. As a secular priest rather than a friar, he was directly associated with colleges rather than with a friary, and in addition held a succession of benefices in various parts of England from about 1361. He began writing his logical works at about the same time, but did not take his doctorate in theology until 1372, after many years of writing and lecturing.

Unlike Ockham, his involvement in political affairs came early rather than late in his academic career, but, like Ockham, he then became embroiled in a dispute between Church and State, in this case between the pope and the king of England. The dispute again concerned the extent of papal power, specifically the pope's right to tax English clergy and to appoint to senior posts in the English Church. English law had already attempted to veto papal presentations to benefices in England via the Statute of Provisors (1351) and the Statute of Praemunire (1353), but the practice continued nevertheless. Wyclif went as part of a delegation to negotiate with the pope in 1374. The outcome was not particularly successful from the point of view of the king's council, but it set Wyclif pondering questions concerning the right to possession and the use of temporal power, as Ockham and others had done before him.[22]

His treatise *De Civili Dominio* [*On Civil Dominion*] attracted the favourable attention of English magnates and the unfavourable attention of the papal court, since both, naturally, had opposing interests on the question of the Church's right to material wealth and power. John of Gaunt summoned Wyclif to London in 1376 to preach against the worldly wealth of the bishops, and Bishop Courtenay of London responded by summoning Wyclif to a tribunal in St Paul's in February 1377. John of Gaunt accompanied him, taking the King's Marshal with him by way of adding to the threat of the secular arm, and the trial broke up amid angry demonstrations by Londoners, resentful of John of Gaunt's intervention.

Wyclif returned to Oxford, and in the meantime Pope Gregory sent bulls to England condemning certain propositions in the work. A combination of chance and royal intervention, however, contrived to prevent the pope's condemnation from being put into effect. Edward III died in June 1377; the succeeding king's mother, the Princess of Wales, widow of the Black Prince, warned the bishops early the next year against harsh treatment of Wyclif; Pope Gregory himself died; and Gregory's death created the circumstances that led to papal schism before the end of 1378.[23]

It was Wyclif's views on the Eucharist – a topic that began to absorb his interest probably from about 1379 – that really brought about his downfall. He challenged the established explanation of transubstantiation, which asserted that the bread ceases to exist once it becomes Christ's body, or, in the philosophical terminology of Wyclif's time, that the accidents remain without a substance. Wyclif thought this explanation absurd, and began to argue against it in his writing. This was dangerous territory. In 1380 the Chancellor of Oxford set up a commission to examine Wyclif's teaching. The commission condemned two of his propositions and threatened anyone teaching them with excommunication and imprisonment. John of Gaunt came to Oxford to try to restrain Wyclif at this point, but Wyclif proceeded to write and publish a defence of his propositions, losing the support of his friends at court.

During the same month as Wyclif published his defence, May 1381, the English Rising was beginning to erupt in the south of England (see chapter 1, pp. 16–19). Contemporary chroniclers, themselves predominantly in holy orders in the orthodox Church, were not slow to link Wyclif's name with the thinking behind the Revolt. Both Knighton and Walsingham associate Wyclif's teaching with that of John Ball, Knighton describing John Ball as preparing the way for Wyclif as John the Baptist did for Christ.[24] The *Fasciculi Zizaniorum*, a Carmelite, and therefore hostile, account of the Lollards, states that John Ball himself confessed 'that for two years he had been a disciple of Wycliffe and had learned from the latter the heresies which he had taught.'[25] It is likely, however, that Ball's 'confession' is a fabrication. As R. B. Dobson argues, the *Fasciculi Zizaniorum* fails to deliver its promise to include the text of the confession, and, if it really existed at the time, 'it is inconceivable that it would not have been exploited by contemporary churchmen and chroniclers'.[26] Wyclif himself, moreover, openly condemned the revolt.[27]

Soon after this, Wyclif left Oxford for Lutterworth in Leicestershire, where he held a living, and continued his writing there, turning with particular venom against the friars, whom he blamed for driving him out of Oxford. Meanwhile, in May 1382, Archbishop Courtenay summoned the Blackfriars council, which condemned ten of Wyclif's propositions as heretical and censured a further fourteen. The council was interrupted by an earthquake. Both parties, naturally enough, read this as a sign: for Wyclif it was a sign of divine anger, but for Courtenay it was indicative of the kingdom breaking wind as it expelled vile heresies. Wyclif was not condemned by name, and not excommunicated, but his followers were forbidden to preach until they had cleared themselves of heresy. Two of them, Hereford and Repington, were excommunicated in July. Wyclif died in 1384 and was buried in Lutterworth churchyard, but he was posthumously condemned by the Council of Constance in 1415, and his bones were dug up and burned in 1428.

Wyclif perceived himself as philosophically opposed to Ockham. In the debate over universals he was a realist, despising the nominalists as mere 'doctors of signs'. He believed, in other words, that the common nature perceptible in individuals of the same species existed in reality, not merely in the mind of the observer, and his most important philosophical work, the *Summa de Ente*, is concerned, as the Latin title indicates, with the nature of being. Yet it is clear that in some respects Wyclif's life and works can be compared with Ockham's. Both became involved, for example, in political dispute between Church and State; both found themselves condemned by the Church and protected by secular lords. Wyclif's argument in his treatise *On Civil Dominion* is broadly similar to Ockham's argument on dominion: a man in sin has no right to dominion; a man in a state of grace possesses all the goods of the universe. For Wyclif, however, this argument led on to virtual communism, which may have contributed to contemporary perceptions of his thinking as linked with the kind of thinking that inspired the Rising of 1381:

All the goods of God should be common. This is proved thus. Every man should be in a state of grace; and if he is in a state of grace, he is lord of the world and all it contains. So every man should be lord of the universe. But this is not consistent with there being many men, unless they ought to have everything in common. Therefore all things should be in common.[28]

The other point about Wyclif that would seem to link him with the aims of the Rising, and which separates him from Ockham, is his insistence in later life on the need to use English in order to reach the widest possible audience, and in particular on the necessity for an English translation of the Bible. Wyclif's use of the vernacular has already been the subject of discussion in chapter 2 above (pp. 39–40), but what needs further emphasis in this context is simply the absolute and single authority of the Holy Scriptures in Wyclif's philosophy. For him the Bible alone contains unassailable truth, and every pronouncement on doctrine made by subsequent commentators, however venerable, must be measured against its evidence. No words are sacred except the Word. He was known to his own contemporaries as *doctor evangelicus* and in Bohemia as the 'fifth Evangelist'.[29]

The importance to Wyclif of making the Bible available to laymen in their own language is the consequence of his redefinition of the church. For him, as for Ockham, the church signifies not the ecclesiastical institution, the visible Church, but the invisible body of the faithful, those whose faith and works proclaim them to be in a state of grace. Wyclif extends this belief to the point where he is ready to dispense with priests as mediators between God and His church, and to lay the responsibility for salvation on the individual soul. Excommunication by the Church, Wyclif argued, was irrelevant, since membership of the true church was a matter between God and the individual soul. It is clear that Wyclif's beliefs on the definition of the church again implied, as did his beliefs on dominion, a radicalism similar to that which inspired the English Rising, regardless of whether Wyclif himself ever considered the social implications of his theology. His ideas were a threat to the conservatism of estates theory, as described in chapter 3, since they muddied the clarity that had previously distinguished layman from cleric, and opened up traditionally male precincts to female participation (see pp. 66–7 above). He called on all 'the faithful . . . in meekness and humility of heart, whether they be clergy or laity, male or female' to read the Bible and draw strength and wisdom from it.[30]

Salvation, according to Wyclif, belonged to the elect, those predestined by God to be the recipients of his grace; yet Wyclif would not have accepted that this belief ruled out the existence of free will. One of the heresies for which his teaching was condemned was the doctrine of necessity, yet he did not in fact believe that the necessity of God's will abrogated the freedom of the individual human will. As he himself argued, if individuals were not free to make their own choices, 'merit and demerit would be eliminated'. Perhaps it was his somewhat implausible explanation of this apparent contradiction that accounted for the failure of his accusers to acknowledge his true position on the question of free will: he argued 'that the volition of God, with respect to the existence of a creature, can be understood as a relationship', that is, that both God's will and the will of the individual stimulated one another simultaneously to the same response.[31]

There was no question, then, of escaping moral responsibility by pointing to the absolute necessity of God's will. On the contrary, Wyclif's system of belief laid a heavy burden on the individual conscience by placing a higher value on the inner life than on the external and communal life of the Church. The Lollards who followed him met privately in each other's houses, read aloud to one another from the Bible, taught one another the skills of literacy so that as many as possible could study the truth of scripture personally, and developed a faith in the priesthood of all believers.

CHAUCER AND *TROILUS AND CRISEYDE*

'Of scepticism, even of Ockhamite scepticism, there is little trace in Chaucer.' This was the stated view of J. A. W. Bennett.[32] But is it really the case that Chaucer's work shows so little engagement with one of most dominant currents of fourteenth-century thinking? In the study of Chaucer's *Troilus and Criseyde* that follows I am not concerned with hunting for direct echoes of the writings of Ockham and Wyclif in order to prove that Chaucer knew their work, since it seems unlikely that he did. Nor am I interested, as a philosopher investigating the writings of Ockham and Wyclif would be, in making clear distinctions between their thinking and the kind of thinking they unwittingly stimulated in their followers. On the contrary, it seems to me that if Chaucer was influenced at all by their work it was in just this rather loose and second-hand way, through contact with their ideas at a popular rather than an academic level. Scepticism and Lollardy, rather than Ockham and Wyclif, represent the currents of thinking with which Chaucer could not have failed to be familiar.

Several times in his work Chaucer makes ironic reference to philosophers in a way that suggests that their work was the subject of discussion at a popular level, though not necessarily understood. The most famous of such allusions is the Nun's Priest's remark concerning whether God's foreknowledge implied the impossibility of free will. There is, says the Nun's Priest,

> greet altercacioun
> In this mateere, and greet disputisoun,
> And hath been of an hundred thousand men.
> But I ne kan nat bulte it to the bren
> As kan the hooly doctour Augustyn,
> Or Boece, or the Bisshop Bradwardyn,
> Wheither that Goddes worthy forwityng [foreknowledge]
> Streyneth me nedely for to doon a thyng –
> 'Nedely' clepe I symple necessitee –
> Or elles, if free choys be graunted me
> To do that same thyng, or do it noght,
> Though God forwoot it er that I was wroght;
> Or if his wityng streyneth never a deel
> But by necessitee condicioneel.
> I wol nat han to do of swich mateere.

> (VII.3237–3251)

The question of free will has been labelled 'the obsession of the century',[33] and Ockham himself testifies that the obsession was not confined to academic circles, but provoked 'laymen and old women' to pursue academics on the subject.[34]

Chaucer again hints at scholastic discussion beyond the skills of his speaker in the *Knight's Tale*, when the Knight speaks of Arcite's death:

> His spirit chaunged hous and wente ther,
> As I cam nevere, I kan nat tellen wher.
> Therfore I stynte; I nam no divinistre [theologian].
>> (I.2809–11)

and again at greater length when the narrator of the Prologue to
The Legend of Good Women meditates on the unknowability of the
after-life:

> A thousand tymes have I herd men telle
> That there is joy in hevene and peyne in helle,
> And I acorde wel that it ys so;
> But natheles, yet wot I wel also,
> That there nis noon dwellyng in this contree
> That eyther hath in hevene or helle ybe,
> Ne may of hit noon other weyes witen
> But as he hath herd seyd or founde it writen;
> For by assay there may no man it preve.
>> (F.1–9)

The first thirty or so lines of the Prologue, though too long to
quote in full, are highly relevant to the question of Chaucer's
engagement with contemporary philosophy. Like Ockham,
Chaucer's narrator argues here that matters which cannot be
observed in the material world are not subject to proof by human
reason; but like Ockham too, his response to his own scepticism
about the limits of reason is to turn to faith. God forbid, he
continues, that men should believe only what they see:

> Men shal nat wenen every thyng a lye
> But yf himself yt seeth or elles dooth;
> For, God wot, thing is never the lasse sooth,
> Thogh every wight ne may it nat ysee.
>> (12–15)

Notably, the text alternates between the individual 'I' and the
collective 'we'. The intensive 'I' of ll. 1–4, which foregrounds, as
Ockham does, the importance of individual observation in
establishing what can be known, gives way first to 'men' and then
to 'we' as the collective inadequacy of human reason is exposed,

and finally returns to 'I' in l. 29 as the narrator returns to the isolated responsibility of personal commitment:

> And as for me, though that I konne but lyte,
> On bokes for to rede I me delyte,
> And to hem yive I feyth and ful credence,
> And in myn herte have hem in reverence.
>
> (29–32)

Poetry here reflects the same tension between faith and reason as pervades Ockham's writing, but with a playfulness that makes the question of the writer's commitment problematic. The most conspicuous gap between poetry and philosophical writing is that a poet does not claim, as a philosopher implicitly does, to be making a true statement of his own beliefs: the speaker is a persona who may slip and slide between points of view in a way that allows the poet to test different statements without committing himself firmly to any. The narrator's statement of faith here, that we should turn, as he does, to books, where there is 'noon other preve' (28), may be a typical piece of irony intended to foreground the unworthiness of books as the object of faith. The discussion in chapter 4 above of Chaucer's conscious pluralism in setting authorities against one another should make us stop short of taking Chaucer at the narrator's word here. How can we accept books as 'proof' of anything if they contradict one another?

Sheila Delany, in another context, has defined Chaucer's scepticism as 'that sense of the unreliability of traditional information which [he] deliberately incorporates into the style and structure of his poetry'.[35] That questioning of 'authority' in the traditional sense of ancient and venerable sources, central to *The Parliament of Fowls*, and rightly perceived by Delany as crucial to *The House of Fame*, becomes in *Troilus and Criseyde* a questioning not only of existing 'authorities' but of the nature of 'authority' in another sense: the inevitable writing of the author *into* the text. Since every text is by definition authored, the words in which it consists are necessarily the result of selection, omission and so on, and thus reflect the authorial subject. If the content of the text claims to be history, thus aligning itself in some special relationship with truth, as though there is an external standard by which such truth can be measured, it becomes even more important to recognise the interference of the writer in the transformation of the real world into the textual world.

Some historical writers were also aware of the problem. Delany quotes Higden, a historical writer contemporary with Chaucer, on the subject of writing history:

> in the writynge of this storie I take nought uppon me to aferme for sooth all that I write, but such as I have seie and i-rad in dyverse bookes, I gadere and write with oute envie, and comoun to othere men. For the apostel seith nought, 'All that is write to oure lore is sooth', but he seith 'Al that is i-write to oure lore it is i-write.'[36]

What Chaucer does in *Troilus and Criseyde* is to remind his audience that writing about experience can never approximate to experience itself. There is no single truth that historical writers transmit; there are only versions of truth, arising out of the individual writer's subject position. The act of reading and the act of writing, in both of which Chaucer is involved, by virtue of reading and rewriting sources, are reminders of the contingency of experience, the absence of a universally acknowledged truth. Just as Ockham's philosophy insisted that the individual mind, not the external world, was the repository of universals, so Chaucer's text insists on its own subjectivity in order to reveal the inadequacy of an essentialist approach to historical truth.[37]

Chaucer's approach to both fiction and history marks a break with more traditional approaches. He divests both of any stable claim to represent a singular truth, a 'sentence' or 'moralitee' that can be lifted free of the material itself. Derek Pearsall, writing about Lydgate's *Troy Book*, has shown how, despite Lydgate's consistent attempt to emulate Chaucer, the significant difference between them is one of approach:

> Systematically . . . and in accord with the best medieval theory and practice, Lydgate empties the story of everything but *sentence* and in so doing restores it to that world of stable truths which fiction always threatens to subvert.
>
> Chaucer treats his story of *Troilus* seriously as a story, giving to his representation of people's lives and feelings a degree of autonomy, and seeking the meaning of the story in that representation and his commentary upon it. In so doing, he

contradicted the traditional medieval assumption that fictions are exemplary, and exist to demonstrate truths outside themselves. Lydgate does not understand that there could be any other assumption.[38]

The first four lines of *Troilus and Criseyde* tell the story in brief. It is clear, then, that the interest of the work will not lie in the story-line, at its simplest level. That much is already known to Chaucer's audience and summarised in this casual way at the beginning. The interest lies instead in *how much* can be known beyond this bare narrative, how much is in fact knowable. The declared theme of the story, as Chaucer tells it, is love. His proem to Book I addresses lovers as the particular audience for the poem; the proem to Book II speaks to those lovers who find that the poem does not accord with their experience, reminding them that every individual experience of love is different; and an impassioned statement by Criseyde's niece Antigone later in Book II, resembling the exploration of the knowable in the Prologue to *The Legend of Good Women*, affirms that perfect love is unknowable to those without individual experience of it:

> But wene ye that every wrecche woot
> The parfit blisse of love? Why, nay, iwys!
> They wenen all be love, if oon be hoot.
> Do wey, do wey, they woot no thyng of this!
> Men most axe at seyntes if it is
> Aught fair in hevene (Why? For they kan telle),
> And axen fendes is it foul in helle.
>
> (II.890–6)

This concern with the limits of knowledge is crucial to the ambivalent depiction of the narrator of *Troilus and Criseyde*. He is a narrator who swings between ignorance and omniscience, but never allows his audience to lose sight of the fact that writers before him have treated the same story, and that every act of writing, or rewriting, distorts. The text is full of reminders that everything in it is subject to selection and interpretation. 'I passe al that which chargeth nought to seye' (III.1576) is a typical reminder to the audience that there is far more to any experience than the written résumé contains, however detailed that account may be. The narrator pauses in Book III to consider the possible expectation that he should outline 'every word, or soonde, or look, or cheere' (492), but replies to his imaginary audience that such a thing not only has never been done, but is impossible: 'And though I wolde, I koude nought, ywys' (I.491ff). The act of writing is constantly restricted, not only by the need to rhyme, as Chaucer often reminds us (for example, at III.90–1), but by the inevitable difference between words and experience. If Ockham recognised the arbitrariness of language as a system of signs, Chaucer's understanding of its failure to communicate the deepest feelings is also an acknowledgement of its artificiality. Regularly he notes its inadequacy to the task in hand:

> This joie may nought writen be with inke;
> This passeth al that herte may bythynke.
> (III.1693–4)

> How myghte it evere yred ben or ysonge,
> The pleynte that she made in hire destresse?
> I not; but, as for me, my litel tonge,
> If I discryven wolde hire hevynesse,
> It sholde make hire sorwe seme lesse
> Than that it was, and childisshly deface
> Hire heigh compleynte, and therfore ich it pace.
> (III.799–805)

> Who koude telle aright or ful discryve
> His wo, his pleynt, his langour, and his pyne?
> Naught alle the men that han or ben on lyve.
> Thow, redere, maist thiself ful wel devyne
> That swich a wo my wit kan nat diffyne;
> On ydel for to write it sholde I swynke,
> Whan that my wit is wery it to thynke.
> (V.267–73)

Not only the words, but the structure, of narrative impose a reading of events that is 'authorised' (specified by a particular writer). Chaucer's five-book structure, echoing Boethius's *Consolation of Philosophy*, endorses both the category of tragedy, which he himself invokes at V.1786, and the theme of the insufficiency of earthly happiness, which is Boethius's subject. But the possibility that the story might be construed in other forms is

constantly presented to us by the references to reading matter
within the narrative. When Pandarus first comes to see Criseyde
she is reading the story of the siege of Thebes with her
companions, though she says a few lines later that it would be
more appropriate for her to be reading saints' lives (II.82–4,
117–19); on the night Criseyde and Troilus are to become lovers at
Pandarus's house, Pandarus tells the story of Wade (III.614); later,
in Criseyde's bedroom, in the company of the lovers, Pandarus
pretends to read 'an old romaunce' (III.980). While one character
reads, for example, history or romance, the author confronts of the
problems of whether to construct his text at any given point as
history or romance.

In Book V references to the artifice of fiction multiply. Troilus
himself sees the literary potential in his experience:

> Whan I the proces have in my memorie
> How thow me hast wereyed on every syde,
> Men myght a book make of it, lik a storie.
>
> (V.583–5)

A sequence of stanzas from l. 1037 onwards transfers responsibility almost obsessively to 'the storie', though the admission
follows that the form into which Chaucer has put the material
highlights a different theme from that of at least one source:

> And if I hadde ytaken for to write
> The armes of this ilke worthi man,
> Than wolde ich of his batailles endite;
> But for that I to writen first bigan
> Of his love, I have seyd as I kan –
> His worthi dedes, whoso list hem heere,
> Rede Dares, he kan telle hem alle ifeere –
>
> (V.1765–71)

His claims to be merely a slavish translator of his source, with
no personal involvement in what he writes (see, for example, the
proem to Book II), function primarily to focus their own untruth.
When it suits him, this narrator claims access to the inner life of
his characters, describing their feelings and motives in analytical
detail, as in portraying first Troilus and then Criseyde weighing
the advantages and disadvantages of love. Elsewhere he casts

doubt on their motives by exaggerated reference to the 'fact' (often bogus) that they are documented in his reading of other writers. Consider how this method subtly undermines the narrator's apparent attribution of 'good entente' to Criseyde when she first assures Troilus, on hearing of the plan to exchange her for Antenor, that she will return to him or die:

> And treweliche, as writen wel I fynde
> That al this thyng was seyd of good entente,
> And that hire herte trewe was and kynde
> Towardes hym, and spak right as she mente,
> And that she starf for wo neigh whan she wente,
> And was in purpos evere to be trewe:
> Thus writen they that of hire werkes knewe.
>
> (IV.1415–21)

More conspicuously, he makes reference to the supposed silence of his 'auctour' on any given point in order to arouse suspicion or doubt in the reader, usually concerning Criseyde. He foregrounds his ignorance, for example, of whether Criseyde believes Pandarus when he tells her Troilus will be out of town on the night he (Pandarus) is inviting her to dinner (III.575–8) and of whether, when Troilus kneels by her bed waiting for her to accept him as a lover, she fails to tell him to rise because sorrow puts it 'out of hire remembraunce' (III.967–73).

Chaucer's choice of a pagan setting, not for the first time, is a further metaphor for restricted knowledge. A Christian writer presenting pagan characters to a Christian audience shares with his audience a belief that these characters lack access to the most crucial truths about the world in which they live, so that, even as the text explores their questioning of that world, the audience is continually aware of the restrictions within which their reason operates. Troilus's famous speech questioning the existence of free will in Book IV (958–1078) is well known both for its indebtedness to Boethius and for its failure to reach Boethius's conclusion that human beings *do* have free will. The extended and literal borrowing from Boethius, together with the divergence from him, would undoubtedly have been perceptible to those among Chaucer's audience who had read Boethius, and would confirm their sense of superior knowledge. Troilus's failure to reach the same conclusion as Boethius is the pagan's failure to see God.

At the same time, however, the restrictions of paganism operate
as a very useful metaphor for the inherent limitations of all human
reason, and as such they help to focus fourteenth-century doubts
about the limits of the knowable. The inconsistent operation of the
pagan metaphor highlights this: Troilus and Criseyde cannot be
dismissed as simple puppets operated by pagan gods. The god of
Love shoots his arrow at Troilus, but this is only one of many
ways in which the question of falling in love is approached. The
shooting of Cupid's arrow is followed by Troilus's withdrawal
into a private chamber and an inner world in order to give full
consideration to the problem of whether to allow himself to
submit to his sudden love. Only after he has interiorised the whole
event, made 'a mirour of his mynde' (I.365) does he reach the
decision to follow his desire:

> Thus took he purpos loves craft to suwe,
> (379)

> . . . he gan fully assente
> Criseyde for to love, and nought repente.
> (391–2)

We are never allowed to see events as moved simply by one
force, whether it be manipulation, Fortune or Providence (human
beings, the gods or God); we are always invited to consider more
than one possibility. As Book III approaches the climactic coming
together of Troilus and Criseyde, Chaucer shows us Pandarus
leaving nothing to chance:

> For he with gret deliberacioun
> Hadde every thyng that herto myght availle
> Forncast and put in execucioun,
> And neither left for cost ne for travaille.
> Come if hem list, hem sholde no thyng faille;
> And for to be in ought aspied there,
> That, wiste he wel, an impossible were.
> (III.519–25)

He then tells us that Troilus was fully aware of 'al this purveiance'
(533), a word laden with irony here, since it is also the word
regularly used for God's foreknowledge (earlier Chaucer writes

that none 'but god and Pandare wist al what this mente' – II.1561). The narrative piles up different angles for the reader to consider in quick succession: Pandarus selects a dark night when rain is certain (III.548–51); the narrator is uncertain as to whether Criseyde believes Pandarus when he assures her that Troilus is out of town (575–8); he invokes the power of *both* Fortune and God to determine events:

> But O Fortune, executrice of wierdes,
> O influences of thise hevenes hye!
> Soth is, that under God ye ben oure hierdes,
> Though to us bestes ben the causez wrie;
> (617–20)

the rainstorm prevents Criseyde from leaving (624–44); Pandarus invents the tale of Horaste, an imaginary rival, as a pretext for admitting Troilus to Criseyde's bedroom; and finally, on Troilus's sudden assertiveness, 'Now yeldeth yow' (1208), Criseyde admits that her own desires were already directing her towards consummation:

> Ne hadde I er now, my swete herte deere,
> Ben yolde, ywis, I were now nought heere!
> (1210–11)

Yet again Chaucer returns us, via uncertainty, to the fact of subjectivity, the isolation of the individual within the inner world of doubt, where the thinking mind itself is the only reality. The poem continually explores the problem of perception, inviting the reader to participate, as do the characters, in the awareness that no two subjects perceive reality in the same way. This concern is at its most conspicuous in the poem's theme of betrayal, where Chaucer's concern is to narrate the tale of betrayal in such a way as to make the simple judgement implied in such a value-laden word seem inadequate. His narrator resists the word and insists on presenting the situation from different angles, stimulating a plural response from the audience.

This world of uncertain values is one that both Ockham and Wyclif helped to create. As Russell Peck, citing the *OED*, has pointed out, it is during the last quarter of the fourteenth century that the word 'conscience' comes to take a plural, developing away from the earlier sense of a natural, shared sense of right and wrong to the sense of a distinct individual conscience.[39] Such a world involves both liberation and imprisonment. It frees the individual to choose her own path, establish her own values ('I am myn owene womman' – II.750), but at the same time it isolates the individual within the limitations of the self, cutting him off from fixed or communal values.

Pandarus responds to such freedom by attempting to adjust the universe to his own specifications. In this, he resembles the narrator and the author and imitates the condition of God (see p. 113 above). His aspiration to play God is of course thwarted, and events prove the limitations of individual human manipulations. Troilus and Criseyde, more insecure than Pandarus, acknowledge their freedom in their agonies over choice. They withdraw into the solitude of private space to consider their positions ('into a closet, for t'avise hire bettre / She wente allone, and gan hire herte unfettre' – II.1215–16), but such private soul-searching yields for them not certainties but doubts. The prominence of the conditional in the *Canticus Troili* of Book I is characteristic:

> If no love is, O God, what fele I so?
> And if love is, what thing and which is he?
> If love be good, from whennes cometh my woo?
> If it be wikke, a wonder thynketh me . . .
>
> (I.400ff.)

Chaucer's Troilus and Criseyde, unable to enclose these empty expanses of uncertainty with the wall of faith, which encircles Christian philosophies, are nevertheless presented simultaneously as shaped by absolutes beyond the self. Despite Troilus's doubts about love, the narrator conveys a sense of love as the absolute, the law of nature which binds the disparate individuals of humankind:

> For evere it was, and evere it shal byfalle,
> That Love is he that alle thing may bynde,
> For may no man fordon the lawe of kynde.
>
> (I.236–8)

The proem to Book III opens with an invocation to Love which makes an explicit connection between Love and the Christian God, suggesting to the Christian audience that even pagan characters are framed by such universal forces regardless of their inability to perceive them:

> God loveth, and to love wol nought werne,
> And in this world no lyves creature
> Withouten love is worth, or may endure.
>
> (III.12–14)

The poem thus slips between pagan and Christian perspectives, between the restricted knowledge of individual characters and the faith that, anachronistically, encloses them for a fourteenth-century audience, so that the concerns of the poem are constantly shifting. The narrator announces his subject at the beginning of the poem as 'the double sorwe of Troilus' (I.1), yet the experience of reading the poem suggests that its narrative content is primarily a vehicle for raising philosophical questions about knowledge and faith. Chaucer's real agenda seems to be the testing of limits, whether of the individual mind or the world it inhabits, and whether that world is perceived to be the pagan world, the Christian universe or the text.

The poem's conclusion is both unsurprising and unsatisfying. It is unsurprising to find that a poem which explores isolation, betrayal and uncertainty ends with an assertion of ultimate stability. There is an inexorable logic in its turning away from the limits of human reason and perception to God, whose goodness and permanence can be accepted on faith without recourse to the ways of reason. Yet it is also profoundly unsatisfying, in that it reaches stability by simply cutting the text loose from the whole arena of exploration it has occupied, so that the conclusion itself becomes something of a betrayal. In moving to resolution (or, perhaps, 'fideistic evasion'),[40] the poem moves out of the perspective it has adopted for its own, the perspective that has encouraged the audience to question, to perceive complexity, to acknowledge doubt. Instead it turns to look at events from an external and eternal perspective, which allows the problems they raised to look unimportant by virtue of their very distance.

This distance is underlined by the curiously detachable quality of the last stanza. It is a self-contained prayer, circular in both language and conception:

Thow oon, and two, and thre, eterne on lyve,
That regnest ay in thre, and two, and oon,
Uncircumscript, and al maist circumscrive,
Us from visible and invisible foon
Defende, and to thy mercy, everichon,
So make us, Jesus, for thi mercy, digne,
For love of mayde and moder thyn benigne.
Amen.

(V.1863–70)

Within the world of the poem all is transient, unclear. One recurrent image for this world, both in *Troilus and Criseyde* and commonly in medieval literature, is the circle of Fortune's wheel, which limits and devalues human endeavour. The audience's foreknowledge of the outcome ensures that they perceive the turning of Fortune's wheel in, for example, Criseyde's response to Diomede, which echoes her dealings with Pandarus and Troilus in Books I and II. God, who is Himself 'uncircumscript', but encloses all earthly circles, offers a refuge from the tyranny of Fortune's wheel.[41] Chaucer's poem ends, as do the philosophical systems of Ockham and Wyclif, at the point where reason defers to faith.

6

'This wrecched world':
The Obsession with Death

I say, then, that the sum of thirteen hundred and forty-eight years had elapsed since the fruitful Incarnation of the Son of God, when the noble city of Florence, which for its great beauty excels all others in Italy, was visited by the deadly pestilence. Some say that it descended upon the human race through the influence of the heavenly bodies, others that it was a punishment signifying God's righteous anger at our iniquitous way of life. But whatever its cause, it had originated some years earlier in the East, where it had claimed countless lives before it unhappily spread westward, growing in strength as it swept relentlessly on from one place to the next.

In the face of its onrush, all the wisdom and ingenuity of man were unavailing. Large quantities of refuse were cleared out of the city by officials specially appointed for the purpose, all sick persons were forbidden entry, and numerous instructions were issued for safeguarding the people's health, but all to no avail. Nor were the countless petitions humbly directed to God by the pious, whether by means of formal processions or in any other guise, any less ineffectual. For in the early spring of the year we have mentioned, the plague began, in a terrifying and extraordinary manner, to make its disastrous effects apparent. It did not take the form it had assumed in the East, where if anyone bled from the nose it was an obvious portent of certain death. On the contrary, its earliest symptom, in men and women alike, was the appearance of certain swellings in the groin or the armpit, some of which were egg-shaped whilst others were roughly the size of the common apple. Sometimes the swellings were large, sometimes not so large, and they were referred to by the populace as *gavoccioli*. From the two areas already mentioned, this deadly *gavocciolό* would begin to spread, and within a short time it would appear at random all over the body. Later on, the symptoms of the disease changed, and many people began to find dark blotches and bruises on their arms, thighs, and other parts of the body, sometimes large and few in number, at other times tiny and closely spaced. These, to anyone unfortunate enough to contract them, were just as infallible a sign that he would die as the *gavoccioló* had been earlier, and as indeed it still was.

Against these maladies, it seemed that all the advice of physicians and all the power of medicine were profitless and unavailing. . . . At all events, few of those who caught it ever recovered, and in most cases death occurred within three days from the appearance of the symptoms we have described, some people dying more rapidly than others, the majority without any fever or other complications.

But what made this pestilence even more severe was that whenever those suffering from it mixed with people who were still unaffected, it would rush upon these with the speed of a fire racing through dry or oily substances that happened to be placed within its reach. . . .

Some people were of the opinion that a sober and abstemious mode of living considerably reduced the risk of infection. They therefore formed themselves into groups and lived in isolation from everyone else. . . .

Others took the opposite view, and maintained that an infallible way of warding off this appalling evil was to drink heavily, enjoy life to the full, go round singing and merry-making, gratify all of one's cravings whenever the opportunity offered, and shrug the whole thing off as one enormous joke. . . .

In the face of so much affliction and misery, all respect for the laws of God and man had virtually broken down and been extinguished in our city. For like everybody else, those ministers and executors of the laws who were not either dead or ill were left with so few subordinates that they were unable to discharge any of their duties. Hence everyone was free to behave as he pleased.

. . . no more respect was accorded to dead people than would nowadays be shown towards dead goats. For it was quite apparent that the one thing which, in normal times, no wise man had ever learned to accept with patient resignation (even though it struck so seldom and unobtrusively), had now been brought home to the feeble-minded as well, but the scale of the calamity caused them to regard it with indifference.[1]

Thus does Boccaccio describe the terrible onslaught of the plague in Europe from 1347–9 and the changing attitudes it produced towards both life and death. The immediate effects of the plague were horrific enough, and many writers, including Boccaccio, describe the unmanageable numbers of corpses, the digging of trenches for communal burial and the curtailment of funeral rites (see, for example, Walsingham on p. 2 above); but the longer-term consequence was repeated epidemics of the disease over the next three centuries. Even during Chaucer's lifetime there were significant outbreaks in England in 1361, 1368–9, 1371, 1375 and 1390.[2]

Not only plague, but famine and warfare cut down the population of fourteenth-century England. The consequence was that death seemed closer than ever before. Literature and the visual arts in the second half of the fourteenth century are dominated by the awareness of death: the personification of death, the dance of death, the meeting of the three living with the three dead, are motifs common to both. Religious treatises preach on how to make a good end, lyrics meditate on the certainty of death, drama derives its shapes from the movement of human life towards the day of judgement. As Philip Ziegler has written, 'death had always been a preoccupation of medieval man; now it became an obsession'.[3] In this chapter I want to look at how various aspects of the late medieval obsession with death are found across a range of Chaucer's texts.

REPRESENTATIONS OF DEATH

A tendency to dwell on the physical details of death as a bodily state is characteristic of the period. The skeleton or decomposing corpse is a familiar image and it is at this time too that death masks are brought into use in the sculpture of effigies.[4] Lazarus's speech from the Towneley cycle catches the macabre mood of numerous lyrics and sermons:

Ilkon [each one] in sich aray with dede thai shall be dight,

And closid colde in clay wheder he be kyng or knyght;
For all his garments gay that semely were in sight,
His flesh shall frete [waste] away with many a wofull wight.
Then wofully sich wightys
Shall gnawe thise gay knyghtys,
Thare lunges and thare lightys,
Thare harte shall frete in sonder;
Thise masters most of myghtys
Thus shall thai be broght under.

Under the erthe ye shall thus carefully then cowche;
The royfe of youre hall youre nakyd nose shall towche;
Nawther great ne small to you will knele ne crowche;
A shete shall be youre pall; sich todys [toads] shall be your
nowche [jewel];
Todys shall you dere [harm];
Feyndys will you fere [frighten];
Youre flesh that fare was here
Thus rufully shall rote;
In stede of fare colore
Sich bandys shall bynde youre throte.[5]

The dance of death, which couples rotting corpses with clothed
human beings, surprised by death, was not only a pictorial theme,
but even the subject of live performance.[6] It encapsulates a bitterly
ironic statement about the inconsequence of social estate in the
face of death and bodily corruption, a statement echoed in literary
and visual forms alike:

> *Sic primus rex Anglice:*
> Kyng I syt and loke aboute,
> Tomorn I may ben withoute.
>
> *Secundus:*
> Wo is me, a kyng I was;
> This world I lovede but that I las [lost].
>
> *Tercius:*
> Nouhth longe gon I was ful ryche
> But nowe is ryche and pore ylyche.

Quartus:
I shal be kynge, that men schulle se
When the wreche ded shal be.[7]

Wreche mon, why art thou prowde
That art of erthe maket?
Hedure ne brouhtest thou no schroude
But pore thou come and naket.
When thy soule is faren out
Of thy body, with erthe yraket,
That body that was so ronke [proud] and loud
Of alle men is hated.[8]

Lollard wills show this same disgust for the body, but in a context that insists more clearly on the separation between body and soul after death. The typical phrase is 'wretched' or 'stinking carrion', and it is linked with an emphatic refusal of funeral pomp. Here, for example, are two extracts from the will of Sir John Cheyne (made in 1413):

my wretched stinking carrion to be buried without the chapel new made within the churchyard of the church of Beckford, my head joining to the wall under the window of the east end of the same chapel. . . .

I pray and charge my surveyors [i.e. overseers] and mine executors as they will answer before God and as all mine whole trust in this matter is in them that on my stinking carrion be neither laid cloth of gold ne of silk but russet cloth price the yard fifteen pence; and one taper at mine head and one other at my feet.[9]

By setting this alongside other wills of the period we may see how more orthodox Christians show their preoccupation with bodily remains through a sense of the *importance* of physical memorials and funeral rites. Thomas Grey, Bishop of London, gives these instructions in 1395:

I will that I be buried before the high altar in the chapel of the Virgin in the church of Holy Trinity, Hadenham. The chapel at my cost to be decorated with painted tiles. I will that a good stone of marble with an image . . . representing a likeness of me

be placed above me. In the north of the chapel I will that a new
and good window . . . be made as wide and as high as the wall
extends, and I will that the story of Jesse be told in glass. And I
will that in one [part] be made a likeness of me kneeling upon
my armorial shield and holding a roll in my hands.[10]

Richard II's orders in the same year for a tomb for himself and
Queen Anne (who had died in 1394) show an extreme interest in
the detail and richness of its adornment, and a lengthy account of
the funeral of the Earl of Salisbury and his son in 1462 documents
a prolonged ritual sequence, involving a chariot led by six horses,
several heralds and bishops and numerous lengths of cloth of
gold. The distance between such elaborate burial rites and the bare
essentials of Sir John Cheyne's funeral is obvious, yet both show a
preoccupation with the body, whether by adorning its resting
place, or rejecting it as a discarded vessel.

Something of the same ambivalence towards death is visible in
Chaucer's *Pardoner's Tale*, which presents death both as a physical
image and as a spiritual state. The passing of a corpse begins the
tale: the rioters, drinking in a tavern, hear 'a belle clynke/Biforn a
cors, was caried to his grave' (VI.664–5). On enquiring how he
died, they are told that he was 'sodeynly . . . yslayn' by 'a privee
theef men clepeth Deeth' (675), who 'hath a thousand slayn this
pestilence' (679). With precise economy, this statement personifies
Death as a sudden slayer, calls up familiar images of the dance of
death, and puts death into the immediate historical context of the
plague. The rioters' determination to slay death is ironic to the
extent that it underlines their unpreparedness for death, and
perhaps also blasphemous, in that the paradox of slaying death by
dying is so strongly associated with Christ. The oath they swear to
live and die for each other is also a parody of Christ's sacrifice,
and the Pardoner notes that their swearing itself tears Christ's
body anew.

Almost at once they meet up with an old man, who, visually at
least, is strongly reminiscent of personifications of death. He is 'al
forwrapped' but for his face (718) – the epithet 'forwrapped'
perhaps suggestive of a winding sheet – and he is visibly
withering:

Lo how I vanysshe, flesshe, and blood, and skyn!

. . . ful pale and welked [withered] is my face.
(732, 738)

Although, allegorically, he cannot be seen as a straightforward personification of death, since he, like the rioters, is a seeker after Death, his iconographical resemblance to death cannot be ignored. Part of his function is to highlight the irony of the rioters' search. He wishes to die, but cannot 'find' death in this sense, though he knows where Death is to be found; the rioters, on the other hand, do not know where to find Death and wish to know, though they do not wish to die. The appearance of the old man, and his directions to them, confirm for the audience that the rioters are already on a certain course to death, though it will still take them, as it traditionally does, by surprise.

Following the old man's directions, the rioters find a heap of gold, and give up the search for Death. The irony is heavily underlined here, since they have of course already found it; but death now ceases to be physically represented and becomes spiritually present in the gold, which provokes them to become the instruments of one another's deaths. The maxim that 'the wages of sin is death' is here made literally true, and death is more subtly explored than the initial iconography of the tale suggests.

The tale not only enacts the maxim but allows it to reflect on the teller. The Pardoner himself, self-confessedly dominated by the same sin of avarice as the rioters of his creation, and in the same state of unrepentant sin, is spiritually dead. Despite his own state, however, the Pardoner is made the spokesman for the truth that embraces a Christian universe, that Christ's pardon is best for the soul.[11] Acknowledgement of the inevitability of judgement and the need for mercy are crucial to the way the fourteenth-century Christian approached the question of death.

DEATH AS JUDGEMENT

Early representations of the end of the world depict the resurrection of the dead without reference to judgement or condemnation. The separation of the saved from the damned begins to appear in twelfth-century art, and the imagery of justice – the scales and the book – becomes prominent in the thirteenth century as part of a widespread depiction of the judgement of all mankind on the last day. Towards the end of the Middle Ages, however, emphasis changes to highlight particular judgement at the close of the individual life, and is depicted in the sick-room rather than in the court of heaven.[12]

Sermons, obviously, play on the fear of sudden death, which brings the sinner unprepared to judgement, without time for repentance. G. R. Owst cites a particularly macabre gesture accompanying the performance of one medieval preacher 'who to strike terror into his audience suddenly displayed the skull of a dead man which he had been carrying under his cloak'.[13] *Everyman* portrays the terrified scrambling of the sinner to find something on the credit side to present before his judgement, and morality plays in general take judgement as the controlling framework for the individual life.

Chaucer's *Friar's Tale* shows quite clearly how death and damnation can suddenly take the sinner unawares. The deceitful summoner in the tale meets a devil disguised as a yeoman, who is quite open about his nature ('I am a feend; my dwellyng is in helle' – III.1448) and his capacity to change shape. He is presented with the same matter-of-factness as any other character in the story. There is nothing unusual in a medieval writer treating devils as literal truth, and numerous sermons attest to their usefulness in frightening a congregation into repentance. Preachers refer to the ghosts of the dead with the same literalism as they refer to devils and for the same ends.[14] A famous story concerning a performance of *Dr Faustus* may serve to remind us of how late such literal belief persisted. The actors, suddenly convinced that

> there was one devell too many amongst them . . . after a little pause desired the people to pardon them, they could go no further with this matter; the people also understanding the thing as it was, every man hastened to be first out of dores. The players . . . contrarye to their custome spending the night in reading and in prayer got them out of the town the next morning.[15]

The summoner and the fiend in Chaucer's tale, swearing to share their winnings, ride together to the house of an old widow, from whom the summoner demands twelve pence. The wording of his refusal to excuse the debt frames an oath in terms of death and damnation:

> the foule feend me fecche
> If I th'excuse, though thou shul be spilt [ruined; put to death]
> (1610–11)

While the widow may be financially ruined, however, it is the summoner who is 'spilt' in the corporal and spiritual senses. The widow, as she confesses, has 'no gilt' (1612): her soul is pure, prepared for death. The summoner's soul, on the other hand, is ripe for damnation. The widow consigns the summoner to damnation by returning him his own oath:

> Unto the devel blak and rough of hew
> Yeve I thy body.
>
> (1622–3)

The summoner's refusal to repent confirms damnation as his punishment: the devil claims his body and soul by right and takes him there and then to hell. The abruptness with which the tale ends is a device that calls attention to the suddenness of death. Death comes without warning, and does not allow space for special pleading. It is therefore best to be in a state of perpetual readiness.

Not only damnation, but death itself, in this tale, is clearly a punishment for sin, and this is another idea widely expressed in Chaucer's time. Death could be meted out as a punishment to the individual sinner, or it could be visited on a nation or on the whole of humankind as a punishment for their corporate sinfulness. The plague itself was widely perceived in this way. Death on this scale could be no accident in a Christian universe. A poem on the earthquake of 1382 (see p. 101 above), for example, cites the earthquake as one of three signs of God's anger with humanity, the other two being the Rising of 1381 and the plague:

> The rysyng of the comuynes in londe,
> The pestilens, and the eorthe-qwake,
> Theose threo thinges, I understonde,
> Beoth tokenes the grete vengaunce and wrake

> That schulde falle for synnes sake,
> As this clerkes conne declare.
> Now may we chese to leve or take,
> For warnyng have we to be ware.[16]

An inscription on the wall of Ashwell Church in Hertfordshire records the same sense of the plague as an act of God, accompanied by signs of violence in the natural world: '1349: plague. 1350: wretched, wild and driven to violence the people remaining become witness at last of a tempest. On St Maur's day this year 1361 it thunders on the earth.'[17]

A common feature of fourteenth-century literature is the prophecy of God's terrible vengeance and the imminence of the last day. Langland scatters such prophecies through *Piers Plowman*:

> Er fyve yer be fulfilled swich famyn shal aryse:
> Thorugh flodes and thorugh foule wedres, fruytes shal faille –
> . . . .
> Thanne shal deeth withdrawe and derthe be justice,
> And Dawe the Dykere deye for hunger –
> But if God of his goodnesse graunte us a trewe.[18]

and shows the coming of Antichrist in the last passus. The fifteen signs of the Last Judgement, taken from the description of the end of the world in the book of Revelations, can still be read in *The Prick of Conscience* (surviving in more manuscripts than any other Middle English poem) and seen in the east window of All Saints Church in York, to name but two of many examples.

The other biblical event called to mind by such prophecies was, of course, the Flood, sent as a punishment for the sins of an entire race, barring Noah's family alone, and Chaucer chooses a prophecy of second flood to place at the centre of the *Miller's Tale*. His tone is very different from the solemn warnings cited above, however, since the tale is a comic tale. The description of Nicholas at the opening of the tale tells us not only that he was devoted to the study of astrology, but that he was 'sleigh and ful privee' [sly and very secretive] (I.3201). The narrative then displays Nicholas's lust for Alison, the wife of the simple carpenter with whom he lodges, and the predictable consequence that Nicholas decides to 'shapen hym a wyle/This sely jalous housbonde to bigyle' (3403–4).

The trick is seen in action before the audience is admitted to the understanding of it. Nicholas keeps to his room and will not answer or come out for over twenty-four hours. The carpenter's thoughts turn to sudden death:

> God shilde that he deyde sodeynly!
> This world is now ful tikel [unstable], sikerly.
> I saugh today a cors yborn to chirche
> That now, on Monday last, I saugh hym wirche.
>   (3427–30)

He sends a servant up to knock at the door and the servant, peeping through a hole in the door, sees Nicholas gaping up towards heaven. Immediately the carpenter blames Nicholas's interest in astronomy and condemns such studies as presumptuous:

> Men sholde nat know of Goddes pryvetee.
> Ye, blessed be alwey a lewed man
> That noght but oonly his bileve kan!
>   (3454–6)

It is difficult to assess how many meanings are intentionally folded into this exclamation. It clearly mocks the carpenter's praise of ignorant faith, since this is what leads him to fall into Nicholas's trap, now in the process of being sprung on him. Yet many serious preachers and writers of Chaucer's time were warning in exactly the same way as John the carpenter against the dangers of presuming to subject all theological mysteries to reason, and Ockham, as we saw in chapter 5 above, taught that certain divine truths were by definition inaccessible to reason, and had to be taken on faith.

When John manages to break into Nicholas's room and sees him apparently in a trance, his response demonstrates the religion of the unlearned in a sequence of superstitious rituals. He makes the sign of the cross over Nicholas to protect him from evil spirits and creatures, says 'the nyght-spel' (3480) all round the house and another charm, 'the white *pater-noster*' (3485), on the threshold. Nicholas then pretends to come to and to tell him, in strictest confidence, what his studies have revealed:

> I have yfounde in myn astrologye,
> As I have looked in the moone bright,
> That now a Monday next, at quarter nyght,
> Shal falle a reyn, and that so wilde and wood
> That half so greet was nevere Noes flood.
> This world,' he seyde, 'in lasse than an hour
> Shal al be dreynt, so hidous is the shour.
> Thus shal mankynde drenche, and lese hir lyf.
> (3514–21)

Nicholas reminds John of how Noah was saved, and instructs him on how they can save themselves and Alison. Alison, of course, knows that this is Nicholas's device for getting John out of the way while he takes Alison to bed, but John is gullible, and Chaucer's irony at the expense of such foolish belief is heavily underlined in this apostrophe and the account of John's behaviour which follows:

> Lo, which a greet thyng is affeccioun!
> Men may dyen of ymaginacioun,
> So depe may impressioun be take.
> This sely carpenter bigynneth quake;
> Hym thynketh verraily that he may see
> Noees flood come walwynge as the see
> To drenchen Alisoun, his hony deere.
> He wepeth, weyleth, maketh sory cheere;
> He siketh with ful many a sory swogh;
> He gooth and geteth hym a knedyng trogh . . .
> (3611–20)

The rhyme on 'swogh' and 'trogh', incongruously linking John's terror with the absurdity of the actions he takes to save himself, confirms Chaucer's invitation to laugh at such behaviour. Indeed, it is the inherent absurdity of John's actions that allows Alison and Nicholas, after they have taken their pleasure, to dismiss the whole event to the neighbours as evidence of John's madness:

> The folk gan laughen at his fantasye;
> Into the roof they kiken [stare] and cape [gape],
> And turned al his harm unto a jape.
> For what so that this carpenter answerde,

It was for noght; no man his reson herde.
With othes grete he was so sworn adoun
That he was holde wood [mad] in al the toun;
For every clerk anonright heeld [agreed] with oother.
They seyde, 'The man is wood, my leeve brother';
And every wight gan laughen at this stryf.

                              (3840–9)

Although the mockery of the ignorant, who believe such prophecies, is unmistakeable, it is less clear whether a rejection of all the threats and prophecies of 'clerks', who support one another's claims, should be read into the tale.

DEATH AS MERCY

Yet Chaucer does not portray all clerks as scheming and corrupt. The content and positioning of the *Parson's Tale* make clear that we should take some clerical utterances very seriously indeed. The preaching of judgement and punishment, both in sermons and in other literary texts, is often qualified by the consolation of mercy. Medieval morality plays, for example, differ most significantly from Marlowe's *Dr Faustus* in the late sixteenth century in that they end with the salvation of the sinner, whereas Faustus is damned.

It is, of course, the Crucifixion that enables justice to be tempered with mercy. Noah's Flood occurs in the Old Testament, the time of judgement; Christ's passion initiates the time of grace. There is a notable concentration on the passion in medieval art and literature, and it is much more prominent than, for example, the Nativity. When the Fourth Lateran Council in 1215 decreed the necessity for each Christian to confess and take Holy Communion at least once a year, the time of that confession was specified to take place around Easter, the most important feast in the Church calendar, and throughout Lent preachers urged the need for confession. And as the Eucharist, the sacrament celebrating Christ's sacrifice, grew in importance within the established Church, a new feast, the feast of Corpus Christi, was introduced to celebrate it.

It is not surprising to find this increasing devotion to the body of Christ reflected in the arts. New genres of literature can be identified with the Church's new emphasis on the importance of penitence, confession and the Eucharist: the growth of the Corpus Christi cycle plays in the late fourteenth century is clearly linked with the establishment of the new feast, while the development of a newly personal literature for purposes of individual meditation, both in prose and in poetry, and the sudden upsurge of mystical writing in the fourteenth century, can be attributed more generally to these changing directions within the Church.

Christians were encouraged to think of their lives as framed by their deaths, and to think of their deaths as framed by the death of Christ. Devotion to the Church in this life, though it could not make salvation secure, could not fail to help the soul on the day of judgement. Wills, again, are a useful source of evidence for the different ways in which the testators show care for the soul:

I bequeath to my beloved wife, Lady of Arundel and Maltravers, a cross containing a large piece of the Holy Cross. This is now in pledge; when it is recovered, each of my children is to have a piece, with the divine blessing and my blessing "ex toto corde meo," but my wife is to have the larger piece for her life. Afterwards the cross and the larger piece of the Holy Cross to go to the church of Stokecours, forever.

Bequests to the new work of the belfry of St Mary-le-Bow and for the purchase of a bell for the same. A tenement . . . to be devoted to the maintenance of chantries in the same church for the good of his soul and the souls of Alice, his late wife, and others, for the service of which he also leaves money for the purchase of a missal, a silver cup weighing forty shillings to be fashioned into a chalice, and divers sums of money for the purchase of vestments, towels, and other ornaments. . . .

For painting an image of the Blessed Mary in the choir and for the purchase of a crown to be placed on her head he leaves sixty shillings.

I bequeath to the church of Weston in Lewes my tablet painted with the story of the Day of Judgment, two curtains painted with angels . . . and one book called Legendary.[19]

The founding of chantries to pray for the soul, the endowment of monasteries, the establishment of religious guilds[20] and the veneration of holy relics were simply some of the ways in which people tried to prepare in life for their deaths.

Some were inspired to more extreme practices, and certainly the terrors of the plague stimulated a frenzied pitch of such behaviour. Boccaccio describes the formation of isolated groups devoted to austere living, and Richard Southern, writing about 'Fringe Orders and Anti-Orders', cites the example of one itinerant flagellant group disrupting the routine of the established Church for a brief period in the summer and autumn of 1349. As Southern argues, 'the chief sources of mass religious movements were disease and despair, and the two generally went together'.[21]

One of the problems, however, with the more moderate devotional practices that the Church encouraged was that the economic foundation of many such practices rendered them open to abuse. Pardons, for example, were originally conceived as remission from temporal punishment for sin rather than as commodities for sale, but since the truly penitent might be expected to demonstrate their penitence by offering money to a pardoner (to be used for charitable ends, such as supporting a hospital), the distinction was impossible to maintain in practice. A whole economy of death developed around the exchange of money for credit in the afterlife, though this is a cynical afterview of a system not necessarily any more corrupt in practice than putting money in a collection box nowadays and feeling self-satisfied as a result.

Popes compounded the problem by tabulating the rewards in the gift of God very specifically, instead of leaving them unspecific. William Wey's description of the system of indulgences operating for those who made the pilgrimage to the shrine of St James of Compostela shows how exact the accounting was:

A third part of all their sins are remitted for anyone who makes a pilgrimage to the church of the blessed James Zebedee at whatever time. If they die on the way there, or at the shrine or returning, if they have repented of their sins, these are all remitted. Item, those who go every Sunday to the procession of the church of St James are given for the procession and consecration forty days of indulgence and are given the same throughout the week. If it is a feast day they are given three hundred more days in addition to the indulgence for a third part of all their sins. Item, on the vigil of St James and on the feast for the dedication of his church they are given six hundred days in addition to the indulgence for a third part of all their sins . . . etc.[22]

The sheer length of the description, of which this is only a part, demonstrates how top-heavy the system of indulgences had become.

Attacks on the corruption of the Church are rife in the literature of the fourteenth century. Chaucer's Pardoner is not an isolated figure, but rather the standard literary type of a pardoner. If you give money to pardoners, says Langland,

> ye gyven youre gold glotons [gluttons] to helpe,
> And leneth it losels that leccherie haunten!
> [hand it to layabouts who spend their time in lechery][23]

It is not only pardoners, however, who come under attack, but all branches of the Church, to the extent that they involve themselves in demands for money. Summoners, as shown above in this chapter, were despised as a group, since their job was to summon offenders to, or collect fines on behalf of, the ecclesiastical courts. Friars, too, were a particular target of attack, since their Rule, which dictated that they should live by begging, was evidently abused as a means of amassing wealth.

Chaucer's *Summoner's Tale*, which recounts the dealings of a friar, brings together in teller and tale two of these most despised ecclesiastical groupings, just as the *Friar's Tale* does in reverse, and in so doing also satirises the general tendency for anti-clerical polemic to be produced from within clerical ranks. Monks, friars and secular orders were each other's worst enemies. The Summoner tells his tale in response to the Friar's wicked jest at the expense of summoners, and begins his description of the friar in his tale with the emphasis firmly on money: the friar preaches and, more emphatically, begs, 'it is no doute' (III.1712). On the day in question the friar has concentrated his sermon particularly on urging the people

To trentals [thirty requiem masses sung for a soul in
purgatory], and to yeve, for Goddes sake,
Wherwith men myghte hooly houses make.

(1717–18)

Here we see the other side of the bargains made in pursuit of
rest for the soul after death. The donor gives money for the saying
of masses and the building of churches because to give in such a
cause is good for the soul. From the point of view of those in
religious orders who receive the money, however, there is a choice:
they can either say the masses and build the churches, or they can
pursue their pleasures. The friar acknowledges both alternatives,
ironically, in his attack on 'possessioners' [those clergy who live on
endowments, rather than by begging]. People should give their
money, he says, to religious orders

Ther as divine servyce is honoured,
Nat ther as it is wasted and devoured,
Ne ther it nedeth nat for to be yive
As to possessioners, that mowen lyve,
Thanked be God, in wele and habundaunce.

(1719–23)

Following this plea for money in the guise of a sermon, the friar
moves tirelessly from one form of begging to the next:

When folk in chirche had yeve him what hem leste,
He wente his wey; no lenger wolde he reste.
With scrippe and tipped staf, ytukked hye,
In every hous he gan to poure and prye,
And beggeth mele and chese, or elles corn.
His felawe hadde a staf tipped with horn,
A peyre of tables [writing tablets] al of yvory,
And a poyntel [stylus] polysshed fetisly,
And wroot the names alwey, as he stood,
Of alle folk that yaf hym any good,
Ascaunces [as if] that he wolde for hem preye.

(1735–45)

He arrives at a house where he is normally very well fed and finds
that Thomas, the man of the house, is sick in bed. Gradually all

the elements of a traditional attack on friars accumulate in the
Summoner's portrayal of this one: gluttony, lechery, hypocrisy and
'glossing' (here a euphemism for 'distorting') the words of Holy
Scripture.

The tale does not immediately proceed to the question of
Thomas's death, as the audience might expect, but allows Thomas's wife to intervene to tell the friar that her child has died within
the last two weeks. The friar does not miss an opportunity, and
immediately tells her:

> His deeth saugh I by revelacioun
>
> . . . .
> I dar wel seyn that, er that half an hour
> After his deeth, I saugh hym born to blisse
> In myn avision, so God me wisse,
>
> (1854–8)

continuing with a long description of the prayers that the friars
then supposedly offered for the dead child. It is the holy life of
apostolic poverty friars lead, he argues, that allows them to see
more 'of Cristes secree thynges' (1871); Jesus, says the friar,
particularly had friars in mind when he said '"Blessed be they that
povere in spirit been"' (1923).

It is clear that Thomas has been a generous donor to the friars
up to this point, but is beginning to be suspicious of any link
between these gifts and his bodily or spiritual health. When the
friar tells Thomas that all the friars are praying for his recovery
day and night, Thomas responds angrily:

> 'God woot,' quod he, 'no thyng therof feele I!
> As help me Crist, as I in fewe yeres,
> Have spent upon diverse manere freres
> Ful many a pound; yet fare I nevere the bet.
> Certeyn, my good have I almoost biset [disposed of].
> Farwel, my gold, for it is al ago!'
>
> (1948–53)

The friar's answer is that Thomas has spread his gifts too widely
among different convents instead of putting all his trust in one.
'Youre maladye', he says 'is for we han to lyte' (1962): *you* are sick

because *we* have too little money. This logic certainly has its origins in the economics of death.

The friar then subjects Thomas to a long sermon against anger, and attempts to hear his confession. When Thomas refuses, on the grounds that he has already made his confession to the curate, the friar unashamedly turns his attention to money again: 'Yif me thanne of thy gold, to make oure cloystre' (2099). Thomas is driven to the limits of his patience, but tells the friar to 'grope wel . . ./Bynethe my buttok' for something hidden which he wishes to give. The gift turns out to be a fart, a fitting response to the outrageous proposition that money can buy salvation.

TRANSIENCE AND CONSOLATION

The didactic insistence of preachers and religious writers that life must always be set against the background of death stimulated an intense feeling for the transience of this life. This world, as more than one medieval writer tells us, is nothing but a cherry fair. The true life is the eternal life, which begins after death. Nothing in earthly life is to be trusted; all is by definition fickle and unstable. This is of course the lesson Troilus learns when he finally sees the world from its true perspective after death, and it is the lesson the narrator finally directs towards the audience of the poem:

> O yonge, fresshe folkes, he or she,
> In which that love up groweth with youre age,
> Repeyreth hom fro worldly vanyte,
> And of youre herte up casteth the visage
> To thilke God that after his ymage
> Yow made, and thynketh al nys but a faire,
> This world that passeth soone as floures faire.
>
> And loveth him the which that right for love
> Upon a crois, oure soules for to beye [buy, redeem]
> First starf [died], and roos, and sit in hevene above;
> For he nyl falsen no wight, dar I seye,
> That wol his herte al holly on hym leye.

> And syn he best to love is, and most meke,
> What nedeth feynede loves for to seke?
>
> (1835–48)

Paradoxically, however, the perspective of eternity, while reminding human beings that life is brief and only given its true shape by
death, does not strip life of all value. Value *is* to be found in the
earthly kingdom, and must be sought in its echoes of the kingdom
of God. Human love, as *Troilus and Criseyde* demonstrates, imitates
divine love; the danger lies in mistaking it as divine in itself.

An early poem of Chaucer's, *The Book of the Duchess*, takes as its
subject the death of a loved one. It is a dream poem in which the
narrator meets a man in black who is lamenting the death of his
lover. The prologue to the dream, however, takes the story of Ceyx
and Alcyone from Ovid's *Metamorphoses*, in order to explore the
relations between love and death before the bereavement of the
dream itself is announced. Ovid's story, in Chaucer's version,
begins with death: King 'Seys' dies in a storm at sea. It is
important to note that Alcyone's distress is due not to death itself,
but to uncertainty, to her ignorance of whether her husband is
dead or alive. She prays to Juno to know, and an image of her
husband then appears to her in a dream with the advice that there
is no sense in her sorrow:

> Let be your sorwful lyf,
> For in your sorwe there lyth no red [good sense, remedy];
> For, certes, swete, I am but ded.
>
> (202–4)

'I am only dead', says Seys, implying that death itself is not so
important, and does not merit sorrow. The implication, perhaps, is
that death begins eternal life, and Alcyone's own death three days
later may suggest their reunion. Chaucer omits Ovid's continuation, which allows the lovers to be transformed into sea-birds
and thus reunited. This, of course, is a pagan solution to the
problem of death. Chaucer's suppression of the ending to this
well-known story allows the audience both to supply their
memory of the reunion after death that concludes Ovid's version,
but to inhibit its specifically pagan transformation and substitute
instead an unstated idea of the Christian afterlife. Seys, though a
pagan, ends his speech with a prayer to the Christian God to

lessen his wife's sorrow. The anachronism acts as a directive to a Christian audience, as so often in *Troilus and Criseyde*.

When the narrator then falls asleep and overhears in his dream the man in black lamenting his sorrow, these ideas – that death is relatively trivial, excessive sorrow pointless and reunion after death possible – are already implanted. Great sorrow is a death in life, a state in which no natural creature can long continue, as the poem repeatedly reminds us. The black knight has become sorrow itself ('For y am sorwe, and sorwe ys y' – 597), so that all that was life for him becomes reversed:

> To derke ys turned al my lyght,
> My wyt ys foly, my day ys nyght,
> My love ys hate, my slep wakynge,
> My myrthe and meles ys fastynge
> (609–12)

No consolation is offered explicitly in the poem, but it is possible that the narrator's understated response to the black knight, when he finally tells him directly that his love is dead, is offered as more appropriate than the knight's immoderate grief: 'Be God, hyt ys routhe [pity]' (1310). 'Routhe' (or 'pitee') is admittedly a much more intense and active concept than Modern English 'pity',[24] yet the narrator's reply is still conspicuously abrupt by contrast with the knight's mourning. It stands as a corrective to the excessive importance that the knight's grief allows to death, a reminder that the death of the flesh must not be allowed to end all life. While eternal life for the dead lady remains an open question, the necessity for the knight to end his own living death, to abandon the solitude of the forest and return to the life of the 'long castel with walles white' (1318) is absolute.

THE PILGRIMAGE OF LIFE

The awareness that true life begins after death is one frequently expressed through the common medieval image of life as a pilgrimage. It forms the structure of several works besides the *Canterbury Tales*: Deguileville's three long pilgrimage allegories, widely translated, Lydgate's *Pilgrimage of the Life of Man*, translated from Deguileville's first book, and Langland's *Piers Plowman* are the best known of such works from the fourteenth and fifteenth centuries. Chaucer's balade 'Truth' advises living in recognition of this metaphor:

> That thee is sent, receyve in buxumnesse [obedience];
> The wrastling for this world axeth a fal.
> Her is non hoom, her nis but wildernesse:
> Forth, pilgrim, forth! Forth, beste, out of thy stal!
> Know thy contree, look up, thank God of al;
> Hold the heye wey and lat thy gost thee lede,
> And trouthe thee shal delivere, it is no drede.
>
> (15–21)

Although the *Canterbury Tales* is unfinished, according to the plan of the *General Prologue*, Alfred David has pointed out that the *Parson's Prologue* seems to suggest the beginning of an ending:

> It is late afternoon, the sun is rapidly setting, and the shadows are lengthening on the ground. Chaucer's shadow is twice the measure of six feet. The shadow points to the earth that is our common inheritance and also suggests the insubstantiality of the body that casts it. The constellation in the sky is Libra, the scales, which recall the Last Judgment.[25]

The Host tells his fellow-pilgrims that this is to be the last tale ('Now lakketh us no tales mo than oon' – X.16) and the Parson himself says that he will tell 'a myrie tale in prose/To knytte up al this feeste and make an ende' (46–7). His tale is not 'merry' in any Modern English sense of the word, yet it contains a message of joy in showing the pilgrims the true end of their pilgrimage: the Parson prays for help

> To shewe you the wey, in this viage,
> Of thilke parfit glorious pilgrymage
> That highte Jerusalem celestial.
>
> (49–51)

The route the Parson recommends is that of penitence, and his tale takes the form of a penitential manual. The fear of judgement, 'drede of the day of doom and of the horrible peynes of helle'

(157), is strongly urged as one of the reasons why sinners should feel contrition, and in that section the Parson cites numerous descriptions of damnation from the Bible. Its most terrible aspect is that it is never-ending: it is both death and not death, a grisly reversal of the joyous paradox of eternal life,

> For, as seith Seint Gregorie,/'To wrecche caytyves shal be deeth withoute deeth, and ende withouten ende, and defaute withoute failynge./For hir deeth shal alwey lyven, and hir ende shal everemo bigynne, and hir defaute shal nat faille.'/And therfore seith Seint John the Evaungelist, 'They shullen folwe deeth, and they shul nat fynde hym; and they shul desiren to dye, and deeth shal flee fro hem.'
>
> (213–15)

Perhaps the old man of the *Pardoner's Tale*, seeking death to no avail, points the rioters more clearly to damnation than to death.

The Parson ends his tale, however, on an optimistic note, describing the victory of eternal life, the fruit of penance:

> Thanne shal men understonde what is the fruyt of penaunce; and, after the word of Jhesu Crist, it is the endelees blisse of hevene,/ther joye hath no contrarioustee [opposite] of wo ne grevaunce; ther alle harmes been passed of this present lyf; ther as is the sikernesse fro the peyne of helle; ther as is the blisful compaignye that rejoysen hem everemo, everich of otheres joye; ther as the body of man, that whilom was foul and derk, is moore cleer than the sonne; ther as the body, that whilom was syk, freele, and fieble, and mortal, is inmortal, and so strong and so hool that ther may no thyng apeyren [harm] it;/ther as ne is neither hunger, thurst, ne coold, but every soule replenyssed [filled] with the sighte of the parfit knowynge of God./This blisful regne may men purchace by poverte espiritueel, and the glorie by lowenesse, the plentee of joye by hunger and thurst, and the reste by travaille, and the lyf by deeth and mortificacion of synne.
>
> (1075–80)

It should come as no surprise, then, to find the writer, as medieval writers so often do, thinking about his own soul at the end of the work. We have already considered the prayer that ends

Troilus and Criseyde (see p. 116 above); at the end of the *Canterbury Tales* Chaucer's prayer is more specifically directed towards God's judgement of his literary endeavours. The title of *Retractions* by which this prayer is usually known comes from within the prayer, since he beseeches his audience

> that ye preye for me that Crist have mercy on me and foryeve me my giltes;/and namely of my translacions and enditynges of worldly vanitees, the whiche I revoke in my retracciouns
>
> (X.1084–5)

He goes on to specify which of his works he considers to be 'worldly vanitees':

> the book of Troilus; the book also of Fame; the book of the xxv. Ladies; the book of the Duchesse; the book of Seint Valentynes day of the Parlement of Briddes; the tales of Caunterbury, thilke that sownen into [tend towards] synne . . . and many another book . . . and many a song and many a leccherous lay.
>
> (1086–7)

He endorses only 'the translacion of Boece de Consolacione, and othere bookes of legendes of seintes, and omelies, and moralitee, and devocioun'. His final prayer is utterly orthodox, a prayer for the grace of true penitence in this life, 'so that I may been oon of hem at the day of doom that shulle be saved' (1092). A poem, like a life, must strive to die well.

7

Reputation and Influence

Throughout this book we have looked at 'Chaucer in his time' without much open acknowledgement of the partial and time-bound nature of such a project. The very process of selection, the attempt to frame history, even intermittently, in narrative form, is, as Chaucer himself knew, a falsification (see chapter 5 above). Narrative, as Hayden White has written in our own time, is not a neutral form of discourse, but a discourse of desire, in the sense that it seeks to find meaning in experience.[1] It imposes an illusory shape and significance on events by representing them as possessing the formal coherence of stories and does so, furthermore, from within a perspective that is not universal, but culture-specific. Writing about the past, even where the writing is non-narrative, or takes as its focus works of literature rather than historical events, is constructed by the writer's own cultural and historical position. There can be no escape from the present in the attempt to focus on the past.

It is important, therefore, in a book of this kind, which claims to look at a past writer in relation to his own time, not only to acknowledge, but to underline, the extent to which such a project is shaped and limited by its own cultural positioning. The most straightforward way of demonstrating the time-bound nature of any one response is to set it alongside the responses of other moments in time, and this chapter begins, therefore, by re-surveying some very familiar ground: the history of Chaucer criticism between Chaucer's time and our own. Following this general survey is a more detailed exploration of one particular instance of the relationship across time: that between Chaucer and Shakespeare.

CHAUCER THE FATHER

Chaucer's own generation already perceived him as a father and mentor. For his immediate contemporaries he was the great poet of love. Thomas Usk, speaking through Love personified in his *Testament of Love* (?1387), has Love direct the narrator to Chaucer's poetry, in particular *Troilus and Criseyde*, for answers to his questions about love:

> myne owne trewe servaunt, the noble philosophical poete in Englissh, whiche evermore him besyeth and travayleth right sore my name to encrease . . . trewly his better ne his pere in schole of my rules coude I never fynde: He (quod she), in a treatise that he made of my servant Troylus, hath this mater touched, and at the ful this questyon assoyled [unravelled] Certaynly, his noble sayinges can I not amende. In goodnes of gentyl manlyche speche, without any maner of nycite of storieres ymagynacion [storyteller's foolish fantasy] in wytte and in good reason of sentence he passeth al other makers. In the boke of Troylus, the answere to thy questyon mayste thou lerne.[2]

John Gower similarly presents the goddess Venus in his *Confessio Amantis* (?1390) acknowledging Chaucer as her disciple.

The next generation, Chaucer's younger contemporaries, quickly began to establish him as first in a new tradition of English poetry.[3] Lydgate's laments for Chaucer's death, for example, repeatedly emphasise his primacy: for him, Chaucer is

> Noble galfride [Geoffrey], poete of breteyne,
> Amonge de englisch that made first to reyne
> The gold dewe-dropis of rethorik so fyne,
> Oure rude langage only tenlwmyne [to illumine].[4]

The impulse to see Chaucer as the well-head of English literary tradition has remained a common, if false, perception into our own time, qualified only by the tendency of fifteenth- and sixteenth-century writers to bracket him with Gower and Lydgate as one of three great initiators.[5]

Lydgate's praise is also representative of the generation that followed Chaucer in its focus on what Chaucer did for the English anguage. Hoccleve, another younger contemporary of Chaucer's, iollows this combination of praising Chaucer both as the first of a 1ew line and as a master of language. He is, writes Hoccleve, 'The iirste fyndere of our faire langage' and the 'flour of eloquence'.[6]

Two aspects of Chaucer's language are most frequently singled)ut for praise in the fifteenth century: his brevity and his elo-juence. Caxton notes both of these in his Prologue to the second :dition of the *Canterbury Tales* (c.1483):

> He comprehended hys maters in short, quyck and hye
> sentences, eschewyng prolyxyte, casting away the chaf of super-
> fluyte, and shewyng the pyked grayn of sentence, uttered by
> crafty and sugred eloquence.[7]

mitators, however, magnified the glories of eloquence at the :xpense of brevity, and gradually an excessively ornate style of liction came to characterise the work of many later fifteenth-:entury writers, perhaps especially in Scotland. Dunbar's tribute o Chaucer is typical both in praising Chaucer's 'anamalit termes :elicall' (literally 'enamelled, heavenly words'), and in conveying iis praise in terms that are themselves more ornate and elaborate han Chaucer's:

> O reverend Chaucere, rose of rethoris all,
> As in oure tong ane flour imperiall
> That raise in Britane evir, quho redis rycht,
> Thou beris of makaris [makers, i.e. poets] the tryumph riall;
> Thy fresch anamalit termes celicall
> This mater could illumynit have full brycht:
> Was thou noucht of oure Inglisch all the lycht,
> Surmounting eviry tong terrestriall
> Alls fer as Mayes morow dois mydnycht?[8]

This straitjacketing of Chaucer's flexible and wide ranging use of anguage into a notion of eloquence defined as elaboration and sugared sweetness is an aspect of what Paul Strohm has described is 'the narrowing of the "Chaucer Tradition"'. As Chaucer's iudience widened from the immediate circle of the court and its servants, Strohm argues, so there was a corresponding narrowing n what the secondary audience valued in his poetry.[9] A gap becomes apparent between 'court poetry' produced literally for a court audience and 'courtly poetry' aspiring to courtly values as perceived by a wider audience.[10]

Part of the reason for this narrowing in appreciation seems to lie in the difficulty Chaucer's originality in language presented to his fifteenth-century audience. Barry Windeatt's careful study of the extant manuscripts of Chaucer's texts has shown fifteenth-century scribes responding to the unusual qualities in the language of their copy-texts by flattening the strange into the familiar, substituting a conventional reading for a difficult one. Windeatt demonstrates that the scribes find problems with Chaucer's diction, syntax and figurative expression. They also tend to make meanings more explicit than Chaucer's text does, thereby suggesting 'the distinctiveness of a style in which the poet intended to leave some of his meaning understated'.[11]

The first attempt at a collected edition of the *Works of Chaucer and others* was Pynson's in 1526, but the first editor to search out and compare different manuscripts, anticipating the methods of modern editors, was William Thynne in 1532. Pynson's edition had advertised its texts as 'newly printed by a trewe copye (*Troilus*), or 'dilygently and truely corrected and newly printed' (*Tales*), but Thynne went further: his son Francis describes how his father was instructed by Henry VIII 'to serche all the liberaries of Englande for Chaucers Workes, so that oute of all the Abbies of this Realme . . . he was fully furnished with multitude of Bookes'.[12] Henry VIII's interest in Chaucer seems to have been part of a conscious propaganda exercise, an attempt to manufacture a 'tradition' in order to lend an air of authority to his programme of Church reform. Lollard pieces, satirising or attacking the established Church of their time, could usefully prime the Tudor audience to accept their own moment as right for reform, and such pieces gained in status and authority if they could leap from ignominious anonymity into the Chaucer canon. Thynne added nineteen new items to his edition.[13]

Skeat argued that the full title of Thynne's edition, *The workes of Geffray Chaucer newly printed, with dyvers workes whiche were never in print before*, indicates that Thynne did not intend to imply that the 'dyvers workes' now added were in fact Chaucer's.[14] While this may or may not be true, Thynne (and Henry VIII) must have been aware that merely printing them in an edition predominantly claiming to be a Chaucer collection could still have the desired effect of bringing these other pieces to unprecedented prominence in the public eye.

An upsurge of interest in Chaucer with the publication of Thynne's edition[15] was followed by a decline in enthusiasm. Although Elizabethan writers rarely failed to make reference to Chaucer, such allusions often have the ring of obligation rather than appreciation. There was, as Ann Thompson has noted, 'a gap between Chaucer's reputation and his real influence'.[16] Those writers loudest in Chaucer's praise (Spenser, Sidney, Harvey, for example), not surprisingly, are the radical Protestants. Chaucer was in this period still widely considered to have been, in Foxe's phrase, 'a right Wiclevian', and Foxe notes reports of readers 'brought to the true knowledge of Religion' by Chaucer's works.[17]

Spenser adopts the persona of Colin Clout, the shepherd-poet, in order to acknowledge Chaucer (Tityrus) as his master:

> The God of shepheards Tityrus is dead,
> Who taught me homely, as I can, to make.
> (*The Shepheardes Calender*, June, 81–2)

In doing so he reaches back to Chaucer through Skelton, from whom he borrows the figure of Colin Clout (an angry critic of Church corruption in the poem that bears his name), thus rooting his respect for Chaucer firmly in the reforming tradition. The metrical roughness and archaic vocabulary that he reproduces as part of his homage to Chaucer ('I wote my rymes bene rough, and rudely drest', confesses Colin in the June Eclogue – 77) are in Spenser's view expressive of an archetypal honesty and straight-forwardness as against the deceit and corruption that may lie hidden under more luxurious language.

It was this same 'roughness' in Chaucer that probably accounted for the decline of interest in his work outside the radical Protestant group. Elizabethans found his language in-creasingly remote, and when Speght brought out his edition of Chaucer's works in 1598, he included, for the first time, a glossary of 'the old and obscure words'. The appearance of Speght's edition, like Thynne's in 1532, may have been the cause of a sudden revival of interest in Chaucer, seen in the appearance of five plays with Chaucerian sources between 1599 and 1602.[18]

Speght was alone at this time, however, in recognising that the apparent roughness of Chaucer's poetry was inherent not in

Chaucer's text, but in the perceptions of sixteenth-century readers. He not only provided a glossary to help Elizabethan readers understand Chaucer's language, but realised that changes in pronunciation had obscured his metrical regularity. 'And for [Chaucer's] verses', he argues, 'although in divers places they seem to us to stand of unequal measures, yet a skilful reader who can scan them in their nature shall find it otherwise.'[19] Such 'mismetring' on the part of later readers was of course exactly what Chaucer himself had predicted (p. 43 above).

Although Spenser may have realised that the archaism and rough metre were born out of the reader's historical position rather than the author's, to acknowledge this would have been to lose a powerful metaphor 'authorising' a tradition of religious and moral plainness. The very fact that Chaucer was a contemporary of Wyclif, making a language for his poetry in the days when the spirit of reform could first be seen emerging, according to the Elizabethan Protestant version of history, seemed to guarantee a purity in his language which could serve as a standard, an uncontaminated source ('well of English undefyled' – *The Faerie Queene*, IV.ii.32) for late sixteenth-century usage. Its apparent, if imaginary, roughness seemed to confirm its purity.

Linguistic archaism, with its connotations of roughness and purity, was drawn into the discourse of nationalism as well as that of religious reform. As debate about how best to enrich the language raged in the sixteenth century, 'Chaucerisms' emerged as an option taken up with a peculiarly nationalistic fervour, set against 'inkhorn terms' and 'oversea language' (the coining of new words from Latin or foreign vernaculars).[20] Gabriel Harvey, for example, rebuked those in favour of borrowing from other languages with a self-righteous xenophobia that is also paradoxically 'democratic' in its opposition to Latin and French as the languages of high culture:

> in Ingland . . . nothinge is reputid so contemptible, and so baselye and vilelye accountid of, as whatsoever is taken for Inglishe, whether it be handsum fasshions in apparrell, or seemely and honorable in behaviour, or choise wordes and phrases in speache, or anye notable thinge else . . . that savorith of our owne cuntrye and is not ether merely or mixtely outlandishe.

Ben Jonson's view that 'Spenser in affecting the ancients writ no language' and E. K.'s argument that Spenser deserves 'special prayse' on account of his attempt 'to restore as to their rightfull heritage such good and naturall English words as have ben long time out of use and almost cleane disherited' show the polarised responses to Spenser's 'Chaucerian' practice. The extent to which their historical position led Elizabethans to read into Chaucer's poetry images of their own prejudice is revealed through a comparison with the subsequent, and already emergent, polemic surrounding Chaucer's language in the seventeenth century, when he was attacked from an opposite direction, for corrupting the language with foreign borrowings. George Chapman's opinion, as stated in 1598, three years after the publication of *The Shepheardes Calender*, was that 'Chaucer (by whom we will needes authorise our true english), had more newe wordes for his time then any man needes to devise now'.[21]

By the late sixteenth century Chaucer was also beginning to acquire a reputation for 'flat scurrilitie', in Sir John Harington's phrase, which is only excused, in Harington's view, by 'the decorum he keepes'.[22] It was during the sixteenth century that a 'Canterbury Tale' came to acquire the meaning of a piece either bawdy or unlikely to be true.[23] It was perhaps partly for this reason that the preference for *Troilus and Criseyde* over the now more popular *Canterbury Tales* remained so marked until the eighteenth century. Sidney's tribute is characteristic in his singling out of this poem for special praise:

> Chaucer, undoubtedly did excellently in hys Troylus and Cresseid, of whom truly I know not, whether to mervaile more, either that he in that mistie time, could see so clearely, or that wee in this cleare age, walke so stumblingly after him.[24]

Caroline Spurgeon points out that up to 1700 the references to *Troilus* are more than double those to the *Canterbury Tales*, and cites Berthelet in 1532 referring to it as Chaucer's 'most speciall warke'.[25]

A paradox comparable with the ambivalent attitude towards Chaucer's language in this period is that while some condemned his work for lewdness, as noted above, others praised his great learning and morality. Praise for his moral standards was, of course, crucial to a Protestant reading of his work. Sir Brian Tuke's letter, prefixed to Thynne's edition, notes Chaucer's 'excellent lernyng in all kyndes of doctrynes and sciences, suche frutefulnesse in wordes, wel accordynge to the mater and purpose, so swete and plesaunt sentences [teachings, maxims]';[26] Gabriel Harvey pays special attention to Chaucer's learning in astronomy and philosophy, adding that 'it is not sufficient for poets to be superficial humanists: but they must be exquisite artists, and curious universal schollers';[27] and William Webbe, in his *Discourse of English Poetrie,* perceives Chaucer's skill in his ability to use the delights of sound to lure his audience into what is in fact a moral discourse, thereby enabling them to perceive the true corruption of their world.[28]

The seventeenth century, by contrast with the sixteenth, showed Chaucer's reputation reaching perhaps its lowest point. There were no editions of his works printed between 1602 and 1687, and the 1687 edition was really only a reprint of the 1602 edition (Speght's second). Indications of interest in Chaucer, where they appear in the seventeenth century, are more eccentric, and swift to acknowledge the increasing sense of distance and difficulty between Chaucer's work and this audience.

Sir Francis Kynaston's translation of *Troilus and Criseyde* into Latin suggests both this difficulty and Kynaston's own distance from his contemporaries in conceiving such a project. The prefatory verses to Kynaston's translation, printed in 1635, celebrate the virtuoso element in the enterprise:

> I'me glad the stomacke of the time's so good,
> That it can relish, can digest strong food:
> That Learning's not absurd; and men dare know,
> How Poets spake three hundred yeares agoe.
> Like travellors, we had bin out so long,
> Oure Native was become an unknowne tongue,
> And homebred Chaucer unto us was such,
> As if he had bin written in High Dutch:
> Till thou the Height didst Levell, and didst Pierce
> The depth of his unimitable verse.[29]

Kynaston translated the whole poem into Latin and wrote a Latin commentary to accompany it, but only the first two books were ever printed. The disparity between the idea and its reception is mirrored in Barker's verse, that praises 'the stomacke of the time' for digesting 'strong food', food which it in fact rejected after the first two mouthfuls.

Richard Brathwait's commentary on the tales of the Miller and the Wife of Bath, published in 1665, shows Brathwait more conscious of his effort as one at odds with the spirit of the time. In an appendix he presents this consciousness as a dialogue with an opponent:

A Critick . . . said 'that he could allow well of Chaucer, if his Language were Better.' – Whereto the Author of these Commentaries return'd him this Answer: 'Sir, it appears, you prefer Speech before the Head piece; Language before Invention; whereas Weight of Judgment has ever given Invention Priority before Language. And not to leave you dissatisfied, As the Time wherein these Tales were writ, rendered him incapable of the one; so his Pregnancy of Fancy approv'd him incomparable for the other.'

Which Answer still'd this Censor, and justified the Author . . .[30]

It is symptomatic of the generally low regard in which Chaucer was held in the seventeenth century that the case for reading his poetry has to be made from an oppositional stance.

Dryden's edition in 1700 of *Fables, Ancient and Modern*, which included translations from the works of Homer, Ovid, Boccaccio and Chaucer, together with the originals, was a landmark in the rise of Chaucer's reputation and also set the fashion for a preference for the *Canterbury Tales* over *Troilus and Criseyde*. It also, of course, set the parameters for eighteenth-century reading of Chaucer by replacing the glossary of hard words with a completely modernised text. 'Chaucer', Dryden wrote, 'is a rough Diamond, and must first be polish'd e'er he shines'.[31] 'Roughness', as we have seen, was a concept associated with Chaucer since the sixteenth century;[32] the notion of modernisation as 'polishing', however, is the hallmark of the late seventeenth and eighteenth centuries, as numerous other texts also testify. Narrative line as well as linguistic 'deficiencies' were subject to 'polishing', and Nahum Tate's version of *King Lear*, for example, which erased Cordelia's death and married her to Edgar, dominated the English stage from 1681 to 1834. Dryden acknowledged that some condemned the work of modernisation as 'Profanation and Sacrilege',[33] but many shared the view that Dryden 'found him [Chaucer] Rubbish, and . . . left him Gold'.[34] A stream of writers, including Pope and Wordsworth, followed Dryden in making their own translations of Chaucer over the next century and a half.

It is interesting to note the continuity from the fifteenth and sixteenth centuries of those characteristics for which Dryden praises Chaucer, even following the relatively barren wastes of seventeenth-century Chaucer criticism before Dryden. Dryden still names Chaucer as 'the Father of English Poetry' and claims as his due 'the same Degree of Veneration as . . . Homer, or . . . Virgil'.[35] He still acknowledges Chaucer's attempts to 'refine' the English language, still singles out his capacity for conciseness, still admires his learning, still respects his 'lashes' against clerical corruption. More specific to Dryden's own time are the standards of nature and good sense: 'Chaucer follow'd Nature every where, but was never so bold to go beyond her'; 'he is a perpetual Fountain of good Sense'.[36]

Above all, perhaps, it is with Dryden that the tradition of admiration for Chaucer's breadth and truth to life in his depiction of character begins. Comparing Chaucer with Ovid, he writes:

> Both of them understood the Manners; under which name I comprehend the Passions, and, in a larger sense, the Descriptions of Persons, and their very Habits . . . I see . . . all the Pilgrims in the Canterbury Tales, their Humours, their Features, and the very Dress, as distinctly as if I had supp'd with them at the Tabard in Southwark.[37]

Dryden's preface also marks the beginning of the critical tradition that would locate Chaucer's genius above and beyond its own time:

> We have our Fore-fathers and Great Grand-dames all before us, as they were in Chaucer's Days; their general Characters are still remaining in Mankind, and even in England, though they are call'd by other Names than those of Moncks, and Fryars, and Chanons, and Lady Abbesses, and Nuns: For Mankind is ever the same, and nothing lost out of Nature, though everything is alter'd.[38]

This is a critical position that was to be highly influential for the next two hundred and fifty years and more,[39] yet, curiously, Caroline Spurgeon, collecting the material for her anthology of Chaucer allusions for publication in 1925, found 'the characteristics which most attract us to him to-day', including 'his close knowledge of human nature', absent from the work of critics before the end of the eighteenth century.[40]

Although Dryden paved the way for a critical response that remained dominant until quite recently, however, it was that minority whose dislike of modernisation Dryden acknowledges in his preface which laid the foundations for the modern study of Chaucer's text. It is perhaps appropriate that this minority should have been most prominently represented by two women, Elizabeth Elstob and Elizabeth Cooper, whose occupation of the margin by virtue of gender is mirrored in the marginality of their projects in their own time. These women were scholars rather than poets, working outside the mainstream of English writing, with the aim of reinstating the work of older poets in its original language and educating a contemporary audience towards an informed understanding of it. In 1715 Elizabeth Elstob published her *Rudiments of Grammar for the English-Saxon Tongue, first given in English: with an Apology for the study of Northern Antiquities. Being very useful toward the understanding our ancient English Poets, and other Writers*, pointing out in her preface the value of a knowledge of 'the English-Saxon Tongue' (Old English) for the understanding of older poets, including Chaucer, whom she quotes, of course, in Middle English. Elstob's recognition of the need for an 'apology' (written defence) for this kind of study indicates her recognition both of the minority interest of the project and of the anomaly of a woman undertaking it. In both her *Grammar* and her earlier edition of Aelfric's Homily on St Gregory's Day she drew attention to gender, dedicating both books to royal women (the *Homily* to Queen Anne and the *Grammar* to the Princess of Wales) and noting in her preface to the *Homily* the hostility with which men typically greeted female learning.[41] Elizabeth Cooper, in 1737, published the Prologue from Chaucer's *Pardoner's Tale* in a volume that aimed, as Elstob did, to rekindle an interest in *English poetry from the Saxons, to the Reign of King Charles II.*

The more scholarly approach to editing initiated by such linguistic research had no influence on an edition of Chaucer until Tyrwhitt's edition of 1775. John Urry's edition of 1721, while not a modernisation, shows no attempt to establish the author's text, but introduces changes at will without acknowledgement. Tyr-whitt's commment in his Appendix to the Preface of his own edition is a measure of the distance between Urry's habits, harking back to scribal practice, and the new standards of the scholarly editor:

> The strange licence, in which Mr. Urry appears to have indulged himself, of lengthening and shortening Chaucer's words according to his own fancy, and of even adding words of his own, without giving his readers the least notice, has made the text of Chaucer in his Edition by far the worst that was ever published.[42]

Tyrwhitt's standards were to set the norm for editions down to the present day. His text is accompanied by the now familiar critical paraphernalia of notes and introduction, together with an essay on the language and versification of Chaucer. In this essay he notes the contradictions pervading the responses of his contemporaries to Chaucer, in a way that reduplicates the terms of the sixteenth-century debate. 'According to one', he writes, 'he is the "well of English undefiled"; according to the other, he has corrupted and deformed the English idiom by an immoderate mixture of French words.' Similarly, he argues, critics praise Chaucer as 'the flour of Poetes' while agreeing that he was 'totally ignorant or negligent of metrical rules'.[43] His essay shows, as did the pioneering work of Elstob and Cooper, a sense of the necessity for research to give solid ground to opinion. He refutes two strands of current opinion by demonstrating their foundation on ignorance, using his own research to argue both for the influence of French upon English outside and before Chaucer's poetry and for the importance of understanding the syllabic and accentual values of his words before making judgements on his metre.

All the best-known writers of the early nineteenth century except Byron (who described Chaucer as 'obscene and contemptible', owing 'his celebrity merely to his antiquity')[44] read and admired Chaucer's poetry. Blake's tribute is the most famous of this period, and his debt to Dryden is obvious:

> The characters of Chaucer's Pilgrims are the characters which compose all ages and nations. . . . Accident ever varies, Substance can never suffer change nor decay . . . some of the names

or titles are altered by time, but the characters themselves for
ever remain unaltered, and consequently they are the physiog-
nomies or lineaments of universal human life, beyond which
Nature never steps.[45]

Admiration for Chaucer expressed through imitation is especially
marked in the work of Keats, who in turn inspired the Pre-
Raphaelite interest in the medieval period. As Caroline Spurgeon
points out, it is in this period too that the name of Chaucer begins
to be regularly linked with that of Shakespeare.

As the century moved on, Romantic devotion to Chaucer
stimulated further scholarly research, and in 1868 the Chaucer
Society was founded 'to do honour to Chaucer, and to let lovers
and students of him see how far the best unprinted manuscripts of
his works differed from the printed texts'.[46] Two of the great
names of nineteenth-century scholarship are linked with this
foundation: that of Frederick J. Furnivall, who founded the Society
and produced its first publication, a parallel text of the six best
manuscripts of the *Canterbury Tales*; and Francis J. Child, who
funded the first work, and to whom Furnivall dedicated his
edition. It was Furnivall's work on the Chaucer manuscripts that
enabled W. W. Skeat to produce the first complete critical edition
of the works in 1894–7.

The flood of work on Chaucer in the twentieth century is
impossible to reduce to the format of this very bare outline, but
has already been well analysed by Lee Patterson.[47] Patterson's
account of the early twentieth century shows the two strands of
historical research and transhistorical appreciation, dominant
opposites within the critical tradition since Dryden's time,
paradoxically becoming unreconciled aspects of individual
scholarship. Root, Kittredge, Manly and others[48] simultaneously
did the historical research that produced so much valuable
extratextual material and wrote those celebrated 'appreciations' of
Chaucer, in the tradition of Dryden and Blake, which left their
historical researches so firmly 'outside' the text. The rise of New
Criticism, with its exclusive emphasis on the text, and Exegetics,
with its privileging of historical theology, may be seen, Patterson
argues, as developing out of the failure of this earlier criticism to
produce any real sense of interface between the text and its
historical moment.

The debate between 'a conditioning historical context and a

transhistorical humanism' implicit in the work of the early twentieth-century critics is one that, as Patterson points out, still preoccupies current criticism, but it is now more explicitly theorised as problematic. In particular, the tendency of earlier critics to attribute to their historical findings the status of objective truth has been called into question, so that New Historicism, now addressing the relationship between the text and its historical moment of production, no longer restricts its explorations to 'the historicity of text', but also acknowledges 'the textuality of history'. The phrasing (now classic) is formulated by Louis Montrose, who goes on to argue that 'if chiastic formulations such as this are now in fashion, it may be because they help to figure a current emphasis on the dynamic, unstable, and reciprocal relationship between the discursive and material domains'.[50]

Developments outside the field of historicism since the mid-century tend either to highlight Chaucer's ambiguity, irony and scepticism or, at the opposite extreme, to produce a 'religious, almost Puritanical Chaucer', linked to, but broader than, the Chaucer of the exegetical school.[51] The attraction of 'the Chaucer religion', as Charles Muscatine has branded this latter movement, is that it 'cleans up the mess',[52] in the sense that it recuperates unity for problematic texts, in particular the *Canterbury Tales*. Muscatine's interest lies in the way such readings, or any readings, reflect their readers, and he sees in them a closing of ranks against the various developments of literary theory which threaten the integrity of the text. 'It seems', he writes,

related to the growth of a Chaucer Industry; to the entry of Chaucer into the class of literary superstars like Homer and Shakespeare and Aristotle and Dante, of whom one does not speak ill, in whom one does not find faults, and whom one can invoke to verify and support one's own innermost values.[53]

As such, I would argue, it is not so much 'new' as a rewriting of earlier nineteenth- and twentieth-century criticism in slightly altered form. It is the rearguard action of canonisation.

CHAUCER AND SHAKESPEARE

Muscatine's choice of Chaucer and Shakespeare as the two English names in his catalogue of superstars is a classic one. Chaucer and Shakespeare are the two authors most firmly established in the canon of English literature. Because both their names carry such resonance it has long been a pursuit of scholars to find points of contact between the two, usually in the form of straightforward source study.[54] Why then choose this same predictable pairing yet again? In part, the answer lies within the question. It is the very inevitability of the pairing, the canonical (and 'canonised') status of the two, that renders an exploration of connections between their work an exploration also of the critical values underpinning this status.

Caroline Spurgeon, whose collection of critical responses to Chaucer underlies the whole first part of this chapter, is an interesting case in point. She chose Chaucer and Shakespeare as the subjects of her two major studies, and her desire to identify genius as transhistorical consistently undermines the historicist framework of her Chaucer project. Here, for example, is the tension between historicism and transhistorical humanism in action:

> We of today are sure that we appreciate to the full all his [Chaucer's] special qualities, and that his position in the history of our literature has been once and for all established. It may be so, but the experience of the past does not confirm it. . . .
>
> To-day, with the record of the opinion of five centuries before us, we can see that the verdict of the most competent critic cannot be wholly trusted until Time has set his seal on it, and that much allowance must always be made, as Hazlitt would have said, 'for the wind,' that is for the prevailing bias of the age, the standards, ideals and fashions, change in which constitutes change in taste.[55]

On the one hand this passage reveals her as more aware than most critics in 1925 of the fact that critical judgements are historically determined; on the other hand, her personification of Time as one who finally sets his seal (thus closing debate) and her repeated use of the word 'evolution' throughout this section of the introduction

express her underlying assumption that criticism 'grows up'
becomes inevitably more competent as time goes on.

It is essentially her belief that 'genius will out' which shapes her
interpretation of shifts in taste along the lines of this evolutionis
model. Not her work on Chaucer alone, she argues, but above al
her comparison of the critical histories of Chaucer and
Shakespeare, have led her to infer 'the existence of a definite
rhythm in the evolution of taste and critical method, as there is a
rhythm in all life'.[56] The use of the singular is important here
Spurgeon is no longer identifying shifts, but finding the
emergence of a single, common rhythm. The genius of Chaucer
and Shakespeare is gradually confirmed, she believes, as 'the
common consciousness of a people becomes enriched with time
and experience'.[57] The historical position of the critic, then, is
fixed predominantly by the stage of 'maturity' in the growing
critical tradition in which she happens to find herself.

In the remaining part of this last chapter I want to raise three
questions: what is the nature of Chaucer's influence on Shakespeare? Is 'influence' the best word to describe the relationship
between their work? How is the perception of that relationship
constructed by the historical positioning of the critic? Before
turning to specific texts, it is necessary to suggest a model for
approach that can be substituted for the approach which works
from the premiss of 'genius'. This model, as we have seen, looks
for 'influence' to link authors in a way that ignores the material
conditions of both and seeks primarily to confirm the continuity of
genius. It is a teleological, even perhaps tautological, approach
which knows its goal before it begins its search: 'genius' is both
the cause that validates the search for 'influence' and the result
that is confirmed by its discovery.

An alternative model that might be used in place of the 'genius'-
directed search for influence is the model of 'intertextuality'
which seeks to demonstrate that any literary text is necessarily
related to vast numbers of earlier texts, absorbing and shaping
them in response to the conditions of its own culture. This model
allows a text to be firmly located within its own time rather than
privileging its author as somehow singled out of time by sheer
genius. It also emphasises that there is no such thing as simple
'borrowing'; every 'borrowing' is a remaking. The concept of
'influence' privileges the first author as 'father', suggesting both
that he has some control over the later text and that the later

author is conscious of a debt. 'Intertextuality', on the contrary, lets go of the notion of fatherhood, and allows a view of the text as a site of plurality, a space in which other texts also play.

Chapter 4 of this book has already approached the question of how the reworking of fragments from earlier texts is part of the meaning of the Chaucerian text. This last chapter now seeks to show how Chaucer's work is itself reproduced and mediated in a Shakespearean text.

A MIDSUMMER NIGHT'S DREAM

As in chapter 4, discussion will centre on one text to allow specificity. *A Midsummer Night's Dream* is appropriate to the purpose because it has so often been studied in relation to Chaucer, and the shape of such studies implicitly raises the question of what is understood by 'influence'. Critics generally, with the exception of Donaldson in 1985, have limited their concern to small, demonstrable points of contact at the expense of any interest in shared, overarching concerns. Straightforward borrowing at the level of narrative and allusion have been well documented. Ann Thompson summarises the influence of four different Chaucerian works briefly thus: '*The Knight's Tale* for the framing action and parts of the main romantic plot, *The Legend of Good Women* for Pyramus and Thisbe and a brief reference to Dido, *The Merchant's Tale* for the quarrel between Oberon and Titania, and perhaps *The Parlement of Foules* for Theseus's reference to St Valentine's day.'[58] At the clearest end of 'influence', then, we can identify Shakespeare's framing story of Theseus and Hippolyta as that of the *Knight's Tale*, though there may have been intermediate stages in the transmission, such as an earlier play of *Palamon and Arcite*.[59] Less clear-cut, because the differences are so substantial, is the analogy between Chaucer's tale of two men in love with the same woman and Shakespeare's plot of two men and two women played upon by magic, so that both men love first one woman, then the other, before the 'right' pairing is finally achieved.

More contentiously, it may be argued that Shakespeare also borrows in tone from the *Knight's Tale*, though here we move further away from the 'provable'. Dorothy Bethurum writes, for example:

The whole conception of Theseus [in *MND*] is Chaucer's. In both stories he is the benevolent ruler, aware of the duties of kingship, aware also of the follies of love and sympathetic to them. In both he furnishes the common sense norm in a world of amorous aberrations.[60]

For her, the tone borrowed is one of consoling certainty, comfortable reliability. She produces the idea of a 'common sense norm' as transhistorical and unproblematic, a shared 'norm' not only between Chaucer and Shakespeare but between both of them and herself.

It is possible, however, comparing in particular the openings of the tale and the play, to argue that what Shakespeare takes from Chaucer here is a tone of *un*certainty. Chaucer's tale begins by recounting, without describing, Theseus's wedding of Hippolyta alongside his conquest of her country, so that she becomes objectified as one of the spoils of war. Theseus was, writes Chaucer,

> swich a conquerour
> That gretter was ther noon under the sonne,
> Ful many a riche contree hadde he wonne;
> What with his wisdom and his chivalrie,
> He conquered al the regne of Femenye,
> That whilom was ycleped Scithia,
> And weddede the queene Ypolita,
> And broghte hire hoom with hym in his contree
> With muchel glorie and greet solempnytee,
>
> (I.862–70)

and the wordplay implicit for the listening ear in the word 'Femenye' underlines the parallel between conquest of the country and of the woman. The opening of *A Midsummer Night's Dream* is set four days *before* the wedding and presents, fleetingly, a tone of apology on Theseus's part:

> Hippolyta, I wooed thee with my sword,
> And won thy love doing thee injuries;
> But I will wed thee in another key:
> With pomp, with triumph, and with revelling.
>
> (I.i.16–19)

Hippolyta's silence, alongside the phallic violence of the first two lines Theseus addresses to her, emphasises the disjunction between the smoothness with which Theseus verbally moves on from the uncomfortable past in an attempt to elide the difference between winning wars and winning love, and the silencing of the woman implicit in the military project. In addition, as Donaldson has pointed out, Theseus's reputation as a treacherous womaniser was well known in Chaucer's time, and, though suppressed in the *Knight's Tale*, is openly alluded to by Oberon in Shakespeare's play.[61] It is self-evident, of course, that this vision of disjunction in the play is as historically and materially determined as is Dorothy Bethurum's more harmonious vision: it is as much the product of the academy of the 1980s and 1990s as Bethurum's is of the 1940s.

Most critics, as Donaldson noted recently, have limited their discussions of influence to the safe confines of verbal parallels. 'The Chaucerian background of *A Midsummer Night's Dream*', he writes,

> is a case in point. Although an excellent start on considering the wider implications of Shakespeare's use of Chaucer was made by Dorothy Bethurum in 1945, discussions since then have usually been limited, rather anachronistically, to matters of detail, to echoes which, though confirming Shakespeare's debt to Chaucer, tell us nothing of real interest about how his imagination responded to and refashioned Chaucer's art.[62]

Donaldson himself widens the scope of analysis to consider 'relationships more subtle and less tangible',[63] in particular suggesting that the interest in self-parody and the scepticism towards romantic love that Shakespeare shows in *A Midsummer Night's Dream* are attitudes shared with Chaucer. He adds Chaucer's *Tale of Sir Thopas* to the catalogue of influences on Shakespeare's play, since its position in relation to the structure of the *Canterbury Tales* is very much that of the play-within-a-play in relation to the whole play of *A Midsummer Night's Dream*.

The question of a shared interest in framing devices as such, however, has been relatively briefly passed over, even by Donaldson. Dorothy Bethurum devotes one sentence of statement and one of explanation to the topic:

In both the play and the romance there is the same effect of a play-within-a-play, illusion within illusion. Chaucer gets it by the contrast of Theseus' real humanity with the stock figures of the two lovers, Shakespeare by the dream.[64]

Alice S. Miskimin, who dedicates her study of *The Renaissance Chaucer* to E. T. Donaldson, takes this somewhat further: she describes the play as one of Shakespeare's most 'Chaucerian', citing its burlesque of the role of the 'playwright-maker' through the figure of Peter Quince, and its framing of 'the dream world and the satyr play within the "real" world of Athens by a series of tacit agreements as to the fictionality of all speakers'.[65] Donaldson's parallel with the *Tale of Sir Thopas* takes it for granted, but he does not go on to suggest that a preoccupation with framing devices that foreground the fictionality of the play or poem is particularly dominant in the work of either writer.

Yet surely it is. And although the limits of this chapter have already been set by the selection of one play, any reader of Chaucer or Shakespeare recognises the device as one familiar throughout the works of both writers. It is not, however, restricted to the work of these two, and does not, *pace* Donaldson, suggest that Shakespeare must have used Chaucer's *Tale of Sir Thopas* as a direct source. This would be to ignore the numerous framed narratives and plays-within-plays found in the work of other medieval and Tudor writers: medieval dream-poetry, for example, and texts such as More's *Utopia* or *Fulgens and Lucrece*, which create second worlds within the world of the text.[66] What it does suggest, I think, is that the interest in framing devices, while not original to either Chaucer or Shakespeare, was particularly foregrounded in their writing, and that Shakespeare, in writing a play so strongly focused on the metadramatic, consciously or unconsciously reworked images of Chaucerian metanarrative. Such an argument can never be satisfactorily 'proved' in the way that verbal echoes can, and yet it surely has more to say to us about *how* one writer read the work of an earlier writer. Verbal echoes can tell us little more than *what* he read. The importance of comparing one writer with another across time lies not merely in proving that the one read the other, but in attempting to reconstruct what he or she saw in that reading and why those particular elements were so conspicuous.

All the Chaucerian works for which evidence has been found in *A Midsummer Night's Dream* are works that play with the narrative frame, and this is no accidental frequency, but the manifestation of a preoccupation everywhere evident in Chaucer's writing. Dorothy Bethurum, in drawing attention to the framing of the Theseus–Hippolita plot, seems to suggest that it operated at an almost accidental level for Chaucer, arising perhaps unintentionally out of a simple contrast between 'real' and stock characters, only maturing beyond the status of mere device in the work of Shakespeare: 'not only the matchless charm of *MND* but also its profoundest meaning lie in Shakespeare's preoccupation throughout with the nature of illusion and the function of imagination'.[67]

This is simply not the case. The *Knight's Tale* is a text that displays its own deep interest in 'the nature of illusion'. It is a romance that explores the conventions of romance, a story in which characters' behaviour is sometimes so conventional as to be patently absurd, and in which pressure is put on the narrative frame by the narrator's intermittent scepticism (see pp. 53–6 above). The story of Theseus and Hippolita is already a frame within a frame, and the other Chaucerian stories Shakespeare uses in *A Midsummer Night's Dream* – the stories of Pyramus and Thisbe (subject of the mechanicals' play) and Pluto and Proserpina (models for Oberon and Titania: Chaucer actually refers to them in the *Merchant's Tale* as king and queen of 'Fairye') – also figure within framed narratives.

Chaucer's retelling of the tale of Pyramus and Thisbe operates, as does the play-within-a-play of Pyramus and Thisbe, as part of a larger framework that manipulates ways of enclosing and determining the significance of the smaller unity, while simultaneously highlighting the arbitrariness and partiality of these very restrictions. Alceste, in Chaucer's *Legend of Good Women,* invites the poet to make up for his injury to women in earlier works (see p. 34 above) by telling tales of women's faithfulness. 'Thus', as Donaldson argues, 'in Chaucer Pyramus must die . . . in order to give Thisbe a chance to prove herself as faithful a lover as he', and the mode of narration enhances the inherent absurdity of this necessity.[68]

Chaucer's project, then, was not dissimilar to Shakespeare's, in so far as both can be seen constructing the tale from a viewpoint that underlines its silliness. The silliness, in the case of the *Legend*, points back to Alceste and, by implication, to those in Chaucer's audience who read his earlier works as reductively as she, as trespasses against womankind. The simplistic reading that demands penance in the form of the

> makynge of a gloryous legende
> Of goode women, maydenes and wyves,
> That were trewe in lovynge al here lyves;
> And . . . of false men that hem betrayen,
> That al here lyf ne don nat but assayen
> How manye wemen they may don a shame
> (G.473–8)

is mocked by the deliberate selection of tales which rebel against the category, and the narrator's last words in the *Legend of Thisbe* draw attention to this ill fit by singling out the *man's* faithfulness:

> Of trewe men I fynde but fewe mo
> In alle my bokes, save this Piramus,
> And therfore have I spoken of hym thus.
> For it is deynte to us men to fynde
> A man that can in love been trewe and kynde.
> Here may ye se, what lovere so he be,
> A woman dar and can as wel as he.
> (917–23)

The mechanicals' play in *A Midsummer Night's Dream* is judged to be silly more by its performance than by its content, yet the process by which the performers repeatedly, yet involuntarily, puncture the theatrical illusion (by making men stand for Wall and Moonshine, by their inability to say their lines correctly and so on) is analogous with the Chaucerian narrator's apparently unwitting introduction of jarring standards in his praise of faithful men within the context of a supposed legend of a good woman.

The complexities of comparison between a performed poem and a play, however, are apparent here. The narrator in Chaucer's text is both a figure within the fiction and the first person 'I' of the performer. As such, his voice is unstable; he is potentially both naïve (a foolish fictional character) and knowing (a performer who may take on this foolish persona with winks and nods to the audience). He thus appears at first sight to occupy the two spaces divided in Shakespeare's play between the mechanicals and the court: the one unconscious and foolish, the other sophisticated, aware of the fictional material as 'the silliest stuff' (V.i.207).

But Shakespeare, like Chaucer, plays with the disruption of those boundaries. The securely knowing space from which Theseus and the court mock the play of Pyramus and Thisbe is rendered unstable by the furthest frame: that of the audience. Theseus and the lovers, despite their clever comments, are after all implicated themselves, as actors, in the project of presenting illusion to an assembled audience; and it is Theseus who speaks the forgiving lines about Peter Quince's company of 'actors': 'the best in this kind are but shadows; and the worst are no worse, if imagination amend them' (V.i.208–9).

Both Chaucer's and Shakespeare's texts become dialogic in performance, acting out open clashes between conflicting modes of perception, and playing with frames as a way of shifting the audience's position of engagement. Both endings refuse to resolve contradiction or to conform to the demands made explicit within the framing device of the fiction. Alceste asks for tales of faithful women and faithless men, yet Chaucer's tale ends with reference to a faithful man; Theseus begs the players, 'No epilogue, I pray you . . . let your epilogue alone' (V.i.346, 352), but *A Midsummer Night's Dream* ends with an epilogue that mischievously echoes, in the phrase 'we shadows' (V.i.413), Theseus's own earlier apology for actors, thus clearly setting him alongside the mechanicals as yet another player.

The analogy between the roles of Pluto and Proserpina in the *Merchant's Tale* and Oberon and Titania in *A Midsummer Night's Dream* is equally suggestive of a common interest in using frames to push the audience towards a highly tuned awareness of the operations of artifice that will allow them to respond with what Brecht calls 'complex seeing'. They are encouraged to engage with the text only provisionally, to be simultaneously conscious of the act of engagement, to recognise that behind every viewpoint that the text constructs there lie other points of view, which may later be revealed. They are in fact invited to 'play' as the texts themselves do.

The *Merchant's Tale*, not unusually among the *Canterbury Tales*, is a narrative of multiple frames. There is, of course, the continuous frame of the pilgrims who tell their tales to one another to while away the journey, and who sometimes seem to select a tale that has a statement to make about them: the Merchant is unhappily

married and tells a tale about a loveless marriage. Within the
Merchant's narrative, there is the semi-frame of the long preamble
in which January asks his two brothers for advice about marriage.
They and he cite numerous biblical texts, often wrenched from
their true context, in a way that insists that the audience consider
the morality of Christian marriage, the numerous ways of distorting and misreading statements of doctrine and the disparity
between ideal and practice. January constructs a further frame
within the story when he builds an enclosed garden that is only
for himself and his wife and to which he holds the only key (until
May has one made for Damian). And within this innermost frame
of the garden Pluto and Proserpina appear to add yet another
framing perspective to the sexual act between May and Damian
that is the culmination of the tale.

Pluto and Proserpina are pagan gods described in this tale as
the fairy king and queen. Either way, they inhabit a different
world from the mortal beings, a world beyond the limitations of
death and Doomsday. So far the moral parameters of the tale have
been set up in a number of ways, all primarily theocentric: by the
consideration of Christian texts and of the first marriage in Eden
in the discussion between January and his brothers; by the priest's
reference to Old Testament marriages in the marriage service,
juxtaposed with the details of the financial transaction that really
underpins the marriage contract; by the garden setting, which
quotes at length from the Song of Songs, widely allegorised as the
spiritual marriage between Christ and his Church on earth; and by
the human practice itself perceived as that of the fallen world:
lustful, deceitful and absurd. The introduction of pagans, or
fairies, seems to insist on another dimension to the complexity of
moral issues in the tale, one that potentially decentres the
Christian frame of reference, and offers a cheap substitute in its
place, a view of the universe as controlled by 'wanton boys' as
trivial in their judgements as mere humans.[69]

Despite their status, Pluto and Proserpina behave in every way
like their mortal counterparts. Although they respectively pull the
strings of January and May – Pluto restoring January's sight at the
climactic moment and Proserpina giving May the clever response
that protects her – their motivations, their marital quarrel, their
struggle for control are purely imitative of the earthly marriage
within the tale. They undermine their own claim to difference, to
the status they claim, even to the point of quoting the Bible, and

operate less as judges of human affairs than as a metaphor for them.

The effect on the audience is complex: the fairy king and queen seem to stand for difference and similarity simultaneously. Their existence contests the Christian framework and suggests the arbitrariness of value-systems, while the fact that they duplicate human behaviour patterns seems to confine them to the fallen world and allow the Christian framework to encircle them. The presence of conflicting centres from which to explain human behaviour functions both to complicate the reader's judgement and to remind her that judgement must nevertheless be made. 'Complex seeing' simultaneously defers judgement and highlights its importance.

A Midsummer Night's Dream works on its audience in parallel ways. Oberon and Titania as fairy king and queen presiding over the enclosed world of the forest are in much the same position as the pagan king and queen within the garden. Like Pluto and Proserpina, their relationship provides a framework within which human relationships are judged; and like Pluto and Proserpina again, their own squabbling undermines their difference from those mortals of whom they are so scornful. Both Chaucer and Shakespeare place their immortals in an intermediate position within the fiction, both framing and framed. The immortal world provides a perspective on the mortal world, but is in turn framed by the wider mortal world of the audience, who are encouraged by the visible shifting of frames to negotiate different forms of engagement with the fiction and to find resolution problematic.

The preoccupation with framing, as I have argued, is neither original to Chaucer or Shakespeare in their time, nor evidence of their shared genius, nor important in confirming the already established fact that Shakespeare read Chaucer. As a broad parallel, and one deeply rooted in the practice of both writers, it points us towards the more historically and materially oriented question of why Shakespeare in the 1590s was particularly sensitive to this anti-monologic quality in Chaucer's poetry. A full comparison between the conditions within which both Chaucer and Shakespeare were writing is not possible in a book of this size, which devotes less than one chapter to comparing the two authors, but a few obvious parallels may be summarised. Both wrote from within societies where the dangers of factionalism were evident, for example, and both sustained long writing careers against a background of changing monarchs and developing power struggles between monarch and parliament. Their foregrounded scepticism, their use of frames to transfer the responsibility for final judgement to the audience may be seen at least partly as a response to the institutions within which they operated, where explicit statement might condemn the writer to lose his hands, if not his head. This leads back into the earlier sections of this book: to Chaucer's life, his professional susceptibility to power shifts between Richard II and the nobles, yet his continuous survival throughout the upheavals outlined in chapter 1; and to his work, his studied avoidance of explicit topical reference, his use of allegory, his exploration of 'authority', his adoption of fictional personae.

Chaucer and Shakespeare are not two points on a line called History. They occupy specific positions in a dialogue that is always in process, interrogating and remaking past and present in the image of each other. Inevitably, then, the position of writing about the past now, in this moment, is also implicated in the process of dialogue. The present casts its own particular shadow: the critic in his or her time attempting to read the workings of intertextuality across two earlier periods is not a passive receiver of 'facts', but an active, determining *factor* (maker of meanings). The text of this chapter, as well as attempting to recognise the 'pastness' of two earlier texts, must itself be recognised as bringing its own 'presentness' and material position to its interrogation of the past.[70] In presenting the view that Shakespeare's attention was drawn to metafictional devices and a playfulness with audience–text relations when he read Chaucer, I am also reflecting a preoccupation of late twentieth-century literary criticism, which characteristically takes pleasure in deconstructing artifice and exploring the play of different surfaces, and which in turn must be related to the social and institutional conditions of its production. There can be no description of Chaucer's 'influence' in the sense of an impartial recording of an existing object. There is no object there. What we describe when we undertake such a project, or the even broader project of locating Chaucer in his time, is the dialogue between ourselves and the textuality of the past.

Chronological Table
1327–1400

Chaucer's life and medieval literature		History	
		1327	Deposition and murder of Edward II Accession of Edward III
1328	William of Ockham excommunicated	1328	Edward's marriage to Philippa
1330–40	Auchinleck Ms Ms Harley 2253		
		1335–8	Wyclif born
		1337	Hundred Years War begins
c.1343	Chaucer born		
1345	Richard de Bury, *Philobiblon*		
		1346	Battle of Crécy
		1348	Edward III founds Order of the Garter
		1348–9	First plague reaches England
1349	William of Ockham dies		
c.1350–2	Boccaccio, *Decameron* Higden, *Polychronicon* Henry of Lancaster, *Livre de Seyntz Medicines*		
		1351	Statute of Labourers
		1356	Battle of Poitiers; capture of French king and hostages
1357	First record of Chaucer: page to the Countess of Ulster		
1359–60	Chaucer on campaign in France and captured		
		1360	Treaty of Calais

Chaucer's life and medieval literature		History	
		1361	Second plague in England Black Prince marries Joan of Kent
		1362	Statute decrees use of English in law courts Black Prince becomes Prince of Aquitaine
1366	Chaucer's journey to Navarre Chaucer's father dies Chaucer marries Philippa de Roet		
1367	Chaucer receives royal annuity	1367	Richard II born
1367–70	Langland, *Piers Plowman: A-text*		
1368	Chaucer overseas, possibly in Italy	1368	Blanche, Duchess of Lancaster dies Lionel of Clarence dies Chancellor first opens Parliament in English
1368–9	Hoccleve born		
1369–72	*The Book of the Duchess*	1369	Third plague in England Queen Philippa dies
1370	Lydgate born		
		1371	John of Gaunt marries Constance of Castile
1372	Chaucer's first recorded journey to Italy		
1373	Boccaccio's lectures on Dante		
1374	Chaucer moves to Aldgate; appointed controller of customs Petrarch dies		
1375	Boccaccio dies		
1376	Chaucer receives payment for 'secret business of the king'	1376	Good Parliament Black Prince dies
1377	Chaucer overseas several times on royal business	1377	Edward III dies Accession of Richard II First poll tax
c.1377–9	Langland, *Piers Plowman: B-text*		

Chaucer's life and medieval literature		History	
1378	Chaucer visits Italy	1378	Papal schism
?1378–80	*The House of Fame*		
		1379	Second poll tax
1380	Cecilia Chaumpaigne case	1380	Third poll tax
1380–2	*The Parliament of Fowls*	1381	English Rising
1382–6	*Troilus and Criseyde, Palamon and Arcite, The Legend of Good Women*	1382	Blackfriars Council Earthquake Richard II's marriage to Anne of Bohemia
		1384	Wyclif dies
1385	Chaucer a member of the Peace Commission for Kent Deschamps's tribute to Chaucer		
c.1385	Gower, *Vox Clamantis*		
1386	Chaucer appointed knight of the shire for Kent Chaucer's wife admitted to the fraternity of Lincoln Cathedral	1386	Wonderful Parliament
c.1386–7	Langland, *Piers Plowman: C-text*		
1387	Trevisa's translation of Higden's *Polychronicon*		
?c.1387	Chaucer begins work on *Canterbury Tales*	1387	Lords Appellant restrict the authority of Richard II
1388	Thomas Usk executed	1388	Merciless Parliament
1389	Chaucer appointed clerk of the king's works		
1390	Construction of the Smithfield lists		
c.1390	Vernon MS		
1390–3	Gower, *Confessio Amantis*		
1391	Chaucer appointed deputy forester for North Petherton forest, Somerset		
		1394	Queen Anne dies

Chaucer's life and medieval literature		History	
		1396	Richard's marriage to Isabella
		1399	John of Gaunt dies
			Deposition of Richard II
			Accession of Henry IV
1400	Chaucer dies	1400	Murder of Richard II

Notes

Chapter 1 Chaucer's Life and Times

1. *Chaucer Life-Records*, ed. Martin M. Crow and Clair C. Olson (Oxford: Clarendon Press, 1966), pp. 370–4. Where quotations concerning Chaucer's life are not attributed they should be assumed to derive from the *Life-Records* (hereafter cited as *LR*). The records are all in either French or Latin, but quotations are usually given here in English translation.
2. While there is obviously room for doubt about which of the Chaucer family's many properties they actually lived in, their residence in Vintry ward between 1341 and 1363 is made virtually certain by the frequency of John Chaucer's name as a witness in the ward. See *LR*, p. 9, nn. 1 and 2.
3. The burdens of taxation are fully discussed by Barbara A. Hanawalt, 'Peasant Resistance to Royal and Seignorial Impositions', in *Social Unrest in the Late Middle Ages*, ed. F. X. Newman, Medieval & Renaissance Texts and Studies, 39 (Binghamton, NY, 1986) pp. 23–48. She notes that contemporary observers feared a peasant revolt in 1341 on account of the tax imposed in that year.
4. Jean Froissart, *Chronicles*, sel., trans. and ed. Geoffrey Brereton, rev. edn (Harmondsworth: Penguin, 1978) p. 92.
5. See, for example, W. M. Ormrod, *The Reign of Edward III: Crown and Political Society in England 1327–1377* (New Haven, Conn. and London: Yale University Press, 1990), p. 21; and Philip Ziegler, *The Black Death* (Harmondsworth: Penguin, rpt 1982) ch. 14.
6. *Historia Anglicana*, ed. H. T. Riley, 2 vols, RS, 28 (1863–4) vol. I, p. 273; quoted in *The World of Piers Plowman*, ed. J. Krochalis and E. Peters (Pennsylvania: University of Pennsylvania Press, 1975) p. 77. John B. Friedman, discussing the portrayal of the plague in the visual arts ('"He hath a thousand slayn this pestilence": Iconography of the Plague in the Late Middle Ages', in Newman, *Social Unrest*, pp. 75–112), notes the emphasis placed on the insufficiency of the living to bury the dead in visual representations as well as written accounts.
7. All quotations from Chaucer's works are taken from the Riverside edition, ed. L. D. Benson, 3rd edn (Oxford: Oxford University Press, 1988).
8. The Statute is cited in full in Krochalis and Peters, *The World of Piers Plowman*, pp. 78–80.
9. The terminology of feudalism throughout the medieval period is inconsistent and confusing. R. H. Hilton discusses the question of medieval serfdom in his book *Bond Men Made Free: Medieval Peasant*

Movements and the English Rising of 1381 (London: Temple Smith, 1973), esp. pp. 55–61. See also Hilton's *The Decline of Serfdom in Medieval England* (London and Basingstoke: Macmillan, 1969) and 'Freedom and Villeinage in England', rpt in *Peasants, Knights and Heretics*, ed. R. H. Hilton (Cambridge: Cambridge University Press, 1976) pp. 174–91.

10. 'Social Change versus Revolution: New Interpretations of the Peasants' Revolt of 1381', in Newman, *Social Unrest*, p. 15.

11. Nicholas Orme, who has written extensively on English medieval schools (*English Schools in the Middle Ages* [London and New York: Methuen, 1973] and *Education and Society in Medieval and Renaissance England* [London and Ronceverte: Hambledon Press, 1989], does not make a distinction between reading and song schools, but considers the terms interchangeable (e.g. *English Schools*, p. 60). Jo Ann Hoeppner Moran, however, insists on a distinction, arguing that 'song schools did not always teach reading' and 'more often reading schools did not teach song' (*The Growth of English Schooling 1340–1548: Learning, Literacy, and Laicization in Pre-Reformation York Diocese* [Princeton, NJ: Princeton University Press, 1985] p. 18).

12. Derek Brewer, in his very readable account of medieval schooling in *Chaucer and his World* (London: Eyre Methuen, 1978), pictures Chaucer learning to read from an English primer (p. 57), but this seems unlikely in the context of both place and date.

13. The full inventory of Ravenstone's collection can be consulted in Edith Rickert's useful collection of fourteenth-century documents, *Chaucer's World*, ed. C. C. Olson and M. M. Crow (London: Geoffrey Cumberlege, Oxford University Press, 1948) pp. 122–6. Rickert points out that library regulations seem to have allowed students to continue to borrow books after they had left the school.

14. Translated in Rickert, *Chaucer's World*, pp. 96–8.

15. The writers on medieval education cited in note 11 above have little to say about the education of girls in fourteenth-century England. Eileen Power has looked at the education of girls in nunneries (*Medieval English Nunneries c.1275 to 1535* [Cambridge: Cambridge University Press, 1922]), but the subject of female education in a wider context awaits full investigation.

16. *Little John of Saintré*, trans. Irvine Gray (London: George Routledge, 1931) p. 33. Derek Brewer (*Chaucer and his World*, pp. 65–7) describes this romance in more detail and also draws attention to the English romance *King Horn* for the similar information it supplies about the duties of a page.

17. D. S. Bland, 'Chaucer and the Inns of Court: A Re-Examination', *English Studies*, vol. 33 (1952) pp. 145–55 has argued that the notion that Chaucer spent some time at the Inns of Court can be considered as 'no more than a plausible theory' (p. 149) and Richard Firth Green (*Poets and Princepleasers: Literature and the English Court in the Late Middle Ages* [Toronto: University of Toronto Press, 1980]) has shown very convincingly that the *familia* of the royal court received a wide-ranging education, and certainly up to

the standard that future service in the king's household offices would require.

18. See, for example, J. I. Wimsatt, *Chaucer and the poems of 'Ch'* (Cambridge: D. S. Brewer, Rowman & Littlefield, 1982). Wimsatt prints some French poems found with the marginal annotation 'Ch'. Although there is no external evidence that these poems are by Chaucer, Wimsatt prints them in order to suggest 'more precisely . . . what Chaucer's French poetry might have been like' (p. 1).

19. Philippa's father was often referred to as Sir Payne (or Paon) de Roet, which seems to have been a nickname from French, meaning either 'peacock' or 'pawn'. 'Pan' may be a form of this name. See *LR*, pp. 17, 69.

20. Paul Strohm, in his recent study, *Social Chaucer* (Cambridge, Mass.: Harvard University Press, 1989) discusses the complexity and fluctuation of late fourteenth-century social class reflected in contemporary usage of the term *'esquier'* (pp. 6–15).

21. Blanche was long believed to have died in September 1369, but evidence discovered by J. N. Palmer ('The Historical Context of the *Book of the Duchess*: A Revision', *Chaucer Review*, vol. 8 [1973–4], pp. 253–61) points to September 1368 as the more likely date. Helen Phillips summarises the reasons for dating the poem 1368–71 in her edition of *The Book of the Duchess* (Durham and St Andrews Medieval Texts, 3, rev. edn, 1984). She also prints summaries and extracts in translation of the French sources cited below.

22. There had been a second outbreak in 1361, which chroniclers reported as particularly affecting children.

23. Deschamps's poem is usually dated 1385–6, and so is no help in dating Chaucer's translation.

24. Prince Lionel, by then Duke of Clarence, married Violante, the daughter of Bernabò Visconti, Lord of Milan, in 1368, so it is possible that Chaucer was involved in negotiations for this marriage.

25. Arguments in favour of the probability that Chaucer knew Italian are discussed in some detail on pp. 190–7 of Howard Schless's article, 'Transformations: Chaucer's Use of Italian', in *Writers and their Background: Geoffrey Chaucer*, ed. Derek Brewer (London: G. Bell, 1974).

26. See David Wallace, 'Chaucer's Continental Inheritance', in *The Cambridge Chaucer Companion*, ed. Piero Boitani and Jill Mann (Cambridge: Cambridge University Press, 1986) p. 21, and J. A. W. Bennett, 'Chaucer, Dante and Boccaccio', in *Chaucer and the Italian Trecento*, ed. Piero Boitani (Cambridge: Cambridge University Press, 1983) pp. 90–1.

27. *The Anonimalle Chronicle: 1333–1381*, ed. V. H. Galbraith (Manchester: Manchester University Press, 1927) pp. 79–80; trans. Rickert, *Chaucer's World*, p. 165.

28. Sermon 69 in M. A. Devlin, ed., *The Sermons of Thomas Brinton, Bishop of Rochester*, 2 vols, Camden 3rd series, 85, 86 (1954). The

translation quoted here is from the introduction, p. xxv. The fable was already popular with earlier writers. The French version, by Nicholas Bozon, is translated in Krochalis and Peters, *The World of Piers Plowman*, pp. 165–6. The allegory originally represented prelates and their parishioners.

29. May McKisack, *The Fourteenth Century 1307–1399* (Oxford: Clarendon Press, 1959) p. 396.

30. This statute is translated in Krochalis and Peters, *The World of Piers Plowman*, pp. 82–3. It is discussed, together with several other attempts by the government to deal with social problems through legislation, by D. W. Robertson, Jr, in an essay entitled 'Chaucer and the Economic and Social Consequences of the Plague', in Newman, *Social Unrest*, pp. 49–76. Barbara Hanawalt, in considering outbreaks of discontent before 1381, has argued for an increased incidence of protest from 1377 onwards (in Newman, *Social Unrest*, pp. 23–48).

31. Froissart, *Chronicles*, p. 194.

32. Ibid., pp. 195–6.

33. *Hist. Ang.*, vol. I, pp. 327–8; cited by Ormrod, *The Reign of Edward III*, p. x.

34. London, Corporation, *Calendar of Letter-Books*, H, pp. 64–6, quoted in Rickert, *Chaucer's World*, p. 45.

35. The *Monk's Tale* may have been written at this early date. See the discussion in the *Riverside* notes, p. 929.

36. 'The Strange Case of Geoffrey Chaucer and Cecilia Chaumpaigne', *Law Quarterly Review*, vol. 63 (1947) pp. 491–515.

37. *Law Quarterly Review.*, vol. 64 (1948) p. 36.

38. Watts cites the strange tenet of medieval English law which affirmed that conception could not occur unless sexual relations had taken place with the woman's consent. Pregnancy, according to Watts, is the most likely explanation of the king's failure to take the case further and of the payment made to Cecilia. Watts goes on to suggest the possibility that 'little Lewis', the son referred to in Chaucer's *Treatise of the Astrolabe*, was Cecilia's son.

39. Quoted in Michael Packe, *King Edward III*, ed. L. C. B. Seaman (London: Routledge and Kegan Paul, 1983) p. 120. Packe cites the relevant extracts from both Le Bel's and Froissart's accounts, and discusses their implications. As he points out (p. 121), there is still room for doubt about the truth. Packe also notes (p. 119) that Le Bel's use of the verb '*efforcha*' to denote rape is capable of the same ambiguity as the Latin '*raptus*', though there is no ambiguity as to its intended meaning in this context.

40. Packe, *King Edward III*, p. 106.

41. See Roland Blenner-Hassett, 'Autobiographical Aspects of Chaucer's Franklin', *Speculum*, vol. 28 (1953) pp. 791–800.

42. *Hist. Ang.*, vol. I, p. 323; cited in R. B. Dobson, *The Peasants' Revolt of 1381* (London: Macmillan, 1970) p. 103. Dobson collects and translates a very good selection from the contemporary chronicles.

43. Dobson prints various accounts of the three taxes, including the

table of graduated taxation for 1379. The Rolls of Parliament stipulate that the 1380 tax is to be collected 'from each lay person of the realm, within franchise or without, both male and female and of whatsoever estate or condition, who have reached the age of fifteen – except for genuine beggars who will be charged nothing. This is on condition that at all times the levy shall be made in due order and form and that each lay person shall be charged equally according to his means in the following manner: that is to say, that for the sum total reckoned for each township, the sufficient shall (according to their means) aid the lesser, provided that the most wealthy do not pay more than sixty groats for themselves and their wives and no one at all should pay less than one groat for himself and his wife' (Dobson, *Peasants' Revolt*, p. 117). As Dobson points out, these arrangements for subsidising those less able to pay 'obviously penalised the inhabitants of poor villages and towns'.

44. John of Gaunt claimed the Spanish throne through his second wife, Constance of Castile. See further Hanawalt, in Newman, *Social Unrest*, p. 28.

45. Walsingham (*Hist. Angl.*, vol. II, p. 32) quotes this couplet in English.

46. *Chronicon*, ed. J. R. Lumby, 2 vols, RS, 92 (1889–95) vol. II, p. 135.

47. Accounts of Wat Tyler's death vary considerably. See Dobson, *Peasants' Revolt*, part III, where the various accounts appear.

48. Walsingham, *Hist. Angl.*, vol. II, p. 18, cited in Dobson, *Peasants' Revolt*, p. 311. I have changed Dobson's translation of the first word from 'rustics' to 'serfs', which I think more clearly conveys the sense of the Latin '*rustici*' to a modern reader.

49. *Polychronicon*, ed. J. R. Lumby, 9 vols, RS, 41 (1865–86) vol. IX, p. 1. See also Dobson, *Peasants' Revolt*, p. 199.

50. *The Major Latin Works of John Gower*, trans. Eric W. Stockton (Seattle: University of Washington Press, 1962) p. 49.

51. The poem is printed in T. Wright's collection *Political Poems and Songs Relating to English History composed during the Period from the Accession of Edward III to that of Richard III*, 2 vols, RS, 14 (1859–61) vol. I, pp. 224–6. It is also reprinted in Krochalis and Peters, *The World of Piers Plowman*, p. 95.

52. See *LR*, pp. 146–7. The evidence is not conclusive, however. All we have is a record of a property transaction made by Chaucer in London the following week. The editors of *LR* use the reference from the *Nun's Priest's Tale* (cited p. 19 below) as evidence for presuming that Chaucer was in London at the time, but this is too insubstantial to suggest an eye-witness account, and the minimal information it contains is no more than would have been common knowledge at the time.

53. Paul Strohm discusses Chaucer's connections with these men in more detail in chapter 2 of *Social Chaucer*, esp. pp. 25–34.

54. See K. B. McFarlane, *Lancastrian Kings and Lollard Knights* (Oxford: Oxford University Press, 1972) for a full account of the careers of these knights and discussion of their Lollard inclinations.

55. Ibid., p. 224.
56. Russell A. Peck, in an article entitled 'Social Conscience and the Poets' (in Newman, *Social Unrest*, pp. 113–48), argues that many of Wyclifs views found their way into poetry of the 1390s, with an emphasis on their implications for society and the individual rather than for theological orthodoxy. See also Anne Hudson, *The Premature Reformation: Wycliffite Texts and Lollard History* (Oxford: Clarendon Press, 1988) ch. 9, 'The Context of Vernacular Wycliffism'.
57. 'Form and Social Statement in *Confessio Amantis* and *The Canterbury Tales*', *Studies in the Age of Chaucer*, vol. 1 (1979) pp. 38–9. Strohm also argues in chapter 1 of *Social Chaucer* that Chaucer's affinity with the king affected his political life.
58. Ormrod, *The Reign of Edward III*, pp. 155–70 gives a good description of the role of knights of the shire in government and the processes of their election.
59. See Knighton, *Chronicon*, vol. II, p. 213 and Walsingham, *Hist. Angl.*, vol. II, p. 148.
60. Anthony Tuck further discusses this threat, together with the possibility that Richard was in fact briefly deposed for a few days in December 1387, in *Richard II and the English Nobility* (London: Edward Arnold, 1973) pp. 102–3.
61. McFarlane gives a full account of the Appellants and the sequence of moves against them in the late 1390s in chapter 2 of *Lancastrian Kings and Lollard Knights*.
62. In the fifteenth century, the office of clerk of the works was apparently ranked fourth among the royal establishments after the household, the chamber and the wardrobe, although the importance of these did vary at different periods (*LR*, p. 476). Strohm again connects this appointment with Richard's re-establishment of his prerogatives from 1389 onwards, although he argues that Chaucer held himself aloof from court factionalism after 1386, which would help to account for the ease with which his privileges were renewed at the time of Henry IV's accession (see 'Form and Social Statement', p. 39).
63. Brereton's selection does not include Froissart's description of Smithfield. Rickert, however, translates extracts from it (*Chaucer's World*, pp. 211–14).
64. *The Regiment of Princes* (878–82), in *Hoccleve's Works*, ed. F. J. Furnivall, 3 vols, EETS, ES, 61, 72–3 (1892–7) vol. II, p. 32.
65. See further Tuck, *Richard II*, pp. 220–5.

Chapter 2 Literary Production and Audience

1. 'The Auchinleck Manuscript and a Possible London Bookshop of 1330–1340', *PMLA*, vol. 57 (1942) pp. 595–627.
2. 'English Books In and Out of Court from Edward III to Henry VII', in *English Court Culture in the Later Middle Ages*, ed. V. J. Scattergood and J. W. Sherborne (London: Gerald Duckworth, 1983) pp. 163–81.

3.	A. I. Doyle and M. B. Parkes have argued that while there is clear evidence for the existence of stationers there is none for the existence of centralised scriptoria ('The Production of Copies of the *Canterbury Tales* and the *Confessio Amantis* in the Early Fifteenth Century', in *Medieval Scribes, Manuscripts and Libraries: Essays presented to N. R. Ker*, ed. M. B. Parkes and A. G. Watson [London: Scolar Press, 1978] pp. 163–203). See also Derek Pearsall's Introduction to *Book Production and Publishing in Britain 1375–1475*, ed. Jeremy Griffiths and Derek Pearsall (Cambridge: Cambridge University Press, 1989) pp. 6–7; and C. Paul Christianson, 'Evidence for the Study of London's Late Medieval Manuscript-Book Trade', in ibid., pp. 87–108.

4.	'The Text of the Canterbury Tales in 1400', *PMLA*, vol. 50 (1935) p. 108.

5.	*Medieval Writers and their Work: Middle English Literature and its Background 1100–1500* (Oxford and New York: Oxford University Press, 1982) p. 27.

6.	See Graham Pollard, 'The Company of Stationers before 1557', *The Library*, 4th ser., vol. 18 (1938) pp. 1–38, and M. B. Parkes, 'The Literacy of the Laity', in *The Medieval World*, ed. David Daiches and Anthony Thorlby (London: Aldus Books, 1973) p. 564.

7.	*The Medieval Library* (Chicago: Chicago University Press, 1939) p. 643.

8.	Derek Pearsall describes this practice in his introduction to the facsimile of the Auchinleck Manuscript, ed. D. Pearsall and I. C. Cunningham (London: Scolar Press, 1979). See further Carol Meale, 'Patrons, Buyers and Owners: Book Production and Social Status', in Griffiths and Pearsall, *Book Production*, pp. 201–38.

9.	Parkes, 'The Literacy of the Laity', p. 564. Janet Coleman also cites the example of the grocers in her discussion of the growth of middle-class literacy in *English Literature in History 1350–1400: Medieval Readers and Writers* (London: Hutchinson, 1981) p. 26.

10.	See, for example, Derek Pearsall, *Old and Middle English Poetry*, Routledge History of English Poetry, vol. I (London: Routledge and Kegan Paul, 1977) esp. ch. 5, and Parkes, 'The Literacy of the Laity', pp. 562–3, 568–70; but see also Julia Boffey and John J. Thompson, 'Anthologies and Miscellanies: Production and Choice of Texts', in Griffiths and Pearsall, *Book Production*, pp. 279–315, who discuss the emergence of new kinds of anthologies in the late fourteenth and fifteenth centuries.

11.	*From Memory to Written Record: England 1066–1307* (London: Edward Arnold, 1979) pp. 60–63; Dorothea Oschinsky (ed.), *Walter of Henley and Other Treatises on Estate Management and Accountancy* (Oxford: Clarendon Press, 1971) pp. 11–50. Clanchy's book documents the changing conditions in which the written word was produced, and how the written word was approached and understood by different classes and at different dates. It is indispensable reading for an understanding of how fourteenth-century conditions grew out of the earlier period.

12.   Although this book was a commonplace book to the extent that it reflected the personal interests of its owner, it had a kind of thematic unity, since Sir John collected in it texts relating to chivalry and referred to it as 'my boke off knyghthod'. See G. A. Lester, *Sir John Paston's 'Grete Boke: A Descriptive Catalogue, with an Introduction, of British Library MS Lansdowne 285* (Cambridge: D. S. Brewer, 1984).

13.   *The Vernon Manuscript*, ed. A. I. Doyle (Woodbridge: D. S. Brewer, 1987) f. i.

14.   *Literary Theory: An Introduction* (Oxford: Basil Blackwell, 1983).

15.   See Doyle and Parkes, in Parkes and Watson, *Medieval Scribes*, pp. 190–1. Elizabeth Salter discusses the multiplicity of the *Canterbury Tales*, together with the disruptiveness of its 'borders' (her analogy throughout the discussion is with manuscript illumination), in *English and International: Studies in the Literature, Art and Patronage of Medieval England*, ed. Derek Pearsall and Nicolette Zeeman (Cambridge: Cambridge University Press, 1988) pp. 253–5.

16.   *Philobiblon*, text and trans. of E. C. Thomas, ed. M. McLagan (Oxford: Basil Blackwell, 1960) pp. 47–9.

17.   See Robert K. Root, 'Publication Before Printing', *PMLA*, vol. 28 (1913) pp. 417–31.

18.   The problems of editing the poem are discussed at length in the preface to the Athlone Press edition of the poem, ed. G. Kane and E. T. Donaldson (London, 1975), and also in chapter 3 of Lee Patterson, *Negotiating the Past: The Historical Understanding of Medieval Literature* (Madison: University of Wisconsin Press, 1987).

19.   See Norman Blake, *The English Language in Medieval Literature* (London: Dent, 1977) p. 23.

20.   Thorlac Turville-Petre, 'The Author of The Destruction of Troy', *Medium Aevum*, vol. 58 (1989) pp. 264–9.

21.   Anne Middleton has recently published an important article on the context and significance of medieval 'signatures', 'William Langland's "Kynde Name": Authorial Signature and Social Identity in Late Fourteenth-Century England', in *Literary Practice and Social Change in Britain 1380–1530*, ed. Lee Patterson (Berkeley, Calif. and Oxford: University of California Press, 1990) pp. 15–82.

22.   *Medieval to Renaissance in English Poetry* (Cambridge: Cambridge University Press, 1985) pp. 105–6. Spearing's distinction between 'work' and 'text' is based on the work of Roland Barthes (see his 'From Work to Text', in *Image, Music, Text*, sel. and trans. Stephen Heath (London: Fontana, 1977) pp. 155–64).

23.   Roland Barthes, 'The Death of the Author', in *Image, Music, Text*, p. 146; cited by Spearing, *Medieval to Renaissance in English Poetry*, p. 105.

24.   *Chaucer Review*, vol. 18 (1983) published several papers from a symposium on Chaucer's audience, including one by Richard Firth Green which raises the question of how many women there might have been in a court audience (pp. 146–54).

25. Jean Froissart, *Chronicles*, sel., trans. and ed. G. Brereton, rev. edn (Harmondsworth: Penguin, 1978) p. 264.

26. Franz H. Bäuml, in an article entitled 'Varieties and Consequences of Medieval Literacy and Illiteracy' (*Speculum*, vol. 55 [1980] pp. 237–65) argues for the use of the term 'quasi-literate' to describe 'those *illiterati* who must and do have access to literacy [and] are, in respect to their dependence on the written word for the exercise of their socio-political function, to be classed with the *litterati*' (p. 246).

27. Psalm 51 according to the numbering of the Authorised Version.

28. For a detailed investigation of the subject see Leona C. Gabel, *Benefit of Clergy in England in the Later Middle Ages*, Smith College Studies in History, vol. 14 (1928–9; rpt New York: Octagon Books, 1969).

29. Clanchy, *From Memory to Written Record*, p. 177. See also Bäuml, 'Varieties and Consequences', pp. 237–9 and Parkes, 'The Literacy of the Laity', *passim*.

30. *Philobiblon*, p. 161.

31. Margaret Deanesly, 'Vernacular Books in England in the Fourteenth and Fifteenth Centuries', *MLR*, vol. 15 (1920) pp. 349–58; and Doyle, 'English Books'.

32. In her examination of 7568 wills Margaret Deanesly (see previous note) found only 338 books recorded. Such a small number is dubious evidence for drawing general conclusions about the predominance of any kind of book in the period, and suggests that a large proportion of books owned were not documented in wills.

33. *Medieval English Nunneries*, p. 247. She points out besides that this progress was exactly echoed in the coronation oaths.

34. But cf. the discussion of *Ancrene Wisse*, a thirteenth-century text, on pp. 72–3 below.

35. *Fourteenth-Century English Poetry: Contexts and Readings* (Oxford: Clarendon Press, 1983) p. 24.

36. *The Vision of Piers Plowman: A Complete Edition of the B-Text*, ed. A. V. C. Schmidt (London: Dent, 1978) XV.370–4.

37. Quoted in Coleman, *English Literature in History 1350–1400*, p. 52.

38. Salter, *English and International*, p. 31. See also Thorlac Turville-Petre, 'Politics and Poetry in the Early Fourteenth Century: The Case of Robert Mannyng's Chronicle', *Review of English Literarture*, n.s., vol. 39 (1988) pp. 1–28.

39. *The Auchinleck Manuscript*, p. viii. See also Vincent Gillespie, 'Vernacular Books of Religion', in Griffiths and Pearsall, *Book Production*, pp. 317–44, where Gillespie argues that the move towards the vernacular in religious manuscripts of the fourteenth century took account not only of the expanding lay audience, but also of the less literate clergy.

40. *Fourteenth Century Verse and Prose*, ed. Kenneth Sisam, 4th edn (Oxford: Clarendon Press, 1970) pp. 148–9.

41. Coleman, *English Literature in History 1350–1400*, p. 19. The evidence she cites on pp. 51–2 of 'the increasing currency of

English . . . to express political and social matters . . . as early a
1327' also seems to me to militate against the view that the cour
continued to speak French in the face of such changes.

42. Froissart, *Chronicles*, p. 408.
43. Juliet Vale, *Edward III and Chivalry: Chivalric Society and its Contex
1270–1350* (Woodbridge: Boydell Press, 1982) pp. 64–5. Thorla
Turville-Petre in a review-article of this book (*Nottingham Medieva
Studies*, vol. 27 [1983] pp. 92–101) also argues that the English cour
must have been English-speaking by Chaucer's time.
44. William Rothwell, 'The Role of French in Thirteenth-Century
England', *Bulletin of the John Rylands Library*, vol. 58 (1975–6
pp. 445–66. For further discussion of this question see R. Berndt
'The Linguistic Situation in England from the Norman Conquest t
the loss of Normandy (1066–1204)', in *Approaches to Historica
Linguistics: An Anthology*, ed. R. Lass (New York: Holt, Rinehart &
Winston, 1969) pp. 369–91; and R. M. Wilson, 'English and Frenc
in England 1100–1300', *History*, vol. 28 (1943) pp. 37–60.
45. *De Officio Pastorali*, ch. xv, rpt in Sisam (ed.), *Fourteenth-century Vers
and Prose*, p. 118. No extant English manuscripts can be certainl
attributed to Wyclif, but Margaret Aston has shown that in his late
years he undoubtedly did produce some writing in English ('Wycli
and the Vernacular', *Studies in Church History*, Subsidia, vol.
[1987] pp. 281–330). The subject of vernacular translations an
ecclesiastical prohibitions against them is very fully discussed b
Margaret Deanesly in *The Lollard Bible and Other Medieval Biblica
Versions* (Cambridge: Cambridge University Press, 1920).
46. This story is edited by C. F. Bühler, *Medium Aevum*, vol. 7 (1938
pp. 167–83. Anne Hudson (*Selected English Wycliffite Writing
[Cambridge: Cambridge University Press, 1978] pp. 167–8) cast
doubt on its truth.
47. Quoted in R. H. Robbins 'Dissent in Middle English Literature: Th
Spirit of (Thirteen) Seventy Six', *Medievalia et Humanistica*, vol.
(1979) p. 40. See also Margaret Aston, 'Lollardy and Seditior
1381–1431', in *Lollards and Reformers: Images and Literacy in Lat
Medieval Religion* (London: Hambledon Press, 1984), p. 11; and Anne
Hudson, *The Premature Reformation*, p. 276, where this same state
ment is cited.
48. Robbins, 'Dissent in Middle English Literature', p. 40. Anne
Hudson examines the association between heresy and the use o
the vernacular in her papers 'Lollardy: the English Heresy?'
reprinted in her collection *Lollards and their Books* (London an
Ronceverte: Hambledon Press, 1985) pp. 141–63 and 'Wyclif an
the English Language', in *Wyclif in his Times*, ed. Anthony Kenn
(Oxford: Clarendon Press, 1986) pp. 85–103. See also Margare
Aston, 'Wyclif and the Vernacular'.
49. See, for example, Coleman, *English Literature in History 1350–1400
ch. 3.
50. Further discussion of Chaucer's interest in the role of the audienc
in constructing the meaning of the text can be found in Janett

Dillon, 'Chaucer's Game in the *Pardoner's Tale*, *Essays in Criticism*, vol. 41 (1991) pp. 208–21.

1. A very full analysis of Chaucer's audience is undertaken by Paul Strohm in his book *Social Chaucer*. See also the publication of the symposium on 'Chaucer's Audience' in *Chaucer Review*, vol. 18 (1983) pp. 137–71 and Strohm's article on 'Chaucer's Fifteenth-Century Audience and the Narrowing of the "Chaucer Tradition"', *Studies in the Age of Chaucer*, vol. 4 (1982) pp. 3–32, which gives brief details of the individuals identifiably associated with Chaucer, some of whom are discussed below.

2. Laila Gross, in the *Riverside* notes, points out the variant 'princesse' in two manuscripts of 'The Complaint of Venus', both Shirley's.

3. Again Gross notes an alternative reading, taking 'prince' as the conventional form of address to the head of a Pui, or poetry-reading group. Given the content of the envoy, however, a political and specific reading of 'prince' seems much more probable.

4. Although the identity of Chaucer's Bukton is not certain, both candidates, Sir Robert of Suffolk and Sir Peter of York, were of similar rank.

5. Derek Pearsall's discussion of 'The *Troilus* Frontispiece and Chaucer's Audience', *Literature and History*, vol. 5 (1977) pp. 26–41, independently analyses Chaucer's audience along similar lines to Strohm. See further his discussion of 'The Chaucer Circle' in *Old and Middle English Poetry* (London: Routledge and Kegan Paul, 1977) pp. 194–7.

6. 'Chaucer's Fifteenth-Century Audience', p. 18.

Chapter 3 Four Estates

1. Cited by G. R. Owst, *Literature and Pulpit in Medieval England*, 2nd edn (Oxford: Basil Blackwell, 1961) p. 554.

2. Jill Mann, who has made a detailed study of the *General Prologue* to the *Canterbury Tales* in the context of other medieval estates literature, draws attention to this point (*Chaucer and Medieval Estates Satire* [Cambridge: Cambridge University Press, 1973] p. 121).

3. Devlin ed., Sermon 44; trans. J. Krochalis and E. Peters, *World of Piers Plowman* (Pennsylvania: University of Pennsylvania Press, 1975) p. 116.

4. Paul Strohm discusses the statute of 1363 in some detail (*Social Chaucer* [Cambridge, Mass.: Harvard University Press] pp. 5–7).

5. See Sylvia L. Thrupp, *The Merchant Class of Medieval London [1300–1500]* (Chicago: University of Chicago Press, 1948) p. 239.

6. See Michael Powicke, *Military Obligation in Medieval England: A Study in Liberty and Duty* (Oxford: Clarendon Press, 1962) p. 173.

7. R. B. Dobson and J. Taylor, *Rymes of Robyn Hood: An Introduction to the English Outlaw*, 2nd edn. (Gloucester and Wolfeboro, NH: Alan Sutton, 1989) p. 82.

8. See Thrupp, *The Merchant Class*, pp. 275–7; T. F. Tout, *Chapters in the*

Administrative History of Medieval England, 6 vols (Manchester: Manchester University Press, 1920–33) vol. III, pp. 479–81; and Caroline M. Barron, 'The Quarrel of Richard II with London 1392–7', in *The Reign of Richard II: Essays in Honour of May McKisack* ed. F. R. H. Du Boulay and Caroline M. Barron (London: Athlone Press, 1971) pp. 173–201.

9. See notes to ll. 323ff in *The Riverside Chaucer* and in F. N. Robinson's edition of Chaucer's *Works*, 2nd edn (Oxford and London: Oxford University Press, 1974).

10. I am grateful to Christopher Dyer for answering my queries on the status of the Ploughman. Dr Dyer agrees that the text offers no evidence concerning the Ploughman's legal status, but points out that his economic and social position seems to be that of a self-sufficient peasant rather than a servant ploughman.

11. Mann, *Chaucer and Medieval Estates Satire*, pp. 72–3. The gap between Chaucer's and Langland's conceptions of the ploughman can be illustrated with reference to John Ball's letters, which used the name of Piers Plowman for political ends, in an attempt to incite rebellion – see R. B. Dobson (ed.), *The Peasants' Revolt of 1381* (London: Macmillan, 1970) pp. 379–83. Chaucer's Ploughman could never have been perceived as a political figure. For different views on the set of meanings associated with the figure of the ploughman before and during the fourteenth century see G. R. Owst, *Literature and Pulpit in Medieval England*, 2nd edn (Oxford: Basil Blackwell, 1961) pp. 549ff; Morton W. Bloomfield (*Piers Plowman as a Fourteenth-Century Apocalypse* (New Brunswick, NJ: Rutgers University Press, 1961) pp. 106–7; Pamela Gradon 'Langland and the Ideology of Dissent', *Proceedings of the British Academy*, vol. 66 (1980) pp. 179–205, esp. pp. 198–9; and Elizabeth D. Kirk, 'Langland's Plowman and the Recreation of Fourteenth Century Religious Metaphor', *Yearbook of Langland Studies*, vol. 2 (1988) pp. 1–21.

12. '"No Man his Reson Herde": Peasant Consciousness, Chaucer's Miller, and the Structure of the *Canterbury Tales*', in *Literary Practice and Social Change in Britain 1380–1530*, ed. Lee Patterson, (Berkeley, Calif. and Oxford: University of California Press, 1990) pp. 113–55. This essay contains a very interesting discussion of how the *Canterbury Tales* encode Chaucer's attitudes to social class, and includes an examination of the unusual scene depicting a confrontation between a lord and a peasant in the *Summoner's Tale*.

13. Ibid., pp. 126, 124.

14. Trans. R. P. Miller (ed.), *Chaucer: Sources and Backgrounds* (New York: Oxford University Press, 1977) p. 138.

15. David Aers discusses political relations in the *Clerk's Tale* in his book *Chaucer* (Brighton: Harvester, 1986), pp. 32–6. I share Aers's view, outlined in chapter 2, 'Chaucer's Representations of Society' that Chaucer depicts his society 'in a manner which encourages critical reflection on the relations between its official ideology

languages and practices, while discouraging simple traditional judgements' (p. 17).

16. *Chaucer*, pp. 24–32.
17. See V. J. Scattergood, 'Chaucer and the French War: *Sir Thopas* and *Melibee*', in *Court and Poet*, ed. Glyn S. Burgess (Liverpool: Francis Cairns, 1981) pp. 287–96 and G. Stillwell, 'The Political Meaning of Chaucer's *Tale of Melibee*', *Speculum*, vol. 19 (1944) pp. 433–44, both of whom speculate about a possible link between the tale and Richard's peace initiatives.
18. The line is also parodied in the *Miller's Tale* at I.3204.
19. *The Paston Letters: A Selection in Modern Spelling*, ed. Norman Davis, 2nd edn (Oxford and New York: Oxford University Press, 1983) p. 24.
20. See, for example, 1 Corinthians 11.9, 14.34; Ephesians 5.22-4; Colossians 3.18-19; 1 Timothy 2.12-15.
21. Accounts of the Beguine movement may be found in Fiona Bowie (ed.), *Beguine Spirituality: An Anthology* (London: SPCK, 1989) and R. W. Southern, *Western Society and the Church in the Middle Ages* (Harmondsworth: Penguin, 1970) pp. 319-31.
22. This was not of course universally true of established churchmen. Matthew Paris, an English monk, mentioned the Beguine movement in each version of his chronicle with apparent approval, and the great English bishop, Robert Grosseteste, openly expressed admiration for their way of life, extolling their self-sufficient poverty in a sermon preached to the Franciscans. See Southern, *Western Society and the Church in the Middle Ages*, pp. 319–20.
23. *The Book of Margery Kempe*, ed. Sanford Brown Meech and Hope Emily Allen, EETS, OS, 212 (London: Oxford University Press, 1940) p. 38.
24. *Holy Feast and Holy Fast: The Religious Significance of Food to Medieval Women* (Berkeley, Calif. and London: University of California Press, 1987).
25. Examples are collected in chapter VIII of Miller's *Chaucer: Sources and Backgrounds*.
26. The importance of glossing as a means whereby the church could retain control over the interpretation of the bible is discussed in chapter 2, p. 40 above.
27. 'The New Reader and Female Textuality in Two Early Commentaries on Chaucer', *Studies in the Age of Chaucer*, vol. 10 (1988) pp. 71–108.
28. Ibid., p. 87.
29. Ibid., p. 84.
30. See ch. 2, p. 35 above.
31. See 1 Corinthians 7.3 and, for example, *Parson's Tale* (X.939).
32. See, for example, G. R. Owst, *Literature and Pulpit in Medieval England*, pp. 388–9; D. W. Robertson, Jr, *A Preface to Chaucer: Studies in Medieval Perspectives* (Princeton, NJ: Princeton University Press, 1962) pp. 317–31; Robert P. Miller, 'The Wife of Bath's Tale* and

Mediaeval Exempla', *ELH*, vol. 32 (1965) pp. 442–56. Since then it has become a critical commonplace.

33. Quoted by Anne Hudson, 'Old Author, New Work: The Sermons of Ms Longleat 4', *Medium Aevum*, vol. 53 (1984) p. 232.

34. *The Form of Preaching*, trans. J. J. Murphy, *Three Medieval Rhetorical Arts* (Berkeley, Calif., 1971) p. 128. The text of this sermon is itself of course translated from Latin. Janet Coleman cites Basevorn in her discussion of the *forma praedicandi*, in order to make the point that the development of such an elaborate formal method was partly due to a conscious effort to exclude the laity from attempting to preach (*English Literature in History*, p. 190).

35. See, for example, *The Pilgrimage of the Life of Man*, ed. F. J. Furnivall, EETS, ES, 77, 83, 92 (1899–1904) vol. I, p. 184, ll. 7029–36.

36. J. A. Burrow and Thorlac Turville-Petre (eds), *A Book of Middle English* (Oxford: Blackwell, 1992) p. 216.

37. See further Ralph Hanna III, 'Sir Thomas Berkeley and his Patronage', *Speculum*, vol. 64 (1989) pp. 878–916.

38. Knighton, *Chronicon*, vol. II, p. 152 (my translation).

39. *The Repressor of Over Much Blaming of the Clergy*, ed. Churchill Babington, 2 vols, RS, 19 (1860) vol. I, p. 123. V. H. H. Green (*Bishop Reginald Pecock: A Study in Ecclesiastical History and Thought* [Cambridge: Cambridge University Press, 1945] p. 87) believes that the *Repressor* was probably written *c.*1449, but not published until five or six years later. Pecock was himself tried for heresy in 1457, and a contemporary, Thomas Gascoigne, believed that he was singled out for prosecution at least partly because he chose to write in English (*Loci e Libro Veritatum*, ed. James E. Thorold Rogers [Oxford: Clarendon Press, 1881] p. 160).

40. *Statutes of the Realm*, ed. A. Luders *et al.*, 9 vols (London, 1810–24) vol. II, pp. 126–7; cited by Margaret Aston, 'Lollardy and Literacy', in *Lollards and Reformers: Images and Literacy in Late Medieval Religion* (London: Hambledon Press, 1984) p. 198.

41. Hudson, 'Longleat 4', pp. 231–2.

42. See, for example, Alcuin Blamires, 'The Wife of Bath and Lollardy', *Medium Aevum*, vol. 58 (1989) pp. 225–39.

43. It is worth noting that the *Canterbury Tales* did attract the attention of the authorities in 1464 during an investigation for heresy. It seems more likely that its use of English rather than its particular content gave rise to suspicion, though we have no information about why it was considered dangerous by the investigators. Perhaps they noticed a possible Lollard element in the Wife of Bath, (see note 42 above), or perhaps they simply spotted the word 'Lollere' in the Epilogue to the *Man of Law's Tale* (II.1173, 1177) and decided to check its context. (The context is in fact the Host's insinuation that the Parson must be a Lollard because he condemns swearing, since Lollards were known for their refusal to swear oaths.)

44. 'The Wife of Bath as Chaucerian Subject', *Studies in the Age of Chaucer: Proceedings*, vol. 1 (1984) pp. 201–10.

Chapter 4 Continental England

1. M. T. Clanchy, *England and its Rulers 1066–1272* (London: Fontana, 1983) p. 44 and chs 1 and 2 in general.
2. M. T. Clanchy, *From Memory to Written Record: England 1066–1307* (London: Edward Arnold, 1979) plate XIV and p. 166.
3. E. J. Dobson, *The Origins of Ancrene Wisse* (Oxford: Oxford University Press, 1976) p. 252.
4. See E. Salter, *English and International: Studies in the Literature, Art and Patronage of Medieval England*, ed. D. Pearsall and N. Zeeman (Cambridge: Cambridge University Press, 1988) ch. 2 and *Fourteenth-Century English Poetry: Contexts and Readings* (Oxford: Clarendon Press, 1983) ch. 2.
5. *Chronicle of the Abbey of Bury St Edmunds*, trans. and intr. Diana Greenway and Jane Sayers (Oxford and New York: Oxford University Press, 1989) p. 37.
6. The poem is written in English; Layamon clearly knew French, since the poem's primary source is Wace's *Roman de Brut*; and Elizabeth Salter has demonstrated the probability that he knew Latin by her study of the poem's stylistic parallels with Latin texts (*English and International*, pp. 60–66).
7. *The Harley Lyrics: the Middle English Lyrics of Ms. Harley 2253*, ed. G. L. Brook, 4th edn (Manchester: Manchester University Press, 1968) no. 19, p. 55.
8. Salter, *English and International*, p. 7.
9. *Philobiblon*, pp. 93–5.
10. *The Evolution of Medieval Thought* (London: Longman, 1962) p. 80.
11. See D. Knowles, *The Evolution of Medieval Thought* (London: Longman, 1962) p. 80.
12. *Medieval Thought* (Harmondsworth: Penguin, 1958) p. 84.
13. *English Friars and Antiquity in the Early Fourteenth Century* (Oxford: Basil Blackwell, 1960) p. 307.
14. Janet Coleman offers a brief picture of the cultural importance of Avignon and England's relations with it in pp. 49–57 of her essay 'English Culture in the Fourteenth Century', in *Chaucer and the Italian Trecento*, ed. Piero Boitani (Cambridge: Cambridge University Press, 1983).
15. See, for example, Gervase Mathew, *The Court of Richard II* (London: John Murray, 1968) pp. 1–3; David Wallace, 'Chaucer and Boccaccio's Early Writings', in Boitani (ed.), *Chaucer and the Italian Trecento*, pp. 145–6.
16. Mathew, *The Court of Richard II* , pp. 16–17.
17. See further Barbara W. Tuchmann, *A Distant Mirror: the Calamitous Fourteenth Century* (Harmondsworth: Penguin, 1979) chs 8 and 9.
18. Juliet Vale, *Edward III and Chivalry: Chivalric Society and its Context 1270–1350* (Woodbridge: Boydell Press, 1982) pp. 49–50 and appendix 9.
19. Numerous critics have written on Chaucer's indebtedness to European tradition. Two helpful, brief introductions to the subject

are D. S. Brewer, 'The Relationship of Chaucer to the English and European Traditions', in *Chaucer and Chaucerians*, ed. D.S. Brewer (London: Nelson, 1966) pp. 1–38, and J. I. Wimsatt, 'Chaucer and French Poetry', in *Writers and their Background: Geoffrey Chaucer*, ed. D. S. Brewer (London: G. Bell, 1974) pp. 109–36. See also Charles Muscatine, *Chaucer and the French Tradition* (Berkeley, Calif.: University of California Press, 1957).

20. *Fourteenth-Century English Poetry*, pp. 121–2.

21. This section as a whole owes a pervasive debt to three works, which the reader should consult for further information concerning the sources of the poem: J. A. W. Bennett, *The Parlement of Foules: An Interpretation* (Oxford: Clarendon Press, 1957); D. S. Brewer (ed.), *The Parlement of Foulys* (London and Edinburgh: Nelson, 1960); and B. A. Windeatt, *Chaucer's Dream Poetry: Sources and Analogues* (Woodbridge: D. S. Brewer, Rowman and Littlefield, 1982).

22. Chaucer uses the phrase to translate the Latin *patriam* or *rem publicam*, and it was regularly used in parliamentary proceedings, although its range is wider than that (see Bennett, *Parlement of Foules*, pp. 33–4, 48–9).

23. Bennett (*Parlement of Foules*, p. 68) thinks that Chaucer was influenced by 'the occasional chafing humour of Virgil's words', but the kind of humour involved in the guide pushing his protégé through the gate seems to me very different from Dante's, almost farcical.

24. *The Parlement of Foulys*, p. 41. Brewer explores the parallel between the garden of Chaucer's poem and the 'good park' of the *Roman* on pp. 39–41.

25. *Fourteenth-Century English Poetry*, p. 135.

26. Gloss to *Teseide*, VII.50–66, trans. Robert P. Miller, *Chaucer: Sources and Backgrounds* (New York: Oxford University Press, 1977) p. 336.

27. Spenser's depiction of the Bower of Bliss and the Garden of Adonis leans heavily on *The Parliament of Fowls*. Bennett discusses this further (*Parlement of Foules*, pp. 113–21).

28. See Brewer, *The Parlement of Foulys*, pp. 17–18.

29. *Boece*, II *metrum* 8, p. 420.

30. See Brewer, *The Parlement of Foulys*, pp. 27–30, and Bennett, *passim*. The name is coined by Arthur O. Lovejoy, *The Great Chain of Being: A Study of the History of an Idea*, 2nd edn (Cambridge, Mass.: Harvard University Press, 1961). These critics have also noted how close to heresy such a philosophy comes.

31. *Summa Contra Gentiles*, II.45; quoted in Bennett, *Parlement of Foules*, p. 141.

32. Not only modern editors, but Chaucer too referred to the poem via its final focus on the parliament. He called it 'the Parlement of Foules' (Prologue to *LGW*, G.407) and 'the book of Seint Valentynes day of the Parlement of Briddes' (Retraction to the *Canterbury Tales*, X.1085). The word could simply mean a conversation, but was already in use also with its modern meaning, which the context seems to call for here.

33. 'The Genre of the "Parlement of Foules"', *MLR*, vol. 53 (1958) pp. 321–6 and *The Parlement of Foulys*, pp. 10–17.
34. See Brewer, *The Parlement of Foulys*, pp. 3–7 and John Fisher, *John Gower: Moral Philosopher and Friend of Chaucer* (London: Methuen, 1965) pp. 78–83.

Chapter 5 *'Greet altercacioun': The Influence of Philosophy*

1.   G. Leff, *Medieval Thought* (Harmondsworth: Penguin, 1958) p. 92; D. Knowles,*The Evolution of Medieval Thought* (London: Longman, 1962) p. 87. I cite these two definitions in particular since both these surveys of medieval philosophy have been formative influences on the writing of this chapter.
2.   See further Knowles, *The Evolution of Medieval Thought*, ch. 13, 'The Origins of the Universities'.
3.   *The Autobiography of Giraldus Cambrensis*, ed. and trans. H. E. Butler, intr. C. H. Williams (London: Jonathan Cape, 1937) p. 97.
4.   There remains some doubt as to whether the Strode who was a fellow of Merton before 1360 was the same man as the Strode who was a London lawyer from 1373 to 1385. The first Strode, if there were two men, is the more likely dedicatee alongside Gower, since he is described as a poet in a late fifteenth-century note to a catalogue of Merton fellows (see *Riverside* note, p. 1058).
5.   See further J. A. W. Bennett, *Chaucer at Oxford and Cambridge* (Oxford and Toronto: Oxford University Press, University of Toronto Press, 1974) ch. 3, 'The Men of Merton'; and F. M. Powicke, *The Medieval Books of Merton College* (Oxford: Oxford University Press, Milford, 1931).
6.   *Defensio Curatorum*, in *Dialogus inter Militem et Clericum etc*, ed. Aaron Jenkins Perry, EETS, OS, 167 (1925) p. 59.
7.   *Medieval Thought*, p. 261.
8.   There is no very accessible modern account of Ockham's life and work. The entry on Ockham in the *Dictionary of the Middle Ages*, ed. Joseph B. Strayer, 13 vols (New York: Charles Scribner's Sons, 1982–9) contains brief details, but in any case not much is known about his life.
9.   See Philotheus Boehner, sel., ed. and trans., *Ockham: Philosophical Writings* (Edinburgh: Thomas Nelson, 1957), pp. xii–xiii.
10. Umberto Eco outlines this debate in his novel, *The Name of the Rose*, trans. William Weaver (London: Secker and Warburg, 1983) see, for example, pp. 12–13, 49–52, 338–43.
11. *De Corpore Christi*, cited by Boehner, *Ockham*, p. xviii.
12. Boehner, *Ockham*, p. xxvii.
13. Quoted in Knowles, *The Evolution of Medieval Thought*, p. 322. A fuller explanation is extracted from Ockham in Boehner, *Ockham*, pp. 41–3.
14. Boehner, *Ockham*, p. 133.

15. Ibid., p. 25.
16. *William of Ockham: The Metamorphosis of Scholastic Discourse* (Manchester and Totowa, NJ: Manchester University Press, Rowman and Littlefield, 1975) p. 8.
17. Knowles, *The Evolution of Medieval Thought*, p. 325.
18. Quoted in Leff, *Medieval Thought*, p. 297. Richard McKeon has drawn attention to the large numbers of manuscripts of Ockham's work in European libraries (*Selections from Medieval Philosophers*, vol. II (New York, Chicago and Boston: Charles Scribner's Sons, 1930) p. 351.
19. These ideas are explained more fully in Leff, *William of Ockham*, ch. 10, 'Society'.
20. Quoted by Leff, ibid., p. 634.
21. Far more is written about Wyclif's life than about Ockham's. The best short account of his life and thought is Anthony Kenny's *Wyclif* (Oxford: Oxford University Press, 1985), to which this summary of Wyclif's life is indebted. See also Anne Hudson's entry on Wyclif in the *Dictionary of the Middle Ages*.
22. This question was the centre of much bitter debate, particularly during the latter half of the fourteenth century – see further Wendy Scase, *Piers Plowman and the New Anti-Clericalism*, Cambridge Studies in Medieval Literature, 4 (Cambridge: Cambridge University Press, 1989).
23. This sequence is outlined in more detail by Anthony Kenny, *Wyclif*, pp. 53–5.
24. Knighton, *Chronicon*, II.151, cited in R. B. Dobson (ed.), *The Peasants' Revolt of 1381* (London: Macmillan, 1970) p. 376.
25. *Fasciculi Zizaniorum*, ed. Walter Waddington Shirley, RS, 5 (1858) pp. 272–4; trans. Dobson, *Peasants' Revolt*, p. 378.
26. Dobson, *Peasants' Revolt*, p. 378.
27. *Tractatus de Blasphemia*, cited in ibid., p. 373.
28. Kenny, *Wyclif* p. 47. See chapter 1 above (p. 17) on the demands of the Rising.
29. See Anne Hudson's entry on Wyclif, *Dictionary of the Middle Ages*, vol. XII, p. 710.
30. *De Veritate Sacrae Scripturae*, cited in Peggy Knapp, *Chaucer and the Social Contest* (New York and London: Routledge, 1990) p. 73.
31. Anthony Kenny devotes a chapter to the discussion of 'Freedom and necessity'. The extracts from Wyclif's writings here are cited from Kenny, *Wyclif*, p. 37.
32. *Chaucer at Oxford and Cambridge*, p. 16. I am aware of only one study that considers Chaucer's debt to Ockhamite thinking at any length: Sheila Delany's *Chaucer's House of Fame: the Poetics of Skeptical Fideism* (Chicago and London: University of Chicago Press, 1974). The influence of Wycliffism on Chaucer has been more frequently considered, ever since John Foxe first described Chaucer as a 'right Wiclevian' (p. 145 below). See, for example, Peggy Knapp, *Chaucer and the Social Contest* and writers listed in ch. 1, n. 56 above.

33. Geoffrey Shepherd, 'Religion and Philosophy in Chaucer', in D. S. Brewer (ed.), *Writers and their Background: Geoffrey Chaucer* (London: G. Bell, 1974) p. 281.
34. *Tractatus contra Benedictum,* iii, in *Guillelmi de Ockham Opera Politica,* vol. III, ed. H. S. Offler, (Manchester: Manchester University Press, 1956) p. 231; cited in B. Smalley, *English Friars and Antiquity in the Early Fourteenth Century* (Oxford: Basil Blackwell, 1960) p. 29.
35. Delany, *Chaucer's House of Fame,* p. 2.
36. Ibid., p. 4.
37. Lee Patterson's book on *Chaucer and the Subject of History* (London: Routledge, 1991), which came to my attention in the final phase of writing this book, deals with the question of Chaucer's own awareness of the problematics of historical writing from a much wider angle of vision, and contains a chapter on *Troilus and Criseyde* which offers a very full account of earlier writings on the matter of Troy.
38. 'Chaucer and Lydgate', in *Chaucer Traditions: Studies in Honour of Derek Brewer,* ed. Ruth Morse and Barry Windeatt (Cambridge: Cambridge University Press, 1990) p. 47.
39. F. X. Newman (ed.), *Social Unrest in the Late Middle Ages,* Medieval and Renaissance Texts and Studies, 39 (Binghamton, NY, 1986) p. 121.
40. Delany, *Chaucer's House of Fame,* p. 26.
41. For a different reading of the importance of images of circularity in the poem see Lee Patterson, *Chaucer and the Subject of History,* ch. 2.

Chapter 6 'This wrecched world': The Obsession with Death

1. Boccaccio, *The Decameron,* trans. G. H. McWilliam (Harmondsworth: Penguin, 1972) pp. 50–6. Boccaccio's account of the plague is worth reading in full; only about one-third is quoted here.
2. Philip Ziegler, *The Black Death* (Harmondsworth: Penguin, 1969; rpt 1984) p. 242.
3. Ibid., p. 136.
4. See Philippe Ariès, *Western Attitudes toward Death from the Middle Ages to the Present,* trans. Patricia M. Ranum (Baltimore and London: John Hopkins University Press, 1974) pp. 47-8.
5. *English Mystery Plays,* ed. Peter Happé (Harmondsworth: Penguin, 1975) pp. 404–5.
6. James M. Clark cites performances at Bruges in 1449 and Besançon in 1453, and mentions a Dance of Death masque produced at Jedburgh as early as 1285 (*The Dance of Death in the Middle Ages and the Renaissance* (Glasgow: Jackson, 1950) pp. 92–4.
7. *Medieval English Lyrics,* ed. Theodore Silverstein (London: Edward Arnold, 1971) p. 81.
8. Ibid., p. 79.
9. K. B. McFarlane, *Lancastrian Kings and Lollard Knights* (Oxford:

Oxford University Press, 1972) p. 211. Cf. Sir Lewis Clifford's will, reprinted in E. Rickert, *Chaucer's World*, ed. C. C. Olson and M. M. Crow (London: Geoffrey Cumberlege, Oxford University Press, 1948) p. 402.

10. Rickert, *Chaucer's World*, p. 418. Rickert prints a number of wills, as well as the orders for Richard II's tomb (pp. 415–17) and the account of the burial of the Earl of Salisbury and his son (pp. 407–10) referred to below.

11. See further J. Dillon, 'Chaucer's Game in the *Pardoner's Tale*', *Essays in Criticism*, vol. 41 (1991) pp. 208–21.

12. Ariès, *Western Attitudes*, pp. 29–38.

13. *Preaching in Medieval England: An Introduction to Sermon Mss of the Period c.1350–1450* (Cambridge: Cambridge University Press, 1926) p. 351.

14. Three medieval ghost stories are translated in *Culture and Belief in Europe 1450–1600: An Anthology of Sources*, ed. David Englander, Diana Norman, Rosemary O'Day and W. R. Owens (Oxford and Cambridge, Mass.: Basil Blackwell with Open University, 1990) pp. 16–18. See also the collection assembled in 'Tales of Saints, Demons, and Relics', in J. Krochalis and E. Peters (ed. and trans.), *World of Piers Plowman* (Pennsylvania: University of Pennsylvania Press, 1975) pp. 143–63.

15. Cited in E. K. Chambers, *The Elizabethan Stage*, 4 vols, 2nd edn (Oxford: Clarendon Press, 1951) vol. III, p. 424.

16. Wright, *Political Poems*, p. 252.

17. The inscription is in Latin, and is cited here in Maurice Hussey's translation (*Chaucer's World: A Pictorial Companion* [Cambridge University Press, 1967] p. 108). A photograph of the inscription appears on p. 109.

18. *Piers Plowman*, VI.323–30; cf. III.325–9 and XIII.152–5. See Bloomfield, *Piers Plowman as a Fourteenth-Century Apocalypse*, who also discusses other writers of prophecy besides Langland.

19. Wills of Richard Poynings, 1428; John de Holegh, hosier, 1352; and John Wodewey, clerk, 1405 (Rickert, *Chaucer's World*, pp. 390, 395).

20. These guilds are not to be confused with professional craft guilds. They were religious foundations for specific purposes, for example to provide a chaplain, to provide candles for a particular shrine or occasion, or to offer prayers to a particular saint or on a particular feast. Rickert cites the certificates of several of such guilds (*Chaucer's World*, pp. 396–400).

21. R. W. Southern, *Western Society and the Church in the Middle Ages* (Harmondsworth: Penguin, 1970) p. 305.

22. Trans. M. L. Kekewich, in *Culture and Belief in Europe*, p. 22.

23. Prologue, 76–7.

24. Jill Mann gives an excellent account of the active force of pity in chapter 1 of her book in the Harvester Wheatsheaf series of Feminist Readings, *Geoffrey Chaucer* (New York, 1991).

25. *The Strumpet Muse: Art and Morals in Chaucer's Poetry* (Bloomington: Indiana University Press, 1976) pp. 236–7.

Chapter 7 Reputation and Influence

1. See Hayden White, 'The Value of Narrativity in the Representation of Reality', rpt as chapter 1 in his collection of essays on the subject of narrative and historiography, *The Content of the Form: Narrative Discourse and Historical Representation* (Baltimore and London: John Hopkins University Press, 1987) pp. 1–25. On Chaucer's own scepticism concerning historiography see also Lee Patterson, *Chaucer and the Subject of History* (London: Routledge, 1991).

2. Caroline F. E. Spurgeon, *Five Hundred Years of Chaucer Criticism and Allusion 1357–1900*, 3 vols (Cambridge: Cambridge University Press, 1925) vol. I, p. 8. I have used this collection throughout on account of its completeness, but many of the same quotations are more easily available in John Burrow (ed.), *Geoffrey Chaucer: A Critical Anthology* (Harmondsworth: Penguin, 1969) and Derek Brewer (ed.), *Chaucer: the Critical Heritage*, 2 vols (London: Routledge and Kegan Paul, 1978). Quotations from Spurgeon are from vol. I unless otherwise stated, and punctuation and typography have been slightly modernised.

3. Barry Windeatt also points this out in his essay on 'Chaucer Traditions', in R. Morse and B. Windeatt (eds) *Chaucer Traditions: Studies in Honour of Derek Brewer* (Cambridge: Cambridge University Press, 1990) p. 2.

4. Spurgeon, *Five Hundred Years of Chaucer Criticism*, p. 24.

5. On the perception of Chaucer as the father, see further A. C. Spearing, *Medieval to Renaissance in English Poetry* (Cambridge: Cambridge University Press, 1985) p. 59 and Patterson, *Chaucer and the Subject of History*, p. 13ff. Patterson's assessment of Dryden's influence on later critical tradition is close to mine on pp. 150–1 below in its emphasis on Dryden's isolation of Chaucer from his time. Caroline Spurgeon prints eight examples of the 'well-established formula' of bracketing Chaucer, Gower and Lydgate together and lists the references (*Five Hundred Years of Chaucer Criticism*, p. xviii, n. 1. Stephen Hawes, she notes, 'is in a minority of one in placing Lydgate above Chaucer'.

6. Spurgeon, *Five Hundred Years of Chaucer Criticism*, pp. 22, 21.

7. Ibid., p. 62.

8. Ibid., p. 66.

9. See P. Strohm, 'Chaucer's Fifteenth-Century Audience and the Narrowing of the "Chaucer Tradition"', *Studies in the Age of Chaucer*, vol. 4 (1982) pp. 3–32, and pp. 42–3 above.

10. This is Derek Pearsall's formulation of the distinction. As he argues, 'the two are often the same, but the sense of a possible distinction is more necessary than ever in the fifteenth century' (*Old and Middle English Poetry*, Routledge History of English Poetry, vol. I [London: Routledge and Kegan Paul, 1977] pp. 212–13).

11. 'The Scribes as Chaucer's Early Critics', *Studies in the Age of Chaucer*, vol. 1 (1979) p. 132.

12. Spurgeon, *Five Hundred Years of Chaucer Criticism*, pp. 75, 151.

13. See Thomas J. Heffernan, 'Aspects of the Chaucerian Apocrypha: Animadversions on William Thynne's Edition of the *Plowman's Tale*', in Morse and Windeatt, *Chaucer Traditions*, pp. 155–67; and two articles by A. N. Wawn: 'Chaucer, Wyclif and the Court of Apollo', *English Language Notes*, vol. 10 (1972) pp. 15–20; and 'Chaucer, *The Plowman's Tale*, and Reformation Propaganda: The Testimonies of Thomas Godfray and *I Playne Piers*', *Bulletin of the John Rylands Library*, vol. 56 (1973–4) pp. 174–92.

14. *Chaucerian and other Pieces* (Oxford: Clarendon Press, 1897) p. ix; cited in Spurgeon, *Five Hundred Years of Chaucer Criticism*, p. 78.

15. The Devonshire manuscript (*c*.1530–40), for example, includes excerpts from *Troilus and Criseyde* standing alone as lyric poems and poems by Sir Thomas Wyatt which show his reading of Chaucer in Thynne's edition. See Windeatt in Morse and Windeatt, *Chaucer Traditions*, p. 11 and nn. 22–4.

16. *Shakespeare's Chaucer: A Study in Literary Origins* (Liverpool: Liverpool University Press, 1978) p. 3. See also Alice S. Miskimin, *The Renaissance Chaucer* (New Haven, Conn. and London: Yale University Press, 1975).

17. Spurgeon, *Five Hundred Years of Chaucer Criticism*, p. 106. Foxe's *Actes and Monuments* was one of the most popular books of its day. First published in 1563 (the references to Chaucer do not appear until the second edition of 1570), it ran into nine editions by 1684.

18. Thompson, *Shakespeare's Chaucer*, p. 30.

19. Quoted by John Burrow in his *Geoffrey Chaucer: A Critical Anthology* (Harmondsworth: Penguin, 1969) p. 63, n. 2. Caroline Spurgeon does not print Speght's comments in full.

20. The debate is discussed in more detail by Albert C. Baugh and Thomas Cable in *A History of the English Language*, 3rd edn (London, Henley and Boston: Routledge and Kegan Paul, 1978) ch. 8, from which the following quotations from Harvey, Jonson and E. K. are cited.

21. Spurgeon, *Five Hundred Years of Chaucer Criticism*, p. 156. See also the views of Richard Verstegan (in ibid., pp. lxxiii–iv).

22. Ibid., p. 134. Cf. Thomas Drant's dismissal of the *Nun's Priest's Tale* as 'the settyng out of the wanton tricks of a payre of lovers' (1567) and John Wharton's reference to the 'stale tales of Chaucer' (1575) (ibid., pp. 100, 111).

23. See ibid., pp. lxxiv–v.

24. Ibid., p. 122.

25. Ibid., pp. lxxvi, 77.

26. Ibid., p. 79.

27. Ibid., p. 128.

28. Ibid., p. 129.

29. Ibid., p. 207.

30. Ibid., p. 242.

31. Ibid., p. 280.

32. Dryden also maintains the view that Chaucer's metre is rough, dismissing Speght's argument for 'the Fault . . . in our Ears' as 'so

gross and obvious an Errour' as to be not worth confuting (ibid., p. 277).

33. Ibid., p. 281.
34. Jabez Hughes, 'Upon Reading Mr Dryden's Fables', ibid., p. 294.
35. Ibid., p. 276.
36. Ibid., p. 276.
37. Ibid., p. 274.
38. Ibid., p. 279.
39. Lee Patterson similarly argues that Dryden's insistence on reading Chaucer as 'an original who stands apart from the entire process [of history] and makes his genius available directly' (*Chaucer and the Subject of History*, p. 14) has been the foundation of modern Chaucer criticism.
40. Spurgeon, *Five Hundred Years of Chaucer Criticism*, p. liii.
41. The title-page of her *Grammar* also carried a challenge to the male intellectual establishment in the form of a quotation taken from a letter written to her by a member of that establishment, a 'Right Reverend Prelate': 'Our Earthly Possessions are truly enough called a PATRIMONY, as derived to us by the Industry of our FATHERS; but the Language that we speak is our MOTHER-TONGUE; And who so proper to play the Criticks in this as the FEMALES'.
42. Spurgeon, *Five Hundred Years of Chaucer Criticism*, p. 354.
43. Ibid., pp. 442–3.
44. Ibid., vol. II. p. 29.
45. Ibid., vol.II, pp. 42–3.
46. Ibid., p. lxix.
47. *Negotiating the Past: the Historical Understanding of Medieval Literature* (Madison: University of Wisconsin Press, 1987) ch. 1. Terms undeveloped here (such as Exegetics) will be found explained by Patterson above, to whom the reader is referred for fuller details of twentieth-century developments.
48. In addition to these three, Patterson names Lowes, Hammond, Tatlock, Patch, Dempster and Malone (ibid., p. 14).
49. Patterson, ibid., p. 14.
50. 'Renaissance Literary Studies and the Subject of History', *ELR*, vol. 16 (1986) p. 8.
51. Charles Muscatine, 'Chaucer's religion and the Chaucer religion', in Morse and Windeatt, *Chaucer Traditions*, p. 250.
52. Ibid., p. 260.
53. Ibid., p. 260.
54. Ann Thompson, who briefly outlines the history of earlier work on Chaucer and Shakespeare in her introduction to the only full-length study of the subject (*Shakepeare's Chaucer: A Study in Literary Origins* (Liverpool: Liverpool University Press, 1978)), describes such work as there has been as 'piecemeal and uncertain' (p. 16).
55. Spurgeon, *Five Hundred Years of Chaucer Criticism*, p. cxxvi.
56. Ibid., p. cxxvi.
57. Ibid., p. cxxix.
58. Thompson, *Shakespeare's Chaucer*, p. 217.

59. Ann Thompson lists two lost plays of 1566 and 1594 on the subject of Palamon and Arcite (ibid., p. 17).
60. 'Shakespeare's Comment on Mediaeval Romance in *Midsummer-Night's Dream*', *Modern Language Notes*,vol. 60 (1945) p. 86.
61. See II.i.74–80 and E. Talbot Donaldson, *The Swan at the Well: Shakespeare Reading Chaucer* (New Haven, Conn. and London: Yale University Press, 1985) pp. 34-6.
62. Donaldson, *The Swan at the Well*, p. 3.
63. Ibid., p. 30.
64. Bethurum, 'Shakespeare's Comment', p. 89.
65. Miskimin, *The Renaissance Chaucer*, p. 112.
66. This is the subject of a number of essays by Harry Berger, collected in his *Second World and Green World: Studies in Renaissance Fiction-Making*, sel. and intr. John Patrick Lynch (Berkeley, Calif. and London: University of California Press, 1988).
67. Bethurum, 'Shakespeare's Comment', p. 89.
68. Donaldson, *The Swan at the Well*, p. 21.
69. Chaucer several times chooses to highlight or insert the problematic framework of pagan gods. *Troilus and Criseyde* (see pp. 111–15 above) and the *Knight's Tale* are the most extended examples of this focus, which seems to suggest a preoccupation with provisionality, a conscious insistence on constructing multiple frames which are mutually deconstructive.
70. The concept of the literary work as existing in a dialogue with each reader in each period is much more fully developed by Hans Robert Jauss (see *Toward an Aesthetic of Reception*, trans. Timothy Bahti [Brighton: Harvester, 1982] esp. ch. 1, 'Literary History as a Challenge to Literary Theory').

Select Bibliography

Throughout the text and bibliography, the abbreviations EETS and RS are used for the Early English Text Society and the Rolls Series.

PRIMARY SOURCES

Chaucer, Geoffrey
The Riverside Chaucer, ed. L. D. Benson, 3rd edn (Oxford: Oxford University Press, 1988).
Works, ed. F. N. Robinson, 2nd edn (Oxford and London: Oxford University Press, 1959).
The Book of the Duchess, ed. H. Phillips, Durham and St Andrews Medieval Texts, 3, rev. edn (Durham, 1984).
The Parlement of Foulys, ed. D. S. Brewer (London and Edinburgh: Nelson, 1960).
Troilus and Criseyde, ed. B. A. Windeatt (London: Longman, 1984).

Alliterative Poetry of the late Middle Ages: An Anthology, ed. T. Turville-Petre (London: Routledge, 1989).
The Anonimalle Chronicle, 1333–1381, ed. V. H. Galbraith (Manchester: Manchester University Press, 1927).
Auchinleck Manuscript, The, intr. D. Pearsall and I. C. Cunningham (London: Scolar Press, 1979).
Boccaccio, G., *The Decameron*, trans. G. H. McWilliam (Harmondsworth: Penguin, 1972).
Brinton,Thomas, Bishop of Rochester (1373–1389), The Sermons of, ed. M. A. Devlin, 2 vols, Camden Society, 3rd series, 85, 86 (1954).
Bryan, W. F. and Dempster G. (eds), *Sources and Analogues of Chaucer's Canterbury Tales* (Chicago: University of Chicago Press, 1941).
Bury, Richard de, *Philobiblon*, trans. E. C. Thomas, ed. M. McLagan (Oxford: Basil Blackwell, 1960).
Crow, M. M. and Olson, C. C. (eds) *Chaucer Life-Records* (Oxford: Clarendon Press, 1966).
Englander, D., Norman, D., O'Day, R. and Owens, W. R. (eds), *Culture and Belief in Europe 1450–1600: An Anthology of Sources*, (Oxford and Cambridge, Mass.: Basil Blackwell with Open University, 1990).
Fasciculi Zizaniorum, ed. W. W. Shirley, RS, 5 (1858).
Fitzralph, Richard, *Defensio Curatorum*, in *Dialogus inter Militem et Clericum etc*, ed. A. J. Perry, EETS, OS, 167 (1925).

Froissart, Jean, *Chronicles*, sel., trans. and ed. G. Brereton, rev. edn (Harmondsworth: Penguin, 1978).

Fourteenth-Century Verse and Prose, ed. K. Sisam (Oxford: Clarendon Press, 1970).

Gascoigne, Thomas, *Loci e Libro Veritatum*, ed. J. E. T. Rogers (Oxford: Clarendon Press, 1881).

Gerald of Wales (see Giraldus Cambrensis).

Giraldus Cambrensis, The Autobiography of, ed. and trans. H. E. Butler., intr. C. H. Williams (London: Jonathan Cape, 1937).

Gower, John, *The Major Latin Works of*, trans. E. W. Stockton (Seattle: University of Washington Press, 1962).

Harley Lyrics, The: The Middle English Lyrics of Ms. Harley 2253, ed. G. L. Brook, 4th edn (Manchester: Manchester University Press, 1968).

Historical Poems of the Fourteenth and Fifteenth Centuries, ed. R. H. Robbins (Oxford: Oxford University Press, 1959).

Hoccleve's Works, ed. F. J. Furnivall, 3 vols, EETS, ES, 61, 72–3 (1892–7).

Jocelin of Brakelond, *Chronicle of the Abbey of Bury St Edmunds*, trans. and intr. D. Greenway and J. Sayers (Oxford and New York: Oxford University Press, 1989).

Kempe, Margery, The Book of, ed. S. B. Meech and H. E. Allen, EETS, OS, 212 (1940).

Knighton, H., *Chronicon*, ed. J. R. Lumby, 2 vols, RS, 92 (1889, 1895).

Krochalis, J. and Peters, E. (ed. and trans.)*The World of Piers Plowman* (Pennsylvania: University of Pennsylvania Press, 1975).

La Sale, Antoine De, *Little John of Saintré*, trans. I. Gray (London: George Routledge, 1931).

Langland, William, *Piers Plowman: the B Version*, ed. G. Kane and E. T. Donaldson (London: Athlone Press, 1975).

Langland, William, *The Vision of Piers Plowman: A Complete Edition of the B-Text*, ed. A. V. C. Schmidt (London: Dent, 1978).

Lydgate, John, *The Pilgrimage of the Life of Man*, ed. F. J. Furnivall, 3 vols, EETS, ES, 77, 83, 92 (1899–1904).

Lyrics, Medieval English, ed. Theodore Silverstein (London: Edward Arnold, 1971).

McKeon, R., *Selections from Medieval Philosophers*, vol. II (New York, Chicago and Boston: Charles Scribner's Sons, 1930).

Miller, R. P., *Chaucer: Sources and Backgrounds* (New York: Oxford University Press, 1977).

Mystery Plays, English, ed. Peter Happé (Harmondsworth: Penguin, 1975).

Ockham: Philosophical Writings, sel., ed. and trans. P. Boehner (Edinburgh: Thomas Nelson, 1957).

Ockham, Guillelmi de, Opera Politica, ed. J. G. Sikes *et al.*, 3 vols (Manchester: Manchester University Press, 1940–56).

Paston Letters, The: A Selection in Modern Spelling, ed. N. Davis, 2nd edn (Oxford and New York: Oxford University Press, 1983).

Pecock, Reginald, *The Repressor of Over Much Blaming of the Clergy*, ed. C. Babington, 2 vols, RS, 19 (1860).

Political Poems and Songs relating to English history composed during the

Period from the Accession of Edward III to that of Richard III, ed. T. Wright, 2 vols, RS, 14 (1859, 1861).

Rickert, E., *Chaucer's World*, ed. C. C. Olson and M. M. Crow (London: Geoffrey Cumberlege, Oxford University Press, 1948).

Robyn Hood, Rymes of: An Introduction to the English Outlaw, ed. R. J. Dobson and J. Taylor, 2nd edn (Gloucester and Wolfeboro, NH: Alan Sutton, 1989).

Spurgeon, C. F. E., *Five Hundred Years of Chaucer Criticism and Allusion 1357–1900*, 3 vols (Cambridge: Cambridge University Press, 1925).

Trevisa, John, trans., *Polychronicon*, ed. J. R. Lumby, 9 vols, RS, 41 (1865–86).

Trevisa, John, *Dialogue between a Lord and a Clerk*, in *A Book of Middle English*, ed. J. A. Burrow and T. Turville-Petre (Oxford and Cambridge, Mass. : Blackwell, 1992).

Vernon Manuscript, The, ed. A. I. Doyle (Woodbridge: D. S. Brewer, 1987).

Walsingham, Thomas, *Historia Anglicana*, ed. H. T. Riley, 2 vols, RS, 28 (1863–4).

Windeatt, B. A. (ed. and trans.), *Chaucer's Dream Poetry: Sources and Analogues* (Woodbridge: D. S. Brewer, Rowman and Littlefield, 1982).

SECONDARY SOURCES

Aers, D. (1980), *Chaucer, Langland and the Creative Imagination* (London: Routledge and Kegan Paul).

Aers, D. (1986), *Chaucer* (Brighton: Harvester).

Aers, D. (1988), *Community, Gender and Individual Identity: English Writing 1360–1430* (London: Routledge).

Ariès, P. (1974), *Western Attitudes toward Death from the Middle Ages to the Present*, trans. Patricia M. Ranum (Baltimore and London: John Hopkins University Press).

Aston, M. (1984), *Lollards and Reformers: Images and Literacy in Late Medieval Religion* (London: Hambledon Press).

Aston, M. (1987), 'Wyclif and the Vernacular', in *Studies in Church History*, Subsidia, vol. 5, pp. 281–330.

Aston, T. H. *et al.* (eds) (1983), *Social Relations and Ideas: Essays in Honour of R. H. Hilton* (Cambridge: Cambridge University Press).

Barron, C. M. (ed.) (1971), see Du Boulay, F. R. H.

Barthes, R. (1977), *Image, Music, Text*, sel. and trans. S. Heath (London: Fontana).

Baugh, A. C. and Cable, T. (1978), *A History of the English Language*, 3rd edn (London, Henley and Boston: Routledge and Kegan Paul).

Bäuml, F. H. (1980), 'Varieties and Consequences of Medieval Literacy and Illiteracy', *Speculum*, vol. 55, pp. 237–65.

Bennett, J. A. W. (1957), *The Parlement of Foules: An Interpretation* (Oxford: Clarendon Press).

Bennett, J. A. W. (1974), *Chaucer at Oxford and Cambridge* (Oxford and Toronto: Oxford University Press, University of Toronto Press).

Berndt, R. (1969), 'The Linguistic Situation in England from the Norman Conquest to the loss of Normandy (1066–1204)', in *Approaches to Historical Linguistics: An Anthology*, ed. R. Lass (New York: Holt, Rinehart and Winston) pp. 369–91.

Bethurum, Dorothy (1945), 'Shakespeare's Comment on Mediaeval Romance in *Midsummer-Night's Dream*', *Modern Language Notes*, vol. 60, pp. 85–94.

Blake, N. F. (1977), *The English Language in Medieval Literature* (London: Dent).

Blamires, A. (1989), 'The Wife of Bath and Lollardy', *Medium Aevum*, vol. 58, pp. 225–39.

Bland, D. S. (1952), 'Chaucer and the Inns of Court: A Re-Examination', *English Studies*, vol. 33, pp. 145–55.

Blenner-Hassett, R. (1953), 'Autobiographical Aspects of Chaucer's Franklin', *Speculum*, vol. 28, pp. 791–800.

Bloomfield, M. W. (1961), *Piers Plowman as a Fourteenth-Century Apocalypse* (New Brunswick, NJ: Rutgers University Press).

Boitani, P. (ed.) (1983), *Chaucer and the Italian Trecento* (Cambridge: Cambridge University Press).

Boitani, P. and Mann, J. (eds) (1986), *The Cambridge Chaucer Companion* (Cambridge: Cambridge University Press).

Bowie, F. (ed.) (1989), *Beguine Spirituality: An Anthology* (London: SPCK).

Brewer, D. S. (1958), 'The Genre of the "Parlement of Foules"', *MLR*, vol. 53, pp. 321–6.

Brewer, D. S. (ed.) (1960), *The Parlement of Foulys* (London and Edinburgh: Nelson).

Brewer, D. S. (1964), *Chaucer in his Time* (London: Nelson).

Brewer, D. S. (ed.) (1966), *Chaucer and Chaucerians: Critical Studies in Middle English Literature* (London: Nelson).

Brewer, D. S. (ed.) (1974), *Writers and their Background: Geoffrey Chaucer* (London: G. Bell).

Brewer, D. S. (1978), *Chaucer and his World* (London: Eyre Methuen).

Brewer, D. S. (ed.) (1978), *Chaucer: the Critical Heritage*, 2 vols (London: Routledge and Kegan Paul).

Burgess, G. S. (1981), *Court and Poet* (Liverpool: Francis Cairns).

Burrow, J. A. (ed.) (1969), *Geoffrey Chaucer: A Critical Anthology* (Harmondsworth: Penguin).

Burrow, J. A. (1982), *Medieval Writers and their Work: Middle English Literature and its Background 1100–1500* (Oxford and New York: Oxford University Press).

Bynum, C. W. (1987), *Holy Feast and Holy Fast: The Religious Significance of Food to Medieval Women* (Berkeley, Calif. and London: University of California Press).

Cable, T. (1978), see Baugh, A. C.

Childs, W. (ed.) (1990), see Taylor, J.

Clanchy, M. T. (1979), *From Memory to Written Record: England 1066–1307* (London: Edward Arnold).

Coleman, J. (1981), *English Literature in History 1350–1400: Medieval Readers and Writers* (London: Hutchinson).

Crosby, R. (1936), 'Oral Delivery in the Middle Ages', *Speculum*, vol. 11, pp. 88–110.

Crosby, R. (1938), 'Chaucer and the Custom of Oral Delivery', *Speculum*, vol. 13, pp. 413–32.

Daiches, D. and Thorlby, A. (eds) (1973), *The Medieval World* (London: Aldus Books).

David, A. (1976), *The Strumpet Muse: Art and Morals in Chaucer's Poetry* (Bloomington: Indiana University Press).

Deanesly, M. (1920), 'Vernacular Books in England in the Fourteenth and Fifteenth Centuries', *MLR*, vol. 15, pp. 349–58.

Deanesly, M. (1920), *The Lollard Bible and Other Medieval Biblical Versions* (Cambridge: Cambridge University Press).

Delany, S. (1972), *Chaucer's House of Fame: the Poetics of Skeptical Fideism* (Chicago and London: University of Chicago Press).

Dillon, J. (1991), 'Chaucer's Game in the *Pardoner's Tale*', *Essays in Criticism*, vol. 41, pp. 208–21.

Dobson, R. B. (ed.) (1970), *The Peasants' Revolt of 1381* (London: Macmillan).

Donaldson, E. T. (1985), *The Swan at the Well: Shakespeare Reading Chaucer* (New Haven, Conn. and London: Yale University Press).

Du Boulay, F. R. H. and Barron, C. M. (eds) (1971), *The Reign of Richard II: Essays in Honour of May McKisack* (London: Athlone Press).

Gradon, P. (1980), 'Langland and the Ideology of Dissent', *Proceedings of the British Academy*, vol. 66, pp. 179–205.

Green, R. F. (1980), *Poets and Princepleasers: Literature and the English Court in the Late Middle Ages* (Toronto: University of Toronto Press).

Green, V. H. H. (1945), *Bishop Reginald Pecock: A Study in Ecclesiastical History and Thought* (Cambridge: Cambridge University Press).

Griffiths J. and Pearsall D. (eds) (1989), *Book Production and Publishing in Britain 1375–1475* (Cambridge: Cambridge University Press).

Hilton, R. H. (1969), *The Decline of Serfdom in Medieval England* (London and Basingstoke: Macmillan).

Hilton, R. H. (1973), *Bond Men Made Free: Medieval Peasant Movements and the English Rising of 1381*, (London: Temple Smith).

Hilton, R. H. (1975), *English Peasantry* (Oxford: Oxford University Press).

Hilton, R. H. (ed.) (1976), *Peasants, Knights and Heretics* (Cambridge: Cambridge University Press).

Hudson, A. (1984), 'Old Author, New Work: The Sermons of Ms Longleat 4', *Medium Aevum*, vol. 53, pp.220–38.

Hudson, A. (1985), *Lollards and their Books* (London and Ronceverte: Hambledon Press).

Hudson, A. (1988), *The Premature Reformation: Wycliffite Texts and Lollard History* (Oxford: Clarendon Press).

Hussey, M. (1967), *Chaucer's World: A Pictorial Companion* (Cambridge: Cambridge University Press).

Jauss, H. R. (1982), *Toward an Aesthetic of Reception*, trans. Timothy Bahti (Brighton: Harvester).

Kenny, A. (1985), *Wyclif* (Oxford: Oxford University Press).

Kenny, A. (ed.) (1986), *Wyclif in his Times* (Oxford: Clarendon Press).

Kirk, E. D. (1988), 'Langland's Plowman and the Recreation of Four-teenth-Century Religious Metaphor', *Yearbook of Langland Studies*, vol. 2, pp. 1-21.

Knapp, P. (1990), *Chaucer and the Social Contest* (New York and London: Routledge).

Knowles, D. (1962), *The Evolution of Medieval Thought* (London: Longman).

Leff, G. (1958), *Medieval Thought* (Harmondsworth: Penguin).

Leff, G. (1975), *William of Ockham: The Metamorphosis of Scholastic Discourse* (Manchester and Totowa, NJ: Manchester University Press, Rowman and Littlefield).

Leicester, H. M. (1984), 'The Wife of Bath as Chaucerian Subject', *Studies in the Age of Chaucer: Proceedings*, vol. 1, pp. 201–10.

Lester, G. A. (1984), *Sir John Paston's 'Grete Boke': A Descriptive Catalogue, with an introduction, of British Library MS Lansdowne 285* (Cambridge: D. S. Brewer).

Loomis, L. H. (1942), 'The Auchinleck Manuscript and a Possible London Bookshop of 1330-1340', *PMLA*, vol. 57, pp. 595–627.

Lovejoy, A. O. (1961), *The Great Chain of Being: A Study of the History of an Idea*, 2nd edn (Cambridge, Mass.: Harvard University Press).

Mann, J. (1973), *Chaucer and Medieval Estates Satire* (Cambridge: Cambridge University Press).

Mann, J. (ed.) (1986), see Boitani, P.

Mann, J. (1991), *Geoffrey Chaucer* (New York: Harvester Wheatsheaf).

Mathew, G. (1968), *The Court of Richard II* (London: John Murray).

McFarlane, K. B. (1972), *Lancastrian Kings and Lollard Knights* (Oxford: Oxford University Press).

McKisack, M. (1959), *The Fourteenth Century 1307–1399* (Oxford: Clarendon Press).

Miller, R.P. (1965), '*The Wife of Bath's Tale* and Mediaeval Exempla', *ELH*, vol. 32, pp. 442–56.

Miskimin, A. S. (1975), *The Renaissance Chaucer* (New Haven, Conn. and London: Yale University Press).

Montrose, Louis (1986), 'Renaissance Literary Studies and the Subject of History', *ELR*, vol. 16, pp. 5–12.

Moran, J. A. H. (1985), *The Growth of English Schooling 1340–1548: Learning, Literacy, and Laicization in Pre-Reformation York Diocese* (Princeton, NJ: Princeton University Press).

Morse, R. and Windeatt, B. (eds) (1990), *Chaucer Traditions: Studies in Honour of Derek Brewer* (Cambridge: Cambridge University Press).

Muscatine, C. (1957), *Chaucer and the French Tradition* (Berkeley, Calif.: University of California Press).

Newman, F. X. (ed.) (1986), *Social Unrest in the Late Middle Ages*, Medieval and Renaissance Texts and Studies, 39 (Binghamton, NY).

Orme, N. (1973), *English Schools in the Middle Ages* (London and New York: Methuen).

Orme, N. (1989), *Education and Society in Medieval and Renaissance England* (London and Ronceverte: Hambledon Press).

Ormrod, W. M. (1990), *The Reign of Edward III: Crown and Political Society in England 1327–77* (New Haven, Conn and London: Yale University Press).

Owst, G. R. (1926), *Preaching in Medieval England: An Introduction to Sermon Mss of the Period c. 1350–1450* (Cambridge: Cambridge University Press).

Owst, G. R. (1961), *Literature and Pulpit in Medieval England*, 2nd edn (Oxford: Basil Blackwell).

Packe, M. (1983), *King Edward III*, ed. L. C. B. Seaman (London: Routledge and Kegan Paul).

Palmer, J. N. (1973–4), 'The Historical Context of the *Book of the Duchess*: A Revision', *Chaucer Review*, vol. 8, pp. 253–61.

Parkes, M. B. and Watson, A. G. (ed.) (1978), *Medieval Scribes, Manuscripts and Libraries: Essays presented to N. R. Ker* (London: Scolar Press).

Patterson, L. (1983), '"For the Wyves love of Bath": Feminine Rhetoric and Poetic Resolution in the *Roman de la Rose* and the *Canterbury Tales*', *Speculum*, vol. 58, pp.656–95.

Patterson, L. (1987), *Negotiating the Past: The Historical Understanding of Medieval Literature* (Madison, Wisconsin: University of Wisconsin Press).

Patterson, L. (ed.) (1990), *Literary Practice and Social Change in Britain 1380–1530* (Berkeley, Calif. and Oxford: University of California Press).

Patterson, L. (1991), *Chaucer and the Subject of History* (London: Routledge).

Pearsall, Derek (1977), 'The *Troilus* Frontispiece and Chaucer's Audience', *Literature and History*, vol. 5, pp. 26–41.

Pearsall, D. (1977), *Old and Middle English Poetry*, Routledge History of English Poetry, vol. I (London: Routledge and Kegan Paul).

Pearsall, D. (ed.) (1989), see Griffiths, J.

Plucknett, T. F. (1948), Note in *Law Quarterly Review*, vol. 64, pp. 33–6.

Pollard, G. (1938), 'The Company of Stationers before 1557', *The Library*, 4th ser., vol. 18, pp. 1–38.

Postan, M. M. (1975), *The Medieval Economy and Society: An Economic History of Britain in the Middle Ages*, 2nd edn (Harmondsworth: Penguin).

Power, E. (1922), *Medieval English Nunneries c. 1275–1535* (Cambridge: Cambridge University Press).

Powicke, M. (1962), *Military Obligation in Medieval England: A Study in Liberty and Duty* (Oxford: Clarendon Press).

Robbins, R. H. (1979), 'Dissent in Middle English Literature: The Spirit of (Thirteen) Seventy Six', *Medievalia et Humanistica*, vol. 9, pp. 25–51.

Root, R. K. (1913), 'Publication Before Printing', *PMLA*, vol. 28, pp. 417–31.

Rothwell, W. (1975–6), 'The Role of French in Thirteenth-century England', *Bulletin of the John Rylands Library*, vol. 58, pp. 445-66.

Rowe, D. (1988), *Through Nature to Eternity: Chaucer's 'Legend of Good Women'* (Lincoln and London: University of Nebraska Press).

Salter, E. (1983), *Fourteenth-Century English Poetry: Contexts and Readings* (Oxford: Clarendon Press).

Salter, E. (1988), *English and International: Studies in the Literature, Art and*

Patronage of Medieval England, ed. D. Pearsall and N. Zeeman (Cambridge: Cambridge University Press).

Scattergood, V. J. and Sherborne, J. W. (ed.) (1983), *English Court Culture in the Later Middle Ages* (London: Gerald Duckworth).

Schibanoff, S. (1988), 'The New Reader and Female Textuality in Two Early Commentaries on Chaucer', *Studies in the Age of Chaucer,* vol. 10, pp. 71–108.

Sherborne, J. W. (ed.) (1983), see Scattergood, V. J.

Southern, R. W. (1970), *Western Society and the Church in the Middle Ages* (Harmondsworth: Penguin).

Smalley, B. (1960), *English Friars and Antiquity in the Early Fourteenth Century* (Oxford: Basil Blackwell).

Spearing, A. C. (1985), *Medieval to Renaissance in English Poetry* (Cambridge: Cambridge University Press).

Stillwell, G. (1944), 'The Political Meaning of Chaucer's *Tale of Melibee*', *Speculum,* vol. 19, pp. 433–44.

Strayer, J. R. (ed.) (1982–9), *Dictionary of the Middle Ages,* 13 vols (New York: Charles Scribner's Sons).

Strohm, P. (1979), 'Form and Social Statement in *Confessio Amantis* and *The Canterbury Tales*', *Studies in the Age of Chaucer,* vol. 1, pp. 17–40.

Strohm, P. (1982), 'Chaucer's Fifteenth-Century Audience and the Narrowing of the "Chaucer Tradition"', *Studies in the Age of Chaucer,* vol. 4, pp. 3–32.

Strohm, P. *et al.* (1983), 'Chaucer's Audience: a Symposium', *Chaucer Review,* vol. 18, pp. 137–71.

Strohm, P. (1989), *Social Chaucer* (Cambridge, Mass.: Harvard University Press).

Tatlock, J. S. P. (1935), 'The Text of the *Canterbury Tales* in 1400', *PMLA,* vol. 50, pp. 100–39.

Taylor, J. and Childs, W. (eds) (1990), *Politics and Crisis in Fourteenth-Century England* (Gloucester and Wolfeboro: Alan Sutton).

Thompson, A. (1978), *Shakepeare's Chaucer: A Study in Literary Origins* (Liverpool: Liverpool University Press).

Thompson, J. W. (1939), *The Medieval Library* (Chicago: Chicago University Press).

Thomson, J. A. F. (1965), *The Later Lollards 1414–1520* (London: Oxford Press).

Thorlby, A. (ed.) (1973), see Daiches, D.

Thrupp, S. L. (1948), *The Merchant Class of Medieval London 1300-1500* (Chicago: University of Chicago Press).

Turville-Petre, T. (1983), Review-article of books by Vale and Scattergood (as listed in this bibliography), *Nottingham Medieval Studies,* vol. 27, pp. 92–101.

Turville-Petre, T. (1988), 'Politics and Poetry in the Early Fourteenth Century: The Case of Robert Mannyng's Chronicle', *Review of English Studies,* n.s., vol. 39, pp. 1–28.

Turville-Petre, T. (1989), 'The Author of *The Destruction of Troy*', *Medium Aevum,* vol. 58, pp. 264–9.

Vale, J. (1982), *Edward III and Chivalry: Chivalric Society and its Context 1270–1350* (Woodbridge: Boydell Press).

Watson, A. G. (ed.) (1978), see Parkes, M. B.

Watts, P. R. (1947), 'The Strange Case of Geoffrey Chaucer and Cecilia Chaumpaigne', *Law Quarterly Review*, vol. 63, pp. 491–515.

White, H. (1987), *The Content of the Form: Narrative Discourse and Historical Representation* (Baltimore and London: John Hopkins University Press).

Wilson, R. M. (1943), 'English and French in England 1100–1300', *History*, vol. 28, pp. 37–60.

Wimsatt, J. I. (1982), *Chaucer and the poems of 'Ch'* (Cambridge: D. S. Brewer, Rowman and Littlefield).

Windeatt, B. A. (1979), 'The Scribes as Chaucer's Early Critics', *Studies in tha Age of Chaucer*, vol. 1, pp. 119–41.

Windeatt, B. A. (ed.) (1990) see Morse, R.

Ziegler, P. (1969; rpt 1984), *The Black Death* (Harmondsworth: Penguin).

Index